NorthStar

Focus on Listening and Speaking

High Intermediate

Tess Ferree
Kim Sanabria

Series Editors
Frances Boyd
Carol Numrich

LONGMAN

NorthStar: Focus on Listening and Speaking, High Intermediate

Pearson Education, 10 Bank Street, White Plains, NY 10606

Editorial director: Allen Ascher
Acquisitions editor: Louisa Hellegers
Director of design and production: Rhea Banker
Development editors: Carolyn Viola-John/Helen Solórzano
Production manager: Marie McNamara
Managing editor: Linda Moser
Production editor: Alice Vigliani
Senior manufacturing manager: Patrice Fraccio
Manufacturing supervisor: Edith Pullman
Photo research: Diana Nott
Cover design: Rhea Banker
Cover illustration: Wassily Kandinsky's *Im Blau* © 1998 Artists Rights Society (ARS), New York/ADAGP, Paris Transparency from Kunstsammlung Nordrhein-Westfalen, Düsseldorf, owner of the painting. Photograph taken by Walter Klein, Düsseldorf.
Text design: Delgado Design, Inc.
Text composition: Preface, Inc.
Photo credits: p. 53, Lown Cardiovascular Research Foundation, Inc.; p. 69, American Red Cross; p. 77, Rueters/Joe Skipper/Archive Photos; p. 93, reprinted with the permission of Co-op America; p. 102, photo by Robert Espier, "Hudson River Mythic"; p. 115, Robert J. Baker, Habitat for Humanity International; p. 121, Oseola McCarty and the University of Southern Mississippi; p. 165, Sojourner®, Mars Rover® and spacecraft design and images copyright © 1996–97, California Institute of Technology. All rights reserved. Further reproduction prohibited; p. 183, courtesy of NASA/Ames Research Center; p. 185, © The Stock Market / Tom and DeeAnn McCarthy, 1996; p. 191, © Stock Boston, Inc. / Gale Zucker, 1994; p. 230, courtesy *House & Garden*. Copyright ©1948 (renewed 1976) by The Conde Nast Publications, Inc.
Art credits: pp., 1, 17, 23, 94, 123, Ron Chironna; pp. 57, 60, 137, 143, Dusan Petricic; p. 70, Lloyd Birmingham; pp. 154, 186, Moffit Cecil.
Listening selections and text credits appear on p. 268.

Library of Congress Cataloging-in-Publication Data
Ferree, Tess.
NorthStar. Focus on listening and speaking, high intermediate/
Tess Ferree, Kim Sanabria.
p. cm. — Northstar
ISBN 0-201-84668-3 (paperback)
1. English language—Textbooks for foreign speakers. 2. English language—Spoken English—Problems, exercises, etc. 3. Listening—Problems, exercises, etc. I. Sanabria, Kim. II. Title. III. Series.
PE1128.F425 1998
428.3'4—dc21 97-43262
CIP

8 9 10—RNT—05 04 03

CONTENTS

INTRODUCTION

NorthStar is an innovative four-level, integrated skills series for learners of English as a Second or Foreign Language. The series is divided into two strands: listening/speaking and reading/writing. There are four books in each strand, taking students from the Basic to the Advanced level. The two books at each level explore different aspects of the same contemporary themes, which allows for reinforcement of both vocabulary and grammatical structures. Each strand and each book can also function independently as a skills course built on high-interest thematic content.

NorthStar is designed to work alongside Addison Wesley Longman's *Focus on Grammar* series, and students are referred directly to *Focus on Grammar* for further practice and detailed grammatical explanations.

NorthStar is written for students with academic as well as personal language goals, for those who want to learn English while exploring enjoyable, intellectually challenging themes.

NORTHSTAR'S PURPOSE

The *NorthStar* series grows out of our experience as teachers and curriculum designers, current research in second-language acquisition and pedagogy, as well as our beliefs about language teaching. It is based on five principles.

Principle One: In language learning, making meaning is all-important. The more profoundly students are stimulated intellectually and emotionally by what goes on in class, the more language they will use and retain. One way that classroom teachers can engage students in making meaning is by organizing language study thematically.

We have tried to identify themes that are up-to-date, sophisticated, and varied in tone—some lighter, some more serious—on ideas and issues of wide concern. The forty themes in *NorthStar* provide stimulating topics for the readings and the listening selections, including why people like dangerous sports, the effect of food on mood, an Olympic swimmer's fight against AIDS, experimental punishments for juvenile offenders, people's relationships with their cars, philanthropy, emotional intelligence, privacy in the workplace, and the influence of arts education on brain development.

Each corresponding unit of the integrated skills books explores two distinct topics related to a single theme as the chart below illustrates.

Theme	Listening/Speaking Topic	Reading/Writing Topic
Insects	Offbeat professor fails at breeding pests, then reflects on experience	Extract adapted from Kafka's "The Metamorphosis"
Personality	Shyness, a personal and cultural view	Definition of, criteria for, success

Principle Two: Second-language learners, particularly adults, need and want to learn both the form and content of the language. To accomplish this, it is useful to integrate language skills with the study of grammar, vocabulary, and American culture.

In *NorthStar,* we have integrated the skills in two strands: listening/speaking and reading/writing. Further, each thematic unit integrates the study of a grammatical point with related vocabulary and cultural information. When skills are integrated, language use inside of the classroom more closely mimics language use outside of the classroom. This motivates students. At the same time, the focus can shift back and forth from what is said to how it is said to the relationship between the two. Students are apt to use more of their senses, more of themselves. What goes on in the classroom can also appeal to a greater variety of learning styles. Gradually, the integrated-skills approach narrows the gap between the ideas and feelings students want to express in speaking and writing and their present level of English proficiency.

The link between the listening/speaking and reading/writing strands is close enough to allow students to explore the themes and review grammar and reinforce vocabulary, yet it is distinct enough to sustain their interest. Also, language levels and grammar points in *NorthStar* are keyed to Addison Wesley Longman's *Focus on Grammar* series.

Principle Three: Both teachers and students need to be active learners. Teachers must encourage students to go beyond whatever level they have reached.

With this principle in mind, we have tried to make the exercises creative, active, and varied. Several activities call for considered opinion and critical thinking. Also, the exercises offer students many opportunities for individual reflection, pair- and small-group learning, as well as out-of-class assignments for review and research. An answer key is printed on perforated pages in the back of each book so the teacher or students can remove it. A teacher's manual, which accompanies each book, features ideas and tips for tailoring the material to individual groups of students, planning the lessons, managing the class, and assessing students' progress.

Principle Four: Feedback is essential for language learners and teachers. If students are to become better able to express themselves in English, they need a response to both what they are expressing and how they are expressing it.

NorthStar's exercises offer multiple opportunities for oral and written feedback from fellow students and from the teacher. A number of open-ended opinion and inference exercises invite students to share and discuss their answers. In information gap, presentation and fieldwork activities, students must present and solicit information and opinions from their peers as well as members of their communities. Throughout these activities, teachers may offer feedback on the form and content of students' language, sometimes on the spot and sometimes via audio/video recordings or notes.

Principle Five: The quality of relationships among the students and between the students and teacher is important, particularly in a language class where students are asked to express themselves on issues and ideas.

The information and activities in *NorthStar* promote genuine interaction, acceptance of differences, and authentic communication. By building skills and exploring ideas, the exercises help students participate in discussions and write essays of an increasingly more complex and sophisticated nature.

DESIGN OF THE UNITS

For clarity and ease of use, the listening/speaking and reading/writing strands follow the same unit outline given below. Each unit contains from 5 to 8 hours of classroom material. Teachers can customize the units by assigning some exercises for homework and/or skipping others. Exercises in sections 1–4 are essential for comprehension of the topic, while teachers may want to select among the activities in sections 5–7.

1. **Approaching the Topic**
   A warm-up, these activities introduce students to the general context for listening or reading and get them personally connected to the topic. Typically, students might react to a visual image, describe a personal experience, or give an opinion orally or in writing.

2. **Preparing to Listen/Preparing to Read**
   In this section, students are introduced to information and language to help them comprehend the specific tape or text they will study. They might read and react to a paragraph framing the topic, prioritize factors, or take a general-knowledge quiz and share information. In the vocabulary section, students work with words and expressions selected to help them with comprehension.

3. **Listening One/Reading One**
   This sequence of four exercises guides students to listen or read with understanding and enjoyment by practicing the skills of (a) prediction, (b) comprehension of main ideas, (c) comprehension of details, and (d) inference. In activities of increasing detail and complexity, students learn to grasp and interpret meaning. The sequence culminates in an inference exercise that gets students to listen and read between the lines.

4. **Listening Two/Reading Two**
   Here students work with a tape or text that builds on ideas from the first listening/reading. This second tape or text contrasts with the first in viewpoint, genre, and/or tone. Activities ask students to explicitly relate the two pieces, consider consequences, distinguish and express points of view. In these exercises, students can attain a deeper understanding of the topic.

5. **Reviewing Language**
   These exercises help students explore, review, and play with language from both of the selections. Using the thematic context, students focus on language: pronunciation, word forms, prefixes and suffixes, word domains, idiomatic expressions, analogies. The listening/speaking strand stresses oral exercises, while the reading/writing strand focuses on written responses.

6. **Skills for Expression**
   Here students practice related grammar points across the theme in both topics. The grammar is practiced orally in the listening/speaking strand, and in writing in the reading/writing strand. For additional practice, teachers can turn to Addison Wesley Longman's *Focus on Grammar*, to which *NorthStar* is keyed by level and grammar points. In the Style section, students practice functions (listening/speaking) or rhetorical styles (reading/writing) that prepare them to express ideas on a higher level. Within each unit, students are led from controlled to freer practice of productive skills.

7. **On Your Own**
   These activities ask students to apply the content, language, grammar, and style they have practiced in the unit. The exercises elicit a higher level of speaking or writing than students were capable of at the start of the unit. Speaking topics include role plays, surveys, presentations, and experiments. Writing topics include paragraphs, letters, summaries, and academic essays.

In Fieldwork, the second part of On Your Own, students go outside of the classroom, using their knowledge and skills to gather data from personal interviews, library research, and telephone or Internet research. They report and reflect on the data in oral or written presentations to the class.

AN INVITATION

We think of a good textbook as a musical score or a movie script: It tells you the moves and roughly how quickly and in what sequence to make them. But until you and your students bring it to life, a book is silent and static, a mere possibility. We hope that *NorthStar* orients, guides, and interests you as teachers.

It is our hope that the *NorthStar* series stimulates your students' thinking, which in turn stimulates their language learning, and that they will have many opportunities to reflect on the viewpoints of journalists, commentators, researchers, other students, and people in the community. Further, we hope that *NorthStar* guides them to develop their own viewpoint on the many and varied themes encompassed by this series.

We welcome your comments and questions. Please send them to us at the publisher:

Frances Boyd and Carol Numrich, Editors
NorthStar
Addison Wesley Longman
10 Bank Street
White Plains, NY 10606-1951
or, by e-mail at:
awlelt@awl.com

ACKNOWLEDGMENTS

We would like to express our deep gratitude to Frances Boyd, who provided support, vision, and insight at each step of the writing process. Our heartfelt thanks also go to Carol Numrich, who, with Frances, created the NorthStar series and who encouraged the best within us.

We also wish to thank our colleagues at Columbia University's American Language Program and our students there, for inspiring us. In addition, special thanks go to Helen Solórzano, Trent Duffy, and Sherry Preiss for their contributions to the manuscript.

At Addison Wesley Longman, we thank Louisa Hellegers for her encouragement and support and Carolyn Viola-John for superbly editing and orchestrating an enormous amount of detail and ideas. We also want to thank Allen Ascher, Penny Laporte, Linda Moser, Alice Vigliani, Diana Nott, and Aerin Csigay for their help and support during the various stages of the project.

We are grateful to the many radio and television producers, hosts, and guests whose contributions have been so vital. For their part, we thank David Alpern of *Newsweek on Air,* Judy Blank of *On the Media,* and Steve Elman of WBUR, Boston. We thank Barbara Walters of NBC, Ken Ulmer of the Advertising Council, Clark Boyd of *The World,* Steve Liquori of Soundtrack Studios, and all the students, teachers, and administrators at the International High School.

Special thanks also go to Joseph Bruchac, David Winston, Oseola McCarty, filmmaker Jonathan Stack, and the Hurricane Hunters. At the Florida Department of Justice, we wish to thank Calvin Ross, Mike Dechman, and Lieutenant Kim Petersen of the Leon County Sheriff's Department Boot Camp.

Finally, we thank Carlos and Jay, Kelly and Victor, Honor and Ed, and all those we love for their strong shoulders, no matter what their size.

Tess Ferree
Kim Sanabria

UNIT 1

No News Is Good News

1 APPROACHING THE TOPIC

A. PREDICTING

Discuss the questions with another student. Then share your ideas with the class.

1. Look at the cartoon. Why do you think the man is so depressed? Why isn't the woman surprised?
2. In your opinion, is the news usually depressing? Does it have to be?
3. The unit title, "No News Is Good News," is a common saying in English. What do you think it means?

B. SHARING INFORMATION

❶ *What news media—newspapers, television, radio, the Internet, magazines—do you use to get your news and information? Complete the survey and check off the news media you use frequently. Then compare your answers in a small group. Discuss the reasons for your choices.*

Where Do You Get News and Information?

Kinds of News	News Media					
	newspapers	television	radio	the Internet	magazines	other people
local news	❑	❑	❑	❑	❑	❑
national news	❑	❑	❑	❑	❑	❑
international news	❑	❑	❑	❑	❑	❑
business news	❑	❑	❑	❑	❑	❑
the weather	❑	❑	❑	❑	❑	❑
the arts/ movie reviews	❑	❑	❑	❑	❑	❑
sports	❑	❑	❑	❑	❑	❑

❷ *Discuss the following question in your group.*

How well does the U.S. media cover news from the countries that interest you?

2 PREPARING TO LISTEN

A. BACKGROUND

Read the information and do the activity that follows.

Americans today are offered many sources of news, some of which are available twenty-four hours a day. Some say that the United States has become a nation of "news junkies," or people who are addicted to the news. In a recent survey of Americans, more than 65 percent responded that they spend from one-half to two hours per day watching, listening to, or reading the news. Twenty percent said they pay attention to the news for more than two hours each day.

With the increased demand for news, serious questions have emerged about the role of the news media in society. There is criticism that the news media in general is increasingly following the lead of the tabloid newspapers and television shows, which focus on negative stories of violence, crime, and scandal. Many critics say that the media is focusing too much on exposing the private lives of celebrities and politicians, and on reporting murder and mayhem. These types of stories help to sell more papers and attract bigger TV audiences.

Critics say that the media's focus on tabloid journalism has a number of serious consequences. For example, as the media pays attention to stories about celebrities, crime, and scandal, it increasingly ignores the more important social, political, and economic issues that we face. Also, some critics fear that media attention to violence might lead people to become less sensitive to its effects or even to act violently themselves.

In a national survey, 1,500 American adults were asked their opinions about the news. Work in pairs to find out the results of the survey. Then, as a class, discuss your reaction to the data.

Student A: Read aloud statements 1 to 5 on page 4. Some of the statements are true, and others are false.

Student B: Look at the graphs on page 4 showing the results of the news survey. Listen to each statement and indicate **T** *for true and* **F** *for false. Use the data to correct the false statements.*

Americans' Opinions About the News

A. Sources of News

_____ 1. Americans get most of their news from newspapers.

_____ 2. Radio is the least common source of news.

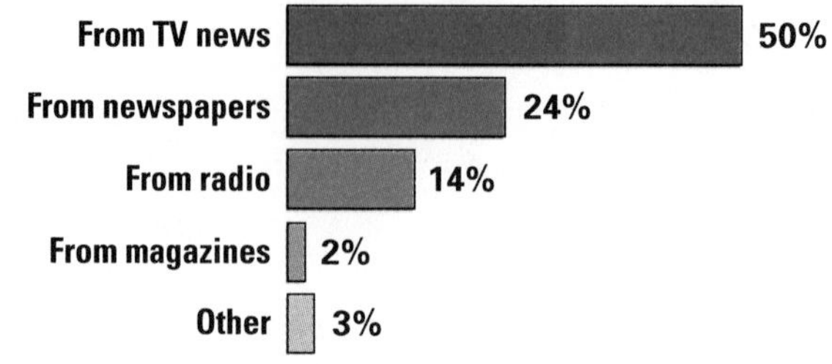

B. Interest in the News

_____ 3. Most Americans are very interested in local news (news from where they live).

_____ 4. Few Americans are interested in news about crime.

_____ 5. People are more interested in news about the arts and political campaigns than in news about the environment and business.

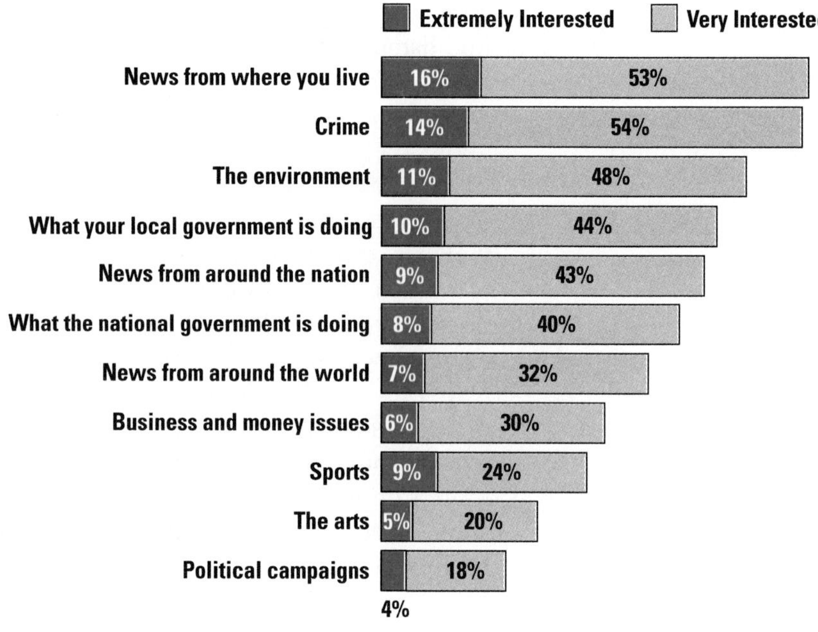

Now switch roles.

Student B: Read aloud statements 6 to 10.

Student A: Look at the graphs on page 5. Listen to each statement and indicate **T** *for true and* **F** *for false. Use the data to correct the false statements.*

C. Quality of News

_____ 6. Most Americans think that radio, TV, and newspaper reporting on the national government is good.

_____ 7. Almost 50 percent of Americans think that reporting on sports and crime is good.

_____ 8. Most people think that reporting on local and national news is not good.

How do you rate the quality of newspaper, TV, and radio reporting on these topics?

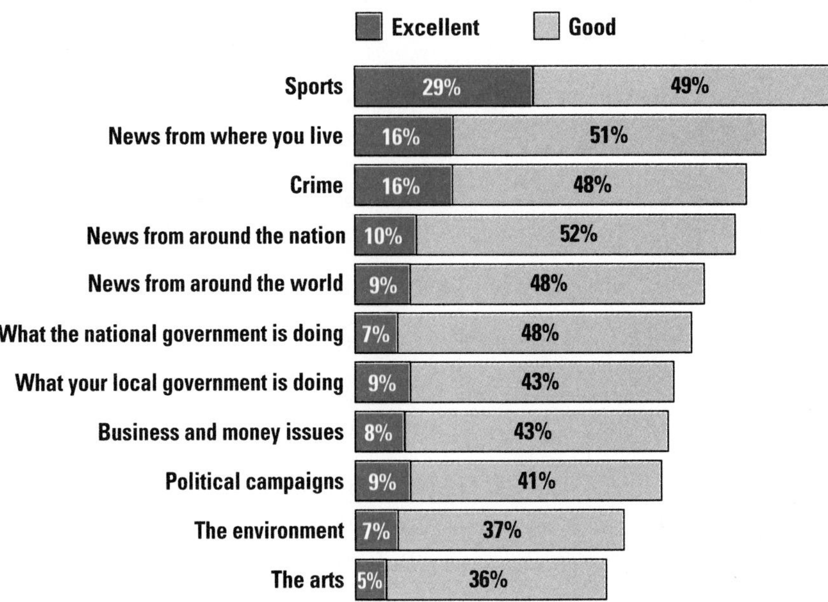

D. Trust in News Reporters

_____ 9. Americans trust lawyers more than they trust newspaper reporters.

_____ 10. People trust corporate executives and medical doctors more than they trust TV reporters.

How much do you trust the following people?

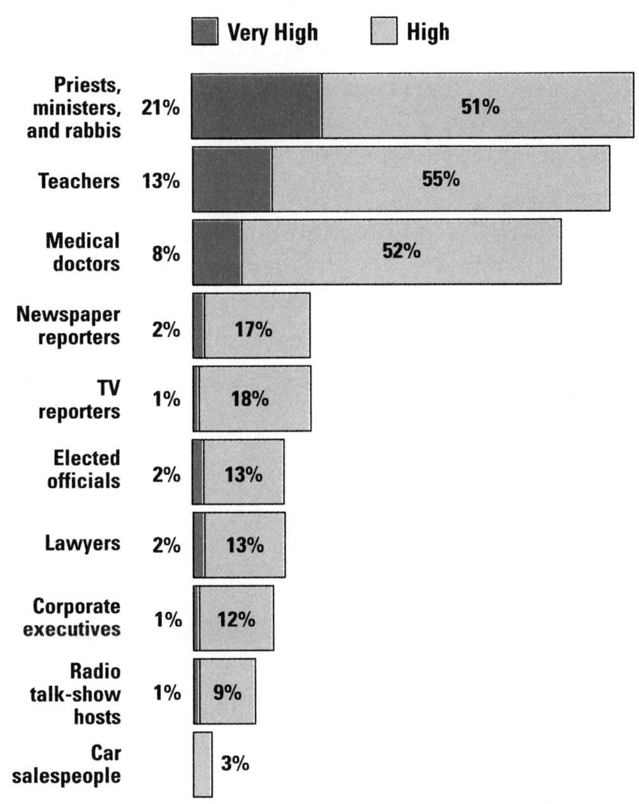

B. VOCABULARY FOR COMPREHENSION

❶ *Work with a partner. Read the sentences and study the underlined words. Then write down your definitions.*

1. Fewer and fewer people are reading serious newspapers these days. Maybe it's because they are fed up with the news.

   fed up with: ______________________________

2. I'm getting tired of the violence I see every time I turn on the TV. I just want to turn the TV off and tune the violence out.

   tune (something) out: ______________________________

3. I've really been enjoying the newspaper lately. It has a lot of articles that are quite interesting. I think that instead of buying it on a day-to-day basis, I might just get a subscription.

   subscription: ______________________________

4. My friend and I decided we were watching too much TV. I took a small step and cut down on how much I watched, but my friend made a quantum leap and sold her TV set!

   quantum leap: ______________________________

5. I'm sick of reading the news because there are never any positive stories. All that seems to be reported is murder and mayhem.

   murder and mayhem: ______________________________

6. You can't believe everything you see in print. You have to be a little bit skeptical and use your own judgment.

   skeptical: ______________________________

7. I like to read a variety of newspapers, both the popular ones and some smaller, alternative papers. That way, I get different views, and I am not so influenced by what I see in the mainstream media.

   mainstream: ______________________________

8. One big problem with the media is the amount of negativity.

   negativity: ______________________________

9. As a young reporter, I have a big assignment: coverage of an entire political campaign.

   coverage: ______________________________

❷ *Working with a partner, match each word on the left with a similar word or expression on the right. Write the appropriate letter in the blank space.*

____ 1. coverage
____ 2. mainstream
____ 3. murder and mayhem
____ 4. negativity
____ 5. skeptical
____ 6. subscription
____ 7. tune . . . out
____ 8. quantum leap
____ 9. fed up with

a. ignore, pay no attention to
b. agreement to buy consecutive issues of a newspaper or magazine
c. reporting
d. disbelieving, doubting
e. widely accepted, usual
f. violence, destruction
g. tired of
h. sudden or dramatic change
i. negative outlook or point of view

3 LISTENING ONE: A New Approach to News

A. INTRODUCING THE TOPIC

You will hear a radio interview by Alex Jones, host of the program *On the Media*. He is speaking to David Hamblin, who decided to start his own newspaper, the *World Times*.

Listen to the introduction to the report, and write short answers to the questions below. Compare your answers with those of your partner.

1. What kind of news might the *World Times* cover?

____

____

2. What are some problems (for example, a low subscription rate) the *World Times* might face?

____

____

B. LISTENING FOR MAIN IDEAS

Read the following statements. Listen to Part One of the interview, and choose the answer that best completes each statement. Then do the same for Part Two. Compare your answers with your partner's.

PART ONE

1. People are fed up with the news because it ______.

   a. is too negative
   b. doesn't have enough details
   c. can't be trusted

2. The interviewer wants to discuss ______.

   a. television news shows
   b. violence in the news
   c. alternative sources of news

3. The *World Times* publishes only ______ news.

   a. local
   b. good
   c. political

PART TWO

4. The *World Times* emphasizes ______.

   a. stories about people helping others
   b. good economic news
   c. the positive side of any story

5. The *World Times* should be ______.

   a. a person's only source of news
   b. more like mainstream media
   c. an alternative source of news

6. Reporting in the *World Times* focuses on ______.

   a. solutions to problems
   b. personal stories
   c. important events

C. LISTENING FOR DETAILS

Read the following statements. Then listen to the report again. Decide if the speakers in each part of the report would agree or disagree with the statements. Write **A** *for agree or* **D** *for disagree. Compare your answers with your partner's.*

PART ONE

Alex Jones would agree or disagree that . . .

_____ **1.** people tune out good news.

_____ **2.** a "good news" newspaper may not contain real news.

_____ **3.** people need alternatives to the murder and mayhem in the news.

_____ **4.** the *World Times* is dedicated to health, growth, liberation, and wholeness.

_____ **5.** a "good news" newspaper is a great idea.

PART TWO

David Hamblin would agree or disagree that . . .

_____ **6.** people need more hope in their lives.

_____ **7.** good news is superficial.

_____ **8.** the *World Times* includes some negative information.

_____ **9.** the *World Times* reports on alternative medicine.

_____ **10.** the *World Times* reports mainly on young people doing incredible things.

D. LISTENING BETWEEN THE LINES

Listen to the excerpts. Notice that the speakers repeat words and phrases to make a point stronger or clearer, or to catch the listener's attention. As you listen, answer the questions. Compare your answers with those of another student.

Excerpt One

1. Alex Jones is saying that . . .

   a. his listeners should stop paying attention to the news.
   b. few people tune out the news.
   c. there is too much bad news these days.

2. What word(s) or phrase(s) did Jones repeat? Why?

   ____

   ____

Excerpt Two

1. David Hamblin is saying that the *World Times* . . .

   a. finds the positive side of the news.
   b. doesn't mention anything negative.
   c. doesn't tell the whole truth.

2. What word(s) or phrase(s) did Hamblin repeat? Why?

   ____

   ____

Excerpt Three

1. Hamblin is saying that the *World Times* . . .

   a. has political articles that talk about problems.
   b. offers positive stories with solutions to problems.
   c. describes the problems senior citizens face.

2. What word(s) or phrase(s) did Hamblin repeat? Why?

   ____

   ____

4 LISTENING TWO: Conversations about the News

A. EXPANDING THE TOPIC

1 *You will hear two conversations about two types of newspapers. Listen to Conversation One. Write down three reasons why one person likes the newspaper. Then listen again. Write down three reasons why the other person doesn't like the newspaper. Then do the same for Conversation Two.*

Conversation One

In this conversation two colleagues, Chen and Tanya, are discussing a "good news" newspaper.

Chen likes reading a "good news" newspaper because . . .

1. ____________________
2. ____________________
3. ____________________

Tanya isn't sure if she likes "good news" newspapers because . . .

1. ____________________
2. ____________________
3. ____________________

Conversation Two

In this conversation two friends, Rita and Mark, are discussing a tabloid newspaper.

Rita likes reading a tabloid newspaper because . . .

1. ____________________
2. ____________________
3. ____________________

Mark doesn't like reading tabloid newspapers because . . .

1. ____________________
2. ____________________
3. ____________________

B. LINKING LISTENINGS ONE AND TWO

Discuss these questions in a small group.

1. What are the arguments you have heard in Listenings One and Two for and against reading a "good news" newspaper? Make a list. Then add arguments of your own and discuss them.

Arguments for Reading a "Good News" Newspaper	**Arguments against Reading a "Good News" Newspaper**
______________________	______________________
______________________	______________________
______________________	______________________
______________________	______________________

2. What is your opinion of "good news" and tabloid newspapers? Do you agree or disagree with the opinions you have heard?

3. What do you think is the future of "good news" newspapers like the *World Times*? Do you think this type of newspaper will become more popular? Why or why not?

5 REVIEWING LANGUAGE

A. EXPLORING LANGUAGE: Using Idiomatic Expressions

❶ *Read the following sentences, and fill in the blanks with an expression from the list below that has a similar meaning.*

come up with	in one sense	right off the bat
first of all	narrow down	sugar-coated
go a step further	pick it up	

1. The interviewer told Hamblin ______________ (immediately) that he was unsure if he would like the newspaper.

2. It's really hard to be a reporter because there are so many details and important decisions you have to make. ________________ (The first one is), you have to decide what news really is.

3. I'm not sure what I think of reporters. ________________ (In a way), everything they write reflects their own opinion.

4. Some people are skeptical of newspapers like the *World Times* and say they give a(n) ________________ (overly positive) version of the news.

5. Many newspapers mention some good news, but I think they should ________________ (do more) and seek out these stories.

6. I've never read a newspaper like the *World Times*. I have to ________________ (buy it) and find out what it's all about.

7. Some people think that newspapers have to cover more types of stories, but I think that they have to ________________ (be more selective in) their coverage.

8. The *World Times* sounds very interesting. I think that Hamblin has ________________ (thought of) a really good alternative to mainstream newspapers.

❷ *Work with a partner.*

Student A: Ask Student B questions 1 through 4.

Student B: Respond to the questions using the expression provided. The first one has been done for you. Then switch roles after question 4.

Student A	**Student B**
1. Did you like the idea of a good news newspaper right away?	1. (right off the bat) "Yes, I liked it right off the bat" or "No, right off the bat I knew I wouldn't like it."
2. In your opinion, what are the main problems with the news?	2. (first of all)
3. If you wanted to start a new newspaper, what would you do?	3. (come up with)
4. I've already bought a paper today. What about you?	4. (pick up)

Now switch roles.

Student B	**Student A**
5. Some local newspapers have expanded their coverage to include national and international news. Can they do all of this well?	5. (narrow down)
6. Many people like news stories about celebrities. What about you?	6. (in one sense)
7. Most papers publish good news stories only occasionally. Do you think that's enough?	7. (go a step further)
8. What do you imagine the coverage is like in the *World Times*?	8. (sugar-coated)

B. WORKING WITH WORDS

❶ *Read the list of adjectives and the sentences. Fill in the blanks with words that have the* **opposite** *meaning from the underlined words.*

alternative	misleading	sensational
depressing	negative	skeptical
innovative	objective	superficial

1. Tabloid news is rarely serious or analytical. In fact, it is usually very ________________.
2. If a glass is filled halfway with water, what do you see? A person with a positive attitude will see that the glass is half full. A person with a(n) ________________ attitude will see that it is half empty.
3. Most news isn't very cheerful. It's often quite ________________.
4. Newspapers are not always truthful, but I don't think they are intentionally ________________ either.
5. I'm not naive. I don't believe everything I read in a newspaper. I think it's better to be a little bit ________________.
6. The problem with television news is that there isn't time for in-depth reporting, so many of the reports are rather ________________.

7. There's nothing wrong with mainstream media, but we should get our news from _______________ sources as well.

8. Most reporting is unoriginal. Reporters are afraid of doing something different, so there is not much _______________ journalism.

9. Newspapers often claim that they are _______________ and are telling both sides of a story. However, editors must make subjective decisions about which facts to include and which ones to leave out.

❷ *Work in small groups. Circle the adjective that you think best describes each type of media listed in the column on the left. Discuss the reasons for your choices. Then add another adjective of your own.*

Tabloid journalism	informative	sensational	shallow	_______________
Television news	objective	cheerful	boring	_______________
Television advertising	exciting	annoying	superficial	_______________
Government-controlled newspapers	comprehensive	misleading	one-sided	_______________
News magazines	subjective	popular	in-depth	_______________
Internet news	analytical	factual	innovative	_______________

6 SKILLS FOR EXPRESSION

A. GRAMMAR: The Passive Voice

❶ *Working with a partner, examine the following sentences and discuss the questions that follow.*

- The *World Times* is designed to provide readers with a positive outlook.
- Some people think that readers have often been misled by the mainstream media.
- The news article about the president's political problems was written by a team of reporters from the *Washington Post.*

a. What do the underlined verb forms have in common?

b. How could these sentences be changed to the active voice?

FOCUS ON GRAMMAR

See The Passive in *Focus on Grammar, High-Intermediate.*

The Passive Voice

Form of the Passive

To form the **passive**, use the verb ***be*** + the past participle. The verb **be** can appear in any tense. If the agent of the action is mentioned, use ***by*** + the name of the agent.

Active	Passive
Many people **read** the *World Times.*	The *World Times* **is read by** many people.
The reporter **discussed** the president's news conference.	The president's news conference **was discussed by** the reporter.
The mainstream media **has covered** the story.	The story **has been covered** by mainstream media.

Use of the Passive

Use the passive voice to shift focus from the agent of the action to the thing or object being described.

◆ The tabloid newspapers **are read** by many people.

Use the passive voice when you do not need to mention the agent of the action, or when the agent is not important.

◆ The news about the robbery **is being reported** in great detail.

Use the passive voice when you want to avoid mentioning the agent, particularly to avoid blaming the agent.

◆ Some factual mistakes **were made** in the article about the murder trial.

❷ *It is very common to use passive structures in a news context when the agent of the action is unknown or not important, or when the speaker wants to avoid saying who the agent is. Complete the following radio reports with the passive voice, using the verbs and verb tenses indicated in parentheses. The first one has been done for you.*

"Hi. I'm Douglas O'Brian, reporting today from the Midwest, where millions of people are being housed (1. house; *present progressive*) in temporary accommodations following a severe storm that has left thousands stranded. Emergency services ______ (2. call; *past*) out late into the night as water levels rose and houses ______ (3. flood; *past*). Many people ______ (4. treat; *present perfect*) for shock, and reports of new panic ______ (5. receive; *present progressive*) as more rain ______ (6. predict; *present*)."

"Could the actress Kelly McKee ______ (7. select; *base form*) as the new sweetheart of Hollywood? Following the movie *Tales of Passion,* which ______ (8. release; *past*) this fall, more than 10,000 fan letters ______ (9. receive; *present perfect*) by her agent. A sequel to the movie ______ (10. plan; *present progressive*) for next year. One thing is certain: Ms. McKee ______ (11. follow; *future*) by photographers wherever she goes. Good luck, Kelly!"

"Francisco Olloa ______ (12. rescue; *past*) by his dog, Ted, last Friday after he fell through the ice into a pond. People ______ (13. warn; *past perfect*) that the ice was thin and that they should not go near the pond, but Francisco did not hear the report. Francisco ______ (14. interview; *past*) on "Good Morning, Nebraska" yesterday. He said that Ted should ______ (15. give; *base form*) a medal for his heroic rescue—and maybe a year's supply of dog bones, too!"

❸ *Work in pairs.*

Student A: Make a statement.

Student B: Respond by using a passive form of the verb and the verb tense indicated.

Switch roles after statement 4.

Student A

1. Hamblin found that traditional news reporting was very negative.
2. These days, many people seem to share his opinion.
3. Since the *World Times* first came out, the publisher has tried to give it a different image.
4. Hamblin feels that there is a lot of good news in our society that we don't hear about.

Student B

1. Yes, I heard that when he was young, he ____________________ (upset; *past*) by the news.
2. That's right. I heard that a lot of subscriptions ____________________ (cancel; *present progressive*).
3. Yes, it ____________________ (not/market; *present perfect*) in the same way as most other papers.
4. Yes, and he said that often the good news ____________________ (not/report; *present*).

Now switch roles.

Student B

5. Hamblin has a different view of "the whole truth."
6. Hamblin gives convincing arguments for buying his newspaper.
7. Photographers are quite aggressive and follow celebrities everywhere to get a picture.
8. Tabloid newspapers are very popular.

Student A

5. He said that he does not want the public ____________________ (mislead; *infinitive*).
6. That's what I think. In my opinion the good news ____________________ (not/report; *present*).
7. Yes, I feel that the photographers should ____________________ (control; *base form*) more strictly.
8. Well, in my neighborhood tabloids are really the only papers that ____________________ (sell; *present*).

B. STYLE: Stating an Opinion

In a conversation or discussion, it is sometimes necessary to state your own opinion or viewpoint clearly. Read the sentences from Listening Two. Notice the phrases that the speakers use to introduce their opinions.

- In my opinion, tabloid papers are a waste of time.
- I feel that it's so interesting! I love gossip.
- Well, I really think famous people have the right to a private life.

Here are some expressions people often use to **state their opinions:**

To express a strong opinion	To express an opinion	If you are unsure what you think
I really think (that) . . .	In my opinion . . .	Hmm, I'm not sure, but . . .
I strongly believe (that) . . .	What I think is (that) . . .	I'm of two minds, but . . .
I'm sure (that) . . .	I feel (that) . . .	Well, I don't know, but . . .
		I can't make up my mind, but . . .

Work in a small group. Take turns presenting and responding to the ten ideas. Use an expression from the box when you give your opinion.

1. I wouldn't read a newspaper like the *World Times*. Would you?

   In my opinion, ______________________________

2. What kind of newspaper do you think is the best?

   I feel that ______________________________

3. I think most reporters are just looking for sensational stories. All they want is to sell more newspapers.

   Hmm, I'm not sure, but ______________________________

4. Do you think that news always has to be bad?

   ____

5. Do you think the news is influenced by advertisers?

   ____

6. I think the news on TV is much better than it used to be.

___

7. I wonder why fewer people read newspapers these days.

___

8. What effect do you think that the Internet is having on newspapers?

___

9. I wonder why so many people read tabloid newspapers.

___

10. It must be really exciting to be a reporter.

___

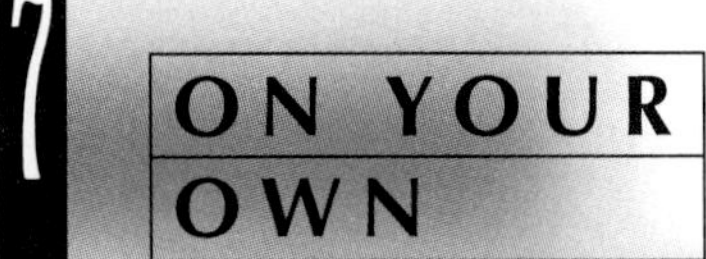

7 ON YOUR OWN

A. SPEAKING TOPICS: Marketing a Newspaper

❶ *Work in small groups. Imagine that you work for a national newspaper, the* News of the Nation, *and that you are trying to boost circulation. Brainstorm ideas to interest different groups of readers in your paper.*

	TYPES OF ARTICLES THAT MIGHT ATTRACT THIS GROUP OF READERS	REASON
city dwellers		
teenagers		
sports fans		
women		
business people		

2 *Choose one of the groups of readers from the chart in Exercise 1 to target. Create a marketing plan. Read the strategies (ideas) below, and select the ones that are most likely to attract your readers. You can also suggest other strategies of your own. Explain how the strategies you choose will attract the reader group you selected.*

Strategy—Focus On	New Feature
Fashion Tips	A special Sunday pull-out offers advice on how to choose clothes that will fit your image and keep you informed of the latest fashion trends.
Health Tips	A twice-weekly supplement educates you about diet, medicine, and common medical problems that you can solve without going to the doctor.
Coupons	Many pages of coupons offer you savings and discounts that are not available anywhere else.
Color Supplements	Sections of the newspaper are completely in color.
Competitions	Every weekend, there is a quiz about the week's news. Readers can send in their answers. Readers who answer correctly are entered into a lottery and might win prizes.
Continuing Stories	Multiple-part serials are included every week. Readers read one chapter of the story per issue.
Readers' Contributions	Readers themselves contribute to the newspaper. They send in personal stories about their lives, and the winners' stories are published in a special edition.
Other Strategy	(Your own)

3 *Present your marketing plan to the class, and explain how it will boost circulation of the* News of the Nation. *Other students should ask questions and express their opinions. Use the passive structures (see Section 6A on pages 15–18) and phrases to introduce opinions (see Section 6B on pages 19–20) that you have learned in this unit to present your ideas.*

B. FIELDWORK: Analyzing the Media

❶ *How negative is the TV or radio news? Watch some TV news (for example, the nightly news or a news channel) or listen to the radio news. Make a list of the stories that are reported. Check whether each one is a good news or bad news story. Discuss the results with the class.*

NEWS STORY	GOOD NEWS?	BAD NEWS?
1. ______	☐	☐
2. ______	☐	☐
3. ______	☐	☐
4. ______	☐	☐
5. ______	☐	☐
6. ______	☐	☐
7. ______	☐	☐
8. ______	☐	☐
9. ______	☐	☐
10. ______	☐	☐

❷ *Visit a local newspaper headquarters, or invite a speaker from the paper to visit your class. Make a list of questions. Ask about the following:*

- readership
- content
- editorial decisions
- strategies to boost circulation
- problems

UNIT 2

Do the Crime, Serve the Time: Teen Boot Camps

1 APPROACHING THE TOPIC

A. PREDICTING

Discuss the questions with another student. Then share your ideas with the class.

1. Look at the picture. Who are the people? Where are they? What are they doing?
2. Look at the title of the unit. What do you think it means? What do you think this unit will be about?

B. SHARING INFORMATION

Work in small groups and discuss your answers to the following questions.

1. The term *boot camp* refers to the first phase of army training. Have you, or anyone you know, ever been in the army? Have you seen a boot camp in the movies or on TV? What was the training experience like? Describe a typical day.

2. Military boot camp training is usually very physically and emotionally difficult for the trainees. What do you think is the purpose of this type of difficult training?

3. Do you think that boot camp training would be an effective punishment for criminals? Why or why not? For what type of criminal would it be most effective?

2 PREPARING TO LISTEN

A. BACKGROUND

Read the newspaper editorial and do the activity that follows.

THE STAR SUN

From the Editor

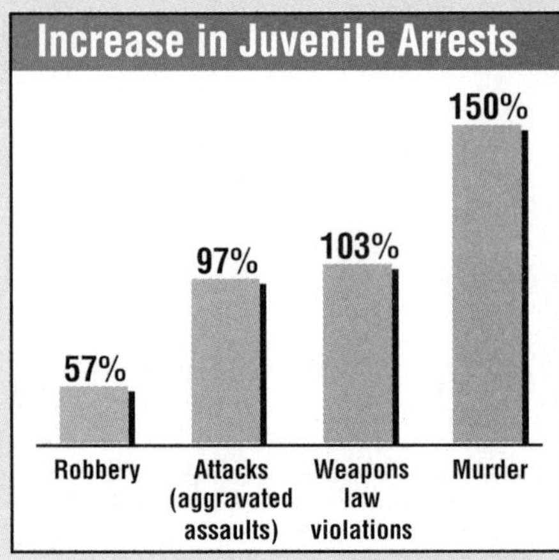

Ronnie has an innocent face, which makes him look younger than his fourteen years. Yet instead of playing with his friends in the schoolyard, he is in court, on trial for attacking another boy with a knife.

Ronnie is one of the thousands of boys and girls who have been arrested for serious, violent crimes in recent years. The trend is disturbing: Although the overall crime rate is decreasing, the number of crimes committed by juveniles is rising. Not only are more juveniles committing crimes, but the crimes they are committing are more violent. As a result, the arrest rate for juveniles has gone up dramatically in the past fifteen years.

What is the cause of this dramatic rise? It may be the high level of violence on the streets, in movies, and on television; the easy availability of guns and drugs; and an increase of single-parent families and families that live in poverty.

Whatever the causes, the justice system is now overwhelmed with young criminals. How should juvenile criminals be punished? It is clear that our current system is not working. One alternative to prison is correctional boot camps. Instead of being locked up in jail, young criminals in boot camps are forced to attend classes and undergo training similar to training for the military. Their strict routine includes many of the features of army training: double-time marching, push-ups, shaved heads, and insults for those who don't obey quickly. Instead of sitting in jail, kids like Ronnie are given a second chance to become useful members of society.

Work in pairs. Look at this schedule of a typical day and some rules for behavior at boot camp (on page 26). Discuss why each activity is included and how useful you think it is. Then fill in the charts with your ideas. The first one has been done for you.

A TYPICAL DAY AT BOOT CAMP		
Daily Schedule		**Purpose and Usefulness**
5:00 - 6:30 a.m.	•Wake up. •Quickly put on uniforms. •Attend roll call. •Make beds. •March to breakfast.	It's good for kids to have clear daily goals. It's also good for them to have an early start to the day and daily chores to do.
6:30 - 8:00 a.m.	•Do rigorous physical training (push-ups, marching, running, military drills, sit-ups).	
8:00 - 3:00 p.m.	•Attend academic classes, counseling, and vocational training. •Take five-minute breaks every half-hour for rigorous physical training. •Take a half-hour lunch break. •Clean up after lunch.	
3:00 - 11:00 p.m.	•Do more physical training and military drills. •Eat dinner. •Attend military ceremony. •Take shower. •Turn out lights by 11:00.	

BOOT CAMP RULES	Purpose and Usefulness

You must <u>not</u>:
•Listen to music or radio.
•Watch movies or TV *except*
  •as a reward for good behavior.
  •for educational purposes.
•Smoke.
•Use the telephone for the first thirty days.
(After that, two five-minute calls are allowed each week—but only to parents, lawyers, or legal guardians.)	

You <u>must</u>: •Have a shaved head. •Address staff as "Sir" or "Ma'am." •Explain why you break a rule *and* •Explain what you think your punishment should be. (Staff may or may not agree.)	

B. VOCABULARY FOR COMPREHENSION

Read the sentences below. Cross out the one word or phrase that does ***not*** *have a similar meaning to the underlined word.*

1. A study is <u>under way</u> to evaluate the effectiveness of the criminal justice system.

a. being considered **b.** being conducted **c.** being done

2. One of the <u>components</u> of the study is an evaluation of the juvenile justice system.

a. parts **b.** lengths **c.** aspects

3. The <u>aim</u> of the study is to find the best way to deal with a growing number of young criminals.

a. goal **b.** purpose **c.** result

4. Although the study hasn't been completed, <u>preliminary</u> findings show that current methods for punishing juveniles are not working.

a. early **b.** conclusive **c.** unfinished

5. It is <u>questionable</u> whether the same methods should be used to punish adults and young offenders.

   a. clear b. arguable c. doubtful

6. They feel that youthful <u>offenders</u> need to be punished differently from adults.

   a. criminals b. citizens c. delinquents

7. In my work with teenage criminals, I have seen a lot of <u>anecdotal evidence</u> showing that the experts may be right.

   a. scientific research b. individuals' stories c. personal impressions

8. The most important reason for punishing young offenders is to <u>deter</u> them from committing more crimes.

   a. delay b. stop c. discourage

9. The high rate of <u>recidivism</u> among young criminals shows that traditional prisons are not working.

   a. returning to jail b. becoming better citizens c. committing another crime

10. Some experts recommend opening more correctional boot camps where physical <u>exertion</u>, such as running and doing push-ups, is used to change behavior.

    a. exercise b. training c. medicine

11. In addition, drug <u>counseling</u> is provided to help young offenders who are drug dependent.

    a. research b. education c. advice

12. This idea may not <u>sell well to</u> the public, who want more prisons to be built so that criminals are kept off the streets.

    a. make money for b. seem like a good idea to c. be popular with

13. Victims want <u>retribution</u> for the pain they and their families have experienced because of crime.

    a. compensation b. payback c. attention

14. But when the study is completed and the <u>hard evidence</u> is in, we may find that there are better alternatives.

    a. difficult evidence b. analytical evidence c. scientific evidence

LISTENING ONE: Do the Crime, Serve the Time

A. INTRODUCING THE TOPIC

You will hear a radio interview from the program *Newsweek on Air*. Host David Alpern discusses correctional boot camps in the United States with *Newsweek*'s Miami correspondent, David González, and Dale Parent, the author of a report on boot camps.

Listen to the introduction to the interview. Then listen to the questions that the interviewer asks during the interview. Predict what the answers might be. Discuss your predictions with a partner.

1. What do they do exactly, beyond the physical exertions and the discipline?
2. Any evidence that they're successful?
3. Isn't there a danger that . . . boot camps for young criminals will do just what boot camps for servicemen are supposed to do—make them tougher, more resourceful, and effective as criminals?

B. LISTENING FOR MAIN IDEAS

Read the following statements. Then listen to Part One of the interview and circle the answer that best completes each statement. Do the same for Part Two. Compare your answers with those of another student.

PART ONE: David González

1. Boot camp programs ______.
   a. mostly emphasize military drill
   b. use only physical exertion and discipline
   c. have several components

2. Boot camps aim to ______.
   a. prepare young offenders for the military
   b. change the way young offenders think
   c. give young offenders a lot of exercise

3. There is not much ______ evidence that boot camps are successful.

   a. analytical
   b. anecdotal
   c. official

4. One purpose of boot camp programs that is *not* mentioned is reducing ______.

   a. overcrowding
   b. recidivism
   c. violent behavior

5. People like the idea of boot camps because they offer ______.

   a. military training
   b. drug counseling
   c. quick retribution

PART TWO: Dale Parent

6. Preliminary findings show that the success rate of boot camps is ______ that of prisons.

   a. much higher than
   b. no different from
   c. much lower than

7. To change criminal behavior, we need to solve basic problems ______.

   a. that cause people to commit crimes
   b. in the criminals' families
   c. within the prison system

C. LISTENING FOR DETAILS

Listen to the interview again. Then read the following statements. Mark them T for true or F for false. Compare your answers with those of another student.

PART ONE: David González

____ 1. David González and Dale Parent both reported on boot camps.

____ 2. There are about fifty boot camp programs in nine states.

____ 3. Military drill, physical training, and drug counseling are all components of boot camp programs.

____ 4. Boot camps try to make young people think differently about their responsibility to their communities.

____ 5. Boot camps have helped some young offenders.

____ 6. There are not enough jail cells in the United States.

____ 7. There is hard evidence that boot camps reduce recidivism and that teenagers who go to boot camp do not commit more crimes.

____ 8. Some people like watching young offenders do push-ups.

____ 9. Politicians and corrections officials agree on the effectiveness of boot camps.

PART TWO: Dale Parent

____ 10. Evaluations of boot camps are under way in several states.

____ 11. We have enough conclusive evidence about boot camps right now.

____ 12. Some people think that boot camps may teach young offenders to be more effective criminals.

____ 13. Deterring people by using extreme discipline is a good idea.

____ 14. People commit crimes because they don't care about others.

____ 15. Many young offenders are also drug dependent.

D. LISTENING BETWEEN THE LINES

Read the questions. Then listen to each excerpt from the interview, and write short answers to the questions. Discuss your answers with a partner and then with the class.

Excerpt One

1. David González uses five adjectives to describe types of evidence: *systematic, analytical, anecdotal, hard,* and *solid.* What are the similarities and differences among these types of evidence?

____

____

2. What types of evidence would he accept to prove the success of boot camps? Where would this evidence come from?

____

____

3. Which type of evidence does he reject? Why do you think he rejects it?

____

____

Excerpt Two

4. David González mentions two groups of people who support boot camps: people who want quick retribution against criminals, and politicians. Why do these two groups share the same viewpoint?

____

____

5. How does he feel about people's desire for retribution? How can you tell?

____

____

6. How does he feel about politicians who support boot camp programs?

____

____

Excerpt Three

7. Dale Parent also uses several adjectives to describe types of evidence: *hard*, *preliminary*, and *conclusive*. What are the differences among these types of evidence?

____

____

8. What type of evidence would Dale Parent accept to prove the success of boot camps? Where would this evidence come from?

____

____

9. Would he agree with David González's view of anecdotal evidence?

____

____

LISTENING TWO: Are Boot Camps Effective?

A. EXPANDING THE TOPIC

Listen to the interview with Thomas Adair, a documentary filmmaker who has closely observed the operation of boot camps. Then read the following statements and circle the best response. Compare your answers with those of another student.

1. Thomas Adair basically ______ the idea of boot camps.
   a. agrees with **b.** isn't sure about
2. He feels that boot camps give kids a ______.
   a. second chance **b.** safe place to live
3. Adair says that adult repeat offenders ______ be easily changed.
   a. can **b.** can't
4. He feels that traditional prison ______ a difference in changing someone's behavior.
   a. helps make **b.** doesn't make
5. Adair says that a reason why many kids become offenders is that they ______ structure and guidance.
   a. ignore **b.** don't have
6. Adair believes that young criminals ______ responsible for all the problems in the United States today.
   a. are probably **b.** can't be
7. He is ______ about the future.
   a. optimistic **b.** pessimistic
8. Adair thinks that boot camps are good because they help to ______ young offenders.
   a. reform **b.** punish

B. LINKING LISTENINGS ONE AND TWO

During the two interviews, the speakers mentioned several different approaches to punish young offenders. These ideas can be summarized in four philosophies of criminal correction:

- **Reform:** to make criminals into good members of society
- **Retribution:** to punish them for doing something wrong
- **Deterrence:** to prevent them and others from committing crimes
- **Protection of the public:** to keep criminals out of society

❶ *Work in pairs. Read the following opinions about criminal correction, and discuss which philosophy or philosophies each quote represents. Indicate your choice(s) in the space provided. Then compare your choices with the class, giving reasons for your decisions.*

1. "People in this neighborhood have the right to go to bed at night and sleep peacefully, knowing that dangerous criminals are behind bars."

   Philosophy(ies): Protection of the public; deterrence

2. "Unless we take strong action now, crime will continue to grow. Criminals see that they can get away with little or no punishment."

   Philosophy(ies): ____________________

3. "Violence is learned behavior. It can be unlearned if criminals are given good models to follow as well as strong discipline."

   Philosophy(ies): ____________________

4. "These are monsters, not kids. We should lock them up and throw away the key."

   Philosophy(ies): ____________________

5. "Many of these kids come from broken homes and are addicted to drugs. They need support and education so they can choose something besides crime as a way of life."

   Philosophy(ies): ____________________

6. "Some of these kids are really victims too, but until they can control themselves we need to prevent them from hurting other people."

   Philosophy(ies): ____________________

❷ *Working in pairs, decide whether David González, Dale Parent, and Thomas Adair would agree or disagree with the ideas expressed in each quote in Exercise 1 on page 33. Write* **A** *for agree or* **D** *for disagree in each column. Use specific examples from the listenings to support your opinion. Then compare your opinions with those of the class.*

	DAVID GONZÁLEZ	DALE PARENT	THOMAS ADAIR
Quote 1			
Quote 2			
Quote 3			
Quote 4			
Quote 5			
Quote 6			

❸ *Discuss these questions in a small group.*

1. Which of the four philosophies of criminal correction are included in boot camp programs? Give specific examples to illustrate your answer.

2. In your opinion, which philosophies are appropriate for punishment of first-time offenders? Which ones are appropriate for juveniles who are repeat offenders?

3. Should juveniles be punished differently from adults? Why or why not?

5 REVIEWING LANGUAGE

A. EXPLORING LANGUAGE: Word Forms

❶ *Working in a small group, fill in the missing forms of the words in the chart. Then say the words aloud with your teacher.*

Noun	Verb	Adjective	Adverb
analysis	analyze		
	X	anecdotal	
		1. correctional **2.** corrective	X
	exert	X	X
insult			insultingly
1. offender **2.** offense	offend		
1. **2.** politician	politicize		
reassessment		reassessed	X
rigor	X		
	systematize		

❷ *Working with a partner, read aloud the dialogues on pages 36–38. Fill in the blanks with the correct form of the word from the chart in Exercise 1 on page 35 as you read. Listen carefully and check each other's answers.*

1. analysis

STUDENT A: Boot camps sound like a good idea, but there's not much (**a**) ________________ of their effectiveness, right?

STUDENT B: Well, I'm not sure I agree. Social scientists seem to take an (**b**) ________________ approach. They're looking beyond simply punishing kids.

STUDENT A: I see what you mean. I guess some people say that a criminal can never change, but maybe they don't really (**c**) ________________ the problem. They probably react with emotion, not reason.

2. anecdote

STUDENT A: It seems there's only (**a**) ________________ evidence that boot camps work. There isn't much scientific information about them.

STUDENT B: Right. By the way, speaking about tough kids, I have a great (**b**) ________________ of my own to tell you sometime.

3. correction

STUDENT A: Boot camps are not the same as prisons, but they are (**a**) ________________ facilities, right?

STUDENT B: Yes, they're designed to (**b**) ________________ destructive behavior and bad habits.

STUDENT A: Boot camp officers must have a tough job. They have to (**c**) ________________ violent behavior.

4. exertion

STUDENT A: Boot camp training involves a lot of physical (a) ________________.

STUDENT B: That's right. I guess that if the kids (b) ________________ themselves all day, they won't have much energy left to get into trouble.

5. insult

STUDENT A: Why do you think certain boot camp officers (a) ________________ the kids so much?

STUDENT B: I guess an (b) ________________ is supposed to make them more respectful or something.

STUDENT A: Well, I think it's really (c) ________________ to treat them like that.

6. offender

STUDENT A: Boot camps usually accept only young, first-time (a) ________________ who have committed crimes.

STUDENT B: That's right. And any (b) ________________ behavior at the boot camp is punished.

7. politics

STUDENT A: I see now that (a) ________________ plays an important role in what happens to these kids.

STUDENT B: You're probably right. It's hard to know if a (b) ________________'s actions are truly for the good of society or if they are simply (c) ________________ moves to get more votes in elections.

8. **reassessment**

STUDENT A: It looks as if people in the United States are (a) ________________ traditional treatment of young criminals.

STUDENT B: Yes, and from what I've heard, (b) ________________ is a good idea.

9. **rigor**

STUDENT A: (a) ________________ physical exercise is a major component in boot camp programs.

STUDENT B: Yes, and the kids follow their academic program (b) ________________, too. If they don't, they have to do more exercises.

10. **system**

STUDENT A: The physical training in boot camps is (a) ________________. It progresses step by step to new levels of difficulty.

STUDENT B: Yes. The idea is that if the kids build new habits (b) ________________, they won't go back to crime when they get out.

B. WORKING WITH WORDS

Read the following article about a boot camp in the United States. Choose a definition for each underlined word or phrase from the list that follows the article. Write the appropriate number next to the definition.

LEON COUNTY BOOT CAMP

A CLOSER LOOK

Lieutenant Kim Petersen works with young offenders in Tallahassee, Florida, at the Leon County Boot Camp, a group of buildings between the police station and the court house. She's been there since the program was (1) initiated in 1983. Almost all the young offenders have drug abuse problems, and most have disruptive and disadvantaged family backgrounds. Lt. Petersen says the (2) rigorous discipline that young offenders (3) go through, combined with education and counseling, (4) deters some of them from returning to crime when they finish the program. The adult-style military atmosphere (5) appeals to many of these tough kids, who feel they are being treated as adults. At first they are (6) reluctant to cooperate, and they (7) come across as hardened (8) punks who want help from no one. Later, though, they often lose their tough-guy attitudes.

The results are mixed. (9) In the short run the eight-month program works, but are the program's supporters (10) fooling themselves? Lt. Petersen is realistic. She says, "Boot camps aren't a cure-all for (11) long-term problems. Eight months isn't very long to change a person's attitudes and lifestyle. That's probably why some boot camp 'graduates' (12) wind up getting into trouble again."

For the most (13) resourceful offenders, the end of the program marks the beginning of a new life. Those few are able to leave the bad environments they came from and start new lives someplace else. For Lt. Petersen, the real successes are those kids who must return to their original environments of poverty and broken homes, but who still manage to (14) turn over a new leaf by going back to school and finding jobs. "Those kids," she says, "have to fight daily against their old temptations. Those are the real success stories, the real heroes. They make our work worthwhile."

____ **a.** not seeing the truth

____ **b.** experience

____ **c.** begun

____ **d.** in the short term

____ **e.** stops, prevents

____ **f.** attracts

____ **g.** strict

____ **h.** unwilling

____ **i.** finally get

____ **j.** begin again in a different way

____ **k.** able, bright

____ **l.** appear to be

____ **m.** rough young people

____ **n.** chronic (lasting a long time)

6 SKILLS FOR EXPRESSION

A. GRAMMAR: Gerunds and Infinitives

1 *Working with a partner, examine the sentences below. Then discuss the questions that follow.*

- Boot camp supporters hope to give young offenders a second chance.
- Boot camps are a way of giving young offenders a second chance.
- People do not want to live in fear of young criminals in their neighborhood.
- People resent living in fear of young criminals in their neighborhood.

a. What is the difference in the forms *to give* and *giving* in the first pair of sentences?

b. In the second pair of sentences, what is similar about the forms *to live* and *living*?

FOCUS ON GRAMMAR

See Gerunds and Infinitives in *Focus on Grammar, High-Intermediate.*

Gerunds and Infinitives

Verbs are often used in the **gerund** or the **infinitive** form.

Gerund

To form the gerund, add ***-ing*** to the base form of the verb:

verb + *-ing*

Use of the Gerund

Use the gerund as the subject of a sentence.	**Throwing** young offenders in prison is not a solution to the problem of juvenile crime.
Use the gerund after prepositions such as ***for, by, of, about, against.***	Boot camps are a way of **giving** young offenders a second chance.
Use the gerund after certain verbs, such as ***advise, avoid, stop, continue, risk, enjoy, keep (on), recommend, require, suggest, support,*** as the object of a sentence.	The judge recommended **sending** the 15-year-old defendant to a correctional boot camp.

Infinitive

To form the infinitive, use ***to*** and the base form of the verb:

to + **verb**

Use of the Infinitive

Use the infinitive to express purpose. — Boot camps were established **to give** young offenders a second chance.

Use the infinitive after a ***be*** + **adjective** combination such as ***happy, old enough, relieved, prepared.*** — He **was happy to go** to boot camp rather than to prison.

Use the infinitive after certain verbs, including ***afford, agree, attempt, decide, deserve, expect, hesitate, hope, learn, manage, need, offer, promise, try, want.*** — The judge **agreed to send** the fifteen-year-old to boot camp because this was his first offense.

2 *These three letters appeared in a local newspaper after it printed a series of articles about boot camps. Read the letters, and fill in the blanks with a gerund or an infinitive form of the verb indicated. Then take turns reading the letters aloud to another student to compare answers.*

To the Editor

Support the Davis Bill

Let's stop __________ (**1.** pamper) criminals and get serious about __________ (**2.** solve) our crime problem. The only way to win is by __________ (**3.** lock up) offenders. The public needs __________ (**4.** know) that delinquents are being punished, no matter what their age. It is practically impossible __________ (**5.** reform) a person after he or she has begun a life of crime.

I'm a state senator, but I'm also a parent and a member of the community. I am prepared __________ (**6.** provide) leadership in the fight against juvenile crime by __________ (**7.** support) the Davis Crime Bill. Discussion of this bill is under way in the Senate right now. If my bill becomes law, it will impose harsher sentences on criminals. Let's finally get tough on crime.

—Senator Davis

To the Editor

Tough on Crime

I was glad ________________ (8. hear) that more young criminals are being sentenced to time in boot camps. I was robbed last year by a 14-year-old who tried ________________ (9. terrorize) me with a knife. Fortunately, a passer-by heard me scream and managed ________________ (10. scare) him away. The punk was caught, but because of his age the judge recommended ________________ (11. release) him in the custody of his parents. Believe me, I was outraged when I learned that he was free ________________ (12. attack) someone else.

I'm absolutely against ________________ (13. deal with) criminals leniently, no matter how young they are. If they're old enough ________________ (14. commit) an adult crime, they're old enough ________________ (15. serve) adult time.

—Mugged in Los Angeles

To the Editor

Rehabilitate Young Offenders

I've worked with the juvenile justice system for the past twenty years, and I'm in favor of ________________ (16. develop) rehabilitation programs. Punishment alone creates a revolving door of prison, crime, and prison again. It doesn't change the criminal. Recidivism needs ________________ (17. be) reduced, and just sending young offenders to prison is not the answer.

It may be expensive ________________ (18. reform) young people, but we can't afford *not* ________________ (19. do) it. These kids are our future. We must avoid ________________ (20. send) them to prison. We should provide education, training, and a second chance. The "tough love" approach works. We risk ________________ (21. lose) so many young people to a life of crime by not ________________ (22. give) them support and encouragement. Let's help young offenders turn over a new leaf.

—Amy Lobens, social worker

B. STYLE: Expressing Some Disagreement

In a conversation, we often use certain phrases or expressions to indicate that we do not fully agree with what the other person is saying or to change the direction of the conversation. In Listening Two, for example, Thomas Adair and the interviewer have this exchange:

ADAIR: [Boot camps are] a way of giving kids a second chance.

INTERVIEWER: I understand what you're saying, but if young people commit the same crimes as adults, why should they be treated differently?

By beginning her reply with "I understand what you are saying, but," the interviewer shows that she understands Adair's ideas but wants to raise another issue.

Here are some phrases that can be used to **express some disagreement** or to **change the direction of a conversation:**

- I understand what you're saying, but . . .
- You have a point, but . . .
- That's an interesting theory, but . . .
- I see what you mean, but . . .
- Yes, I see, but . . .
- Well, that might be true, but . . .

Work in pairs.

Student A: You are in the "Hot Seat." Argue one of the positions from the "Hot Seat Opinions" list.

Student B: Express some disagreement with Student A, using phrases from the box.

Student A: Respond to Student B's opinion, using phrases from the box.

Switch roles after opinion 4. The first one has been done for you.

HOT SEAT OPINIONS

Student A	Student B	Student A
1. How can you expect crime to go down when movies and TV shows are full of guns and violence?	1. **Example** "You have a point, but obviously not everyone who sees violence on TV commits a crime."	1. **Example** Response: "I understand what you're saying, but TV violence really *does* influence young kids."
2. Divorce is the main problem. If there were fewer divorces, there would be less crime.	2. Well, that might be true, but . . .	2. Response: I see what you mean, but . . .
3. Boot camp doesn't sound all that tough to me. I think that we should be much less lenient with juvenile criminals.	3. (Choose expressions from the list.)	3. Response: (Choose expressions from the list.)
4. Teachers should be allowed to hit students who misbehave.	4.	4.

Now switch roles.

Student B	Student A	Student B
5. The main reason for crime is poverty. There aren't enough jobs in poor neighborhoods.	5. (Choose expressions from the list.)	5. Response: (Choose expressions from the list.)
6. It's easy for young people to choose the wrong friends and make mistakes. It's really important to give people a second chance when they commit a crime.	6.	6.
7. I don't care how old they are, criminals should go to prison for their crimes.	7.	7.

7 ON YOUR OWN

A. SPEAKING TOPICS: What Should We Do with These Young Criminals?

❶ *Before you read the case studies in Exercise 2, match the name of the crime on the left with the definition on the right. Write the letter in the blank.*

_____ 1. arson	a. buying alcohol while under the legal drinking age
_____ 2. vandalism	b. stealing a car or truck
_____ 3. motor vehicle theft	c. setting fire to a building
_____ 4. burglary	d. destroying property
_____ 5. weapons law violation	e. breaking into a building to steal something
_____ 6. liquor law violation	f. illegally carrying or using a gun
_____ 7. drug violation	g. selling or using illegal drugs

❷ *Working in small groups, read the six case studies that follow. Decide on an appropriate punishment or treatment for each crime. Use the information from this unit and your own knowledge to make recommendations. Some possible options are:*

- prison or detention center
- boot camp
- probation (released from prison or boot camp, but must report weekly to officials who check behavior)
- community service (must do useful work for the town or state, such as cleaning parks or roadways)
- other alternative sentencing (for example, punishing parents for their children's crimes)

1. **Arson**

   Kevin, a thirteen-year-old, is playing with matches and sets fire to his family's apartment. The apartment is so badly damaged that the family has to move out. He has been warned before not to play with matches.

   Recommendation: ______________________________

2. **Vandalism**

   A gang of adolescents breaks into a library in a small town and damages most of the electronic equipment at the front desk. They also rip pages out of expensive books and pull other books from the shelves. They are caught leaving the library through a window.

   Recommendation: ______________________________

3. **Motor vehicle theft**

   An eighteen-year-old is caught driving a stolen vehicle to another state. He seems to be heading for a garage and is probably planning to take the car apart and sell it for parts.

   Recommendation: ______________________________

4. **Burglary**

   A couple of sixteen-year-olds break into a supermarket after it closes. They steal $46 from the cash registers and try to get into the safe. They are caught as they exit the building.

   Recommendation: ______________________________

5. **Weapons law violation**

   A teenage girl is caught with a gun in her school locker. She says it is not hers. Apparently it belongs to her boyfriend. She says he asked her to take care of the gun, but she doesn't know where he is.

   Recommendation: ______________________________

6. **Liquor law violation**

   A group of sixteen-year-olds goes to a liquor store. They use fake identification to purchase vodka. A policeman sees them drinking on the street outside of the store, examines their identification, and takes them to the police station.

   Recommendation: ______________________________

❸ *Present your group's recommendations to the class. As you listen to the other groups, ask questions about their ideas. In your discussion, try to use infinitives and gerunds (see the grammar box on pages 40–41 in Section 6A) and phrases that express some disagreement (see the box on page 43 in Section 6B).*

B. FIELDWORK: Roving Reporter

A roving reporter asks several people their opinions on a current issue in a very short interview. The reporter "roves," or moves from person to person, in order to solicit opinions.

❶ *Working with a partner, interview at least three people on the topic of punishments for young offenders. Before you begin your interviews, come up with a list of three or four questions. The list has been started for you.*

1. In certain states, military-style boot camps are being used to punish young people who break the law. Do you think this is a good idea?
2. Some people claim that jail turns young offenders into worse criminals. What is your view?
3. ______________________________
4. ______________________________

❷ *While you interview, take notes on the interviewees' answers to the questions.*

❸ *Present a summary of your findings to the class.*

UNIT 3

The Doctor-Patient Relationship

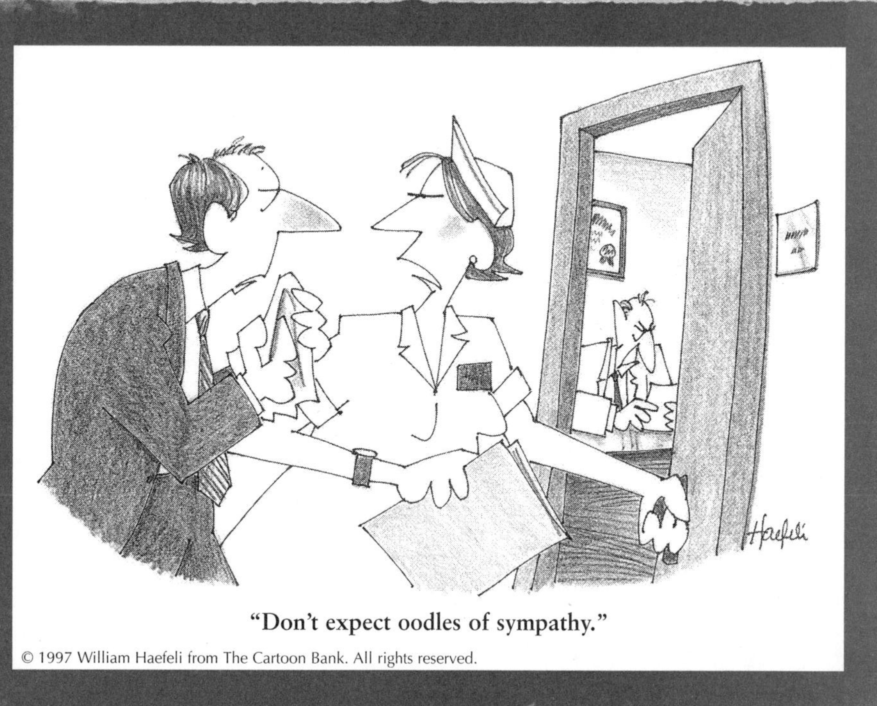
"Don't expect oodles of sympathy."

1 APPROACHING THE TOPIC

A. PREDICTING

Discuss the questions with another student. Then share your ideas with the class.

1. Look at the cartoon. A patient is about to enter a doctor's office. Why is the receptionist warning the patient not to expect "oodles," or lots, of sympathy from the doctor? What do you think will happen when the patient enters the doctor's office? Why?
2. In your opinion, how important is it to have a doctor who is sympathetic and listens to what you say?
3. There are a lot of doctor jokes in English. Why do you suppose people make jokes about doctors?

B. SHARING INFORMATION

Work in a small group. Read the following quotation about the relationship between doctors and patients. Then answer the questions.

> "Many physicians . . . may want to give you the feeling of participating in decisions without the reality of true participation. They are not used to viewing patients as partners or as equals."
>
> —Lawrence C. Horowitz, physician

1. What do you think the phrase "give you the feeling of participating in decisions" means? Do most patients make decisions with their doctors? Should they?

2. Why don't doctors view patients as "partners or as equals"? Should doctors and patients be equal? Explain.

3. How would you explain this quote in your own words?

2 PREPARING TO LISTEN

A. BACKGROUND

Read the information and do the activity that follows.

Many people believe that there is a crisis in health care in the United States today. Unlike the situation in many countries, many people in the United States do not have adequate health care because medical insurance is very expensive. Many Americans who do not have jobs that provide health insurance cannot afford to buy insurance themselves.

Another problem is the quality of health care. Although Americans spend far more on health care than people in most Western countries do, many patients are not satisfied with the treatment they receive. They often feel that the quality of medical care they receive depends on how much and what kind of insurance they have.

Health care has become a big business. Now that corporations run large health maintenance organizations (HMOs), many patients feel that money and technology have replaced the relationships they used to have with their doctor. They feel that human interaction is essential to the doctor-patient relationship and that it is being lost today.

Work in a small group. Read the chart, which lists a doctor's responsibilities, and indicate how important you think each one is by checking the appropriate box. Then discuss your answers.

IT IS IMPORTANT FOR A DOCTOR TO:	VERY IMPORTANT	SOMEWHAT IMPORTANT	NOT IMPORTANT
1. make patients feel comfortable			
2. diagnose and treat illness skillfully			
3. have polite, helpful nurses and secretaries			
4. have a comfortable waiting room, exam room, and office			
5. clearly explain diagnosis and treatment to patients			
6. ask patients what kind of treatment they prefer and try to adjust treatment to fit patients' requests			
7. be available when the office is closed			
8. be sensitive to the cost of health care			
9. talk to other doctors who are also involved in a patient's care			

B. VOCABULARY FOR COMPREHENSION

❶ *Complete the sentences with the correct word or phrase from the list. The first one has been done for you.*

adverse reaction	dying breed	long for
anxieties	earmarks	rough and tumble
array	healing	specialist
chief complaint	hospitalization	symptoms
critical	inefficient	trivial
diagnosis		

1. Patience, education, and the ability to sympathize with a patient are just some of the ____earmarks____ of a good doctor.
2. Some ________________ of a cold are runny nose, headache, and fever.
3. It seems that fewer and fewer doctors are prepared to listen carefully to their patients. Many experts worry that our ideal doctors are a(n) ________________ that will soon no longer exist.
4. Doctors prescribe medicine to treat illness, but ________________ a patient takes more than medicine. It also takes communication and sensitivity.
5. Studies have shown that patients really ________________ a chance to explain their problems in detail. They have a strong desire to ask questions and express their concerns.
6. Doctors gather information from various tests and from an interview with the patient about the patient's history. They use the information to make a(n) ________________.
7. If there is a problem that the doctor cannot solve, the patient might be referred to a(n) ________________, another doctor who has more training in a particular area.

8. When prescribing medicine, doctors try to avoid creating new problems. For example, the patient might have a(n) ________________ to a particular medicine, so doctors often ask about a patient's allergies and other medications being taken.

9. Many illnesses can be treated by a doctor in the office. Some are more serious and require ________________.

10. If you have a headache, go to a pharmacy. You'll find a shelf full of remedies, a whole ________________ of products that can be used to treat your problem.

11. The doctor's task is to listen to the patient's ________________, or main concern. However, the real problem might be something the patient is completely unaware of.

12. Some people think that the health care system is costly and ________________. It requires too much money and too much time.

13. Many complaints are not serious, but actually ________________. However, the doctor still has an important role: to calm patients and give them some peace of mind.

14. Some people go to the doctor when they don't really need to. They have minor aches and pains that are part of the ________________ of everyday living.

15. Most patients think that a doctor's ability to give them information is ________________ to a good doctor-patient relationship. Though patients think this is vital, many doctors don't inform them adequately.

16. When people are sick, they often worry. Patients bring to the doctor's office not only physical illnesses, but a lot of ________________, too.

❷ *Match the words and expressions on the left with a definition or synonym on the right. Write the appropriate letter in the blank. Then compare your answers with those of another student.*

_____	1. adverse reaction	a. difficulties and accidents
_____	2. anxieties	b. curing an illness
_____	3. array	c. group or collection
_____	4. chief complaint	d. medical finding or conclusion
_____	5. critical	e. most serious problem or concern
_____	6. diagnosis	f. negative physical response
_____	7. dying breed	g. doesn't produce good results quickly
_____	8. earmarks	h. not serious or important
_____	9. healing	i. old-fashioned; a type that is disappearing
_____	10. hospitalization	j. physical signs of illness
_____	11. inefficient	k. identifying features; signs
_____	12. long for	l. someone who works in a specific area
_____	13. rough and tumble	m. a stay in the hospital
_____	14. specialist	n. very important
_____	15. symptoms	o. want very much
_____	16. trivial	p. worries

3 LISTENING ONE: Is Healing a Lost Art?

A. INTRODUCING THE TOPIC

You will hear an unrehearsed radio conversation with Dr. Bernard Lown, author of *The Lost Art of Healing*. He is interviewed by Christopher Lydon, host of *The Connection*, a Boston radio show.

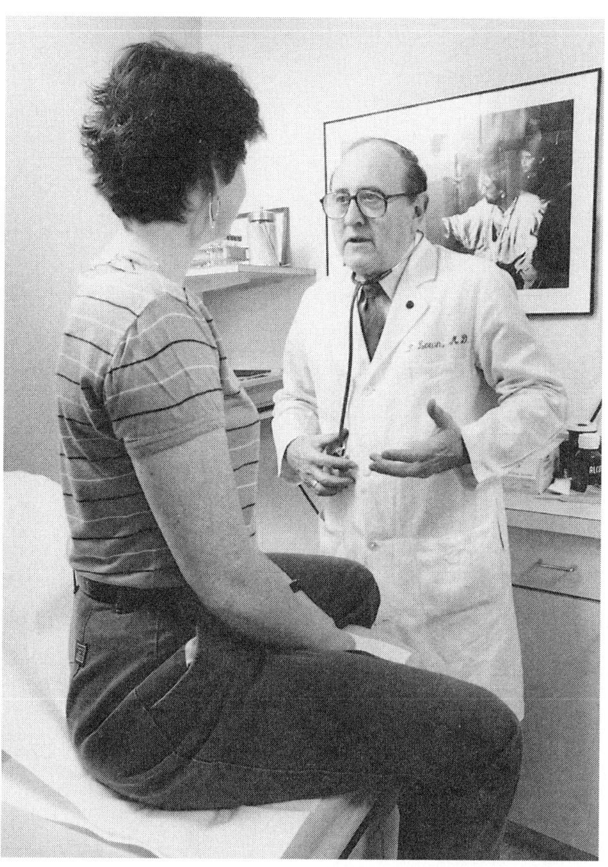

Born in Lithuania, Dr. Lown was trained in the United States at Johns Hopkins University School of Medicine. He accepted the Nobel Peace Prize in 1985 for the International Physicians for the Prevention of Nuclear War.

Listen to a comment by Dr. Bernard Lown about "earmarks . . . of trouble" in the doctor-patient relationship. Then discuss the following questions with another student.

1. According to Dr. Lown, what behavior on the part of the doctor gives patients a bad impression?

2. What do you think Dr. Lown will say are the earmarks, or signs, of a good doctor-patient relationship? Write down your predictions, then compare them to what Dr. Lown says in Listening One.

____

____

____

____

____

B. LISTENING FOR MAIN IDEAS

Read the pairs of sentences. Then listen to the interview. As you listen, check the sentence in each pair that best summarizes the main ideas of the interview.

1. ____ **a.** The doctor-patient relationship is in danger because of too little human contact.

   ____ **b.** The doctor-patient relationship is in danger because of too much machinery.

2. ____ **a.** The doctor-patient relationship can and must be saved.

   ____ **b.** The medical system can and must be saved.

3. ____ **a.** Taking a patient's history takes too much time.

   ____ **b.** Taking a patient's history helps a doctor.

4. ____ **a.** The most valuable information about patients comes from listening.

   ____ **b.** The most valuable information about patients comes from examinations and lab tests.

5. ____ **a.** Insurance companies allow less than fifteen minutes to take a patient's history.

   ____ **b.** Insurance companies think listening to a patient is inefficient and costly, but in fact it is efficient.

6. ____ **a.** Many patients go to the doctor with trivial complaints.

   ____ **b.** More patients should ask their doctors about trivial problems.

7. ____ **a.** Tension and anxiety cause an array of medical problems.

   ____ **b.** Not seeing a doctor causes an array of medical problems.

8. ____ **a.** Some doctors today don't listen to patients enough.

   ____ **b.** Some doctors today don't understand their patients' symptoms.

C. LISTENING FOR DETAILS

Read the statements below. Listen to the interview again. Then circle the best answer. Compare your answers with those of another student.

1. Dr. Bernard Lown believes that curing and healing ______ the same thing.

   a. are b. are not

2. The medical crisis began when ______.

   a. doctors distanced themselves from patients b. too many specialists became involved

3. People long for doctors to ______.

   a. focus on their illness b. see them as a whole person

4. Listening to patients is ______.

   a. easy b. difficult

5. ______ percent of a doctor's valuable information comes from listening.

   a. Fifty b. Seventy-five

6. ______ percent of a doctor's valuable information comes from modern medical technology.

   a. Five b. Twenty-five

7. Good listening by doctors will decrease the use of drugs that cause ______.

   a. medical costs to rise b. adverse reactions and hospitalizations

8. Dr. Lown quotes Norman Cousins as saying that "Americans think they're going to live forever until they get a cold, and then they think they'll ______."

   a. be dead within the next ten minutes b. need hospitalization

9. These days, most doctors don't have enough ______.

   a. time b. technology and equipment

10. In the old days, family members used ______ to help cure illness.
    a. chicken soup
    b. hot tea

11. Doctors today don't listen to patients because ______.
    a. they are not trained or rewarded for it
    b. their patients don't ask them to listen

12. Dr. Lown describes himself as ______.
    a. an incurably sick man
    b. an optimist

13. The most important quality for a doctor to have is ______.
    a. concern for patients
    b. medical knowledge

D. LISTENING BETWEEN THE LINES

Read the following questions. Listen to each excerpt from the interview. Write short answers to the questions on a separate piece of paper. Next, discuss your answers with a partner. Then discuss your answers with the class.

Excerpt One

1. What is the interviewer's attitude toward the doctor-patient relationship?
2. How does his choice of words reflect this attitude?

Excerpt Two

1. What is the interviewer's attitude toward machinery in medicine?
2. How do his tone of voice and choice of words reflect this attitude?

Excerpt Three

1. Dr. Lown quotes the writer Norman Cousins. How does Norman Cousins describe Americans' attitudes toward health?
2. Why does Dr. Lown quote Norman Cousins?

Excerpt Four

1. According to Dr. Lown, what change in American society has affected people's health?
2. How does Dr. Lown feel about that change? How do his tone of voice and choice of words reflect that attitude?

4 LISTENING TWO: *Body Talk*–A Call-In Show

A. EXPANDING THE TOPIC

❶ *Listen to this excerpt from a radio call-in show,* Body Talk. *Three callers describe the problems they have had with medical treatment in the past. As you listen, take notes on what they say. Then compare your notes with those of another student.*

	WHAT MEDICAL PROBLEM DID THIS PERSON HAVE?	HOW DID THE DOCTOR TREAT THIS PATIENT?	WAS THE EXPERIENCE SATISFACTORY?	DID THE PATIENT TRY AN ALTERNATIVE TREATMENT?	WAS THIS TREATMENT SUCCESSFUL?
Shelley Travers					
Linda Jenkins					
Ray Ishwood					

❷ *If you had a medical problem, would you call a doctor on a radio call-in show? Explain.*

❸ *Work with a partner. Discuss an experience you or a family member has had with a doctor. Was it a negative or positive experience? If negative, how could the experience have been better?*

B. LINKING LISTENINGS ONE AND TWO

❶ *Work with a partner. Plan a doctor-patient role play. After you read the instructions, take a few minutes to think about what you are going to say, and create a dialogue. Try to use the ideas and vocabulary from the listenings.*

Student A: You are one of the patients who called Body Talk *in Listening Two. Tell Dr. Ideal about your problem. When the doctor asks you questions, use your imagination and add details about your complaint.*

Patients

Shelley Travers, a secretary who suffers from back pain

Linda Jenkins, a person who has a large wart on her foot

Ray Ishwood, an elderly person with arthritis

Student B: You are Dr. Ideal. Take time to listen to your patient. Ask lots of questions so that you can make an accurate diagnosis.

❷ *In a small group, discuss the following questions.*

1. Should doctors give patients all the information about their conditions, even when the news is bad?
2. Traditionally, U.S. insurance companies have not paid for alternative treatments such as acupuncture,[1] herbal remedies, and chiropractic.[2] Do you think they should?
3. Many people think new doctors should be trained to be polite and sensitive toward their patients. How could this be done?

---

[1] *Acupuncture:* a Chinese medical practice in which illness is treated by the insertion of needles in specific places on the body.

[2] *Chiropractic:* a method of treatment by which the segments of a person's spine are adjusted.

5 REVIEWING LANGUAGE

A. EXPLORING VOCABULARY: Pronouncing Elongated Stressed Syllables

You may find that sometimes your English pronunciation is not easy to understand, even when you pronounce each sound carefully and correctly. This may happen because you are not **elongating**, or holding, the stressed syllable. In other words, native English speakers hold the stressed syllables in a word.

❶ *Listen to the words in the list below. For each word, underline the syllable that the speaker holds longer than others. The first one has been done for you. Then listen again and repeat aloud after the speaker, taking care to hold the stressed syllable.*

1. al<u>ter</u>native
2. acupuncturist
3. intensive
4. diagnosis
5. symptoms
6. medical
7. educated
8. trivial
9. anxieties
10. remedies
11. chiropractor
12. interesting
13. specialist
14. embarrassing
15. reaction
16. natural
17. ailments
18. allergies
19. physician
20. injections

❷ *Form two teams to play this pronunciation game: What's the Word? Then read the rules and scoring procedures. The team with the most points wins.*

Rules: Someone from Team A chooses a word from Exercise 1 and writes it down for his or her team members to see. The team quietly discusses five clues to describe the meaning of the word without saying the word. One by one, the members of Team A give the clues to Team B. Team B tries to guess the secret word.

Then, reverse roles and Team B chooses a word from Exercise 1. Reverse roles for each new word.

Scoring: Each team starts with 30 points.

For each wrong answer, the team loses a point.

For each word pronounced with the wrong stress, the team loses another point.

The chart below shows how the two teams would discuss and guess the secret word *acupuncturist*.

WHAT'S THE WORD?

Team A	Team B
Clue 1: This is a person.	Physician?
No, that's not the word. You lose one point. **Clue 2:** This person practices a special kind of medicine.	Specialist?
No. You lose another point. **Clue 3:** This person uses needles.	Acupuncturist!
Yes, that's it, but you didn't pronounce it right. You have lost 3 points in total.	

SCORES

Team A	Team B

B. WORKING WITH WORDS

Work in groups of four. Read aloud the panel discussion about health care. Fill in the blanks with the correct word or phrase from the list below. Use an appropriate tone of voice for each role.

acupuncture	chief complaint	put a premium on
ailments	diagnosis	revolt
allay	hospitalization	tend to
alternative	long for	treatment
array		

HMOs: Helping or Hurting?

Moderator: In recent years, medical costs have been rising at an alarming rate. Mathematical predictions showed that if costs had continued to rise at the same rate for forty years, medical costs would have become higher than the entire U.S. gross national product.[1] As part of a general (1) ________, patients, employers, and politicians turned to HMOs (health maintenance organizations) to keep costs down. An HMO usually requires that the patient see only certain doctors. Those doctors must agree to obey the HMO rules regarding treatments and tests. HMOs are now very successful at controlling medical costs in the United States, but patients, doctors, and employers have an (2) ________ of complaints about the new system. Some people even (3) ________ the old system, in which they could choose any doctor they liked and doctors could provide any service they thought necessary. Let's start with Dr. Gruber. What's your (4) ________ about the new managed care system?

Dr. Robert Gruber: I want to do what's right for my patients, but I am limited by the HMO rules. For instance, to make a (5) ________ I sometimes need to run expensive tests, but I have to argue for approval from an HMO administrator who knows nothing about my patient's (6) ________ or about medicine. When I prescribe a treatment I have to do the same thing—argue for approval with some businessperson. And (7) ________ treatments such as (8) ________ and chiropractic, which some of my patients want, are not covered. No offense, Bill, but you know that many administrators out there don't know much or care much about medicine.

Moderator: Bill Jackson, you work for an HMO. Do you want to defend people in your profession?

Mr. Jackson: Well, I like to think I'm not that kind of administrator [laughs]. But, seriously, you have a point. The HMO I work

(continued on page 62)

[1] *Gross national product:* the total dollar value of all the goods and services produced by a country.

(continued)

for does (9) ________ keeping costs down. You know, many of these expensive tests are just not necessary. And besides, who is going to pay for them? Patients and employers have demanded that HMOs lower medical costs in this country, and that's exactly what we've done.

Patient: Can I say something about that? I had to pay more for medical care and insurance before I joined an HMO, but now I'm not so sure that changing was the right thing. I mean, I had leg surgery a few months ago, serious surgery. Do you know that because my HMO limits (10) ________, they sent me home from the hospital on the same day! I couldn't believe it!

Dr. Gruber: And that's not the worst of it. A colleague of mine was stopped by his HMO from telling a cancer patient about an expensive new (11) ________ Can you imagine? The HMO wouldn't even allow a discussion of the topic.

Bill Jackson: I agree with you there. The HMO was not acting ethically, but as I said before, not all HMOs are the same. People (12) ________ get nervous because of stories about the bad ones. We at the responsible HMOs need to (13) ________ those anxieties.

Moderator: Well, let's take a break here. Thank you all for joining us.

SKILLS FOR EXPRESSION

A. GRAMMAR: Present Unreal Conditionals

1 *Read this excerpt from another call to the* Body Talk *radio show. Then discuss the questions with a partner.*

CALLER: I believe that if education of medical students were different, doctors would be better listeners.

BILL: Why would they be better listeners?

CALLER: If they received training on how to listen to patients, they wouldn't be afraid of it. They might realize how important it is.

BILL: You're right. Training doctors to listen could make a difference.

a. According to the caller, how do doctors feel about listening to patients?

b. Is the speaker happy with the current system of medical education? Why or why not?

c. What verb form helped you answer the questions above?

FOCUS ON GRAMMAR

See Unreal Conditionals in *Focus on Grammar, High-Intermediate.*

Present Unreal Conditionals

Use the **present unreal conditional** to talk about something that is untrue, impossible, or imagined. The ***if*-clause** tells about the condition, and the **main clause** tells about the result.	If my doctor **listened** to me, she **would understand** my problem. Meaning: My doctor doesn't listen to me, so she doesn't understand my problem.
To form the present unreal conditional, use the *past form* of the verb in the *if*-clause. Use ***would*** + ***base form*** of the verb in the main clause to describe a definite result. Use ***might*** or ***could*** to describe a possible result.	If doctors **didn't request** so many medical tests, health care costs could go down. If doctors **received** better training, they **would know** how to listen. If doctors **learned** to listen, they **might avoid** requesting so many medical tests.
To make a question, use question order in the main clause. The *if*-clause is not needed if the condition is understood by the listener.	If medical education were different, **would doctors be** better listeners? Why **would they be** better doctors?
For the verb ***be,*** use ***were*** for all subjects.	If I **were** a doctor, I would listen to my patients.
You can begin the sentence with either the *if*-clause or the main clause. When writing, put a comma between the clauses in sentences that start with the *if*-clause.	**If I had a better doctor,** I would feel better. (comma) I would feel better **if I had a better doctor.** (no comma)

❷ *Linda is unhappy with her doctor. Read the statements about her complaints. Combine the statements into one sentence using the present unreal conditional and make the necessary changes. Compare your answers with those of another student. The first one has been done for you.*

Condition	**Result**
1. My doctor's telephone line is always busy.	I can't reach her office.

If my doctor's telephone line weren't always busy, I could reach her office.

2. My doctor is in the office two days a week.	It's difficult to make an appointment with her.

____

3. She's late for my appointments.	I miss more time from work.

____

4. She rushes during my appointment.	She doesn't have time to listen to me.

____

5. My insurance doesn't pay for alternative treatments.	I can't try acupuncture.

____

6. My doctor doesn't know about alternative treatments.	She only recommends surgery.

____

❸ *Working in a small group, use the present unreal conditional to discuss the following topics. Also try to use vocabulary from the listenings.*

PART ONE

Discuss problems with the medical system in the United States. Read the list of problems. Discuss how the system could be different. Use the present unreal conditional to ask each other questions about the problems and to offer possible solutions.

Example: Doctors aren't trained to listen to patients.

STUDENT A: If doctors were trained to listen to patients, the patients would be more satisfied.

STUDENT B: I agree. I also think that medical costs would go down.

STUDENT C: Why would they go down?

STUDENT B: They'd go down because the doctors wouldn't need to give so many expensive tests.

Problems with the U.S. Medical System

1. It's easier for doctors to request medical tests than to listen to patients.
2. Medical schools don't teach doctors about alternative treatments such as acupuncture.
3. Patients don't feel comfortable talking to their doctors.
4. Patients often have to change doctors because they move, change jobs, or change health insurance.
5. Doctors don't explain things clearly to patients.
6. Insurance companies pressure doctors to spend only a short time with each patient.
7. Medical tests are often very expensive.
8. Doctors have to ask insurance companies to approve the medical treatment they recommend.
9. Medical insurance is provided by private companies, not by the government.
10. Many patients don't ask their doctors questions when they should.

PART TWO

Discuss problems with the medical system where you live. Make a list of four problems, using the present tense. Compare your list with those of the other students in your group. Then use the present unreal conditional to discuss how the medical systems could be different.

Problems with the Medical System in ______________________

1. ______________________________
2. ______________________________
3. ______________________________
4. ______________________________

B. STYLE: Interrupting Politely to Ask Questions

At times it is important to interrupt a speaker to ask a question about something that you did not hear or understand. For example, in Listening Two, at times the speaker doesn't speak clearly or can't be heard because of background noise, so the host interrupts. At one point the host says, "Sorry to interrupt you, Linda. What did you say?"

Here are some expressions that can be used to **interrupt a speaker**:

- I'm sorry to interrupt you. What did you say?
- Umm, excuse me. Do you mean . . .
- Sorry, could you repeat that?
- Wait a minute. I didn't catch that.
- Sorry, what was that?
- I didn't hear you. What was that?

Work in pairs and do the following exercise. Take turns listening and interrupting, using the expressions from the box.

Student A: Cover the right-hand column, and tell your partner about the medical problem listed below. As you are speaking, your partner will interrupt to ask questions.

Student B: Cover the left-hand column, and begin to listen to your partner's problem. Politely interrupt your partner to ask a question or to ask him or her to repeat something you didn't understand.

Student A	Student B
1. I had a terrible earache. The doctor said I had <u>otitis media</u>, but not a serious case. Anyway, he prescribed some ear drops. (NOTE: Otitis media is an infection of the ear canal.)	**1.** Sorry, could you repeat that?
2. When I had a bad cold, I went to the health food store. The clerk told me to try <u>echinacea</u> [eh-kin-ee-sha]. She told me that it would help me feel better. (NOTE: Echinacea is a herbal remedy.)	**2.** (Choose an expression.)

Student A	**Student B**
3. I get a lot of nosebleeds. It may be an <u>old wives' tale</u>, but I always do what my mother told me—lean back and put a coin on my forehead. It seems to work fine. (NOTE: An old wives' tale is folklore. It may or may not be true.)	3.
4. (Your own idea)	4.

Now switch roles.

Student B	**Student A**
5. I've heard that drinking a glass of red wine every day can cut down on your risk of <u>cardiac arrest</u>. Anyway, I'm not sure what I think about that, but it seems like a good remedy. (NOTE: Cardiac arrest is the same thing as a heart attack.)	5.
6. I heard about some new pills that contain a strong <u>stimulant</u> to reduce your appetite. I'm overweight, so I'm thinking of trying them. (NOTE: A stimulant is a chemical that affects your energy level.)	6.
7. (Your own idea)	7.

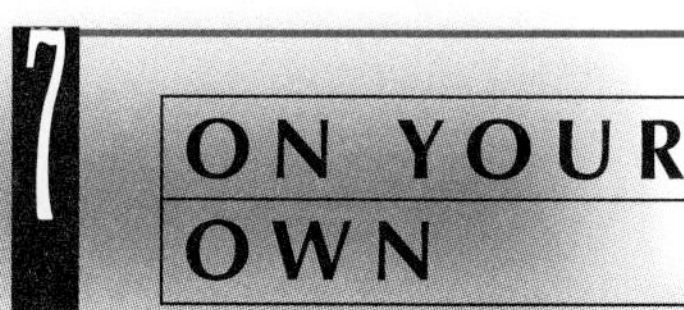

7 ON YOUR OWN

A. SPEAKING TOPICS: Paraphrasing Ideas about the Doctor-Patient Relationship

❶ *Form three groups, one for each set of quotations below and on page 68. Choose one set of quotations for your group to work on. Read the quotations. Paraphrase the ideas they present, and discuss them.*

Set A

"May I never forget that the patient is a fellow creature in pain. May I never consider him merely a vessel of disease."

—Maimonides, ancient philosopher and physician

"What would please me most would be a doctor who enjoyed me. I want to be a good story for him. . . . If a patient expects a doctor to be interested in him, he ought to try to be interesting."

—Anatole Broyard, essayist

Set B

"It's supposed to be a secret, but I'll tell you anyway. We doctors do nothing; we only encourage the doctor within."

—Dr. Albert Schweitzer, humanitarian, physician, Nobel Peace Prize winner

"Americans think they are going to live forever until they get a cold. Then they think they'll be dead within the next ten minutes."

—Norman Cousins, writer

Set C

"My husband just changed doctors. The first one had no TV in his waiting room."

"It is almost impossible to find a doctor who is poor, even though there are many poor doctors."

"Doctor, my wife's got laryngitis. What can she take that will clear it up in a year or two?"

—old doctor jokes

❷ *Present your paraphrases and opinions to the class. As you listen to the other groups present their paraphrases, interrupt them to ask questions when you do not understand or can't hear what they are saying. Use expressions from Section 6B (on page 66), and use vocabulary from the unit.*

B. FIELDWORK: An In-Depth Interview

1. Do an in-depth interview of one person. Find out about this person's relationship with his or her doctor. Working with a partner, come up with a list of questions. You may want to refer to the items in the chart on page 49. The list has been started for you.

   - The last time you went to your doctor, how long did you have to wait to get an appointment?
   - Was there a long wait in the waiting room?
   - How would you describe your relationship with your doctor?

2. Take notes as you interview the person.

3. Report to a small group. What did you learn about this person's relationship with his or her doctor? Would Dr. Lown consider this physician an ideal doctor?

UNIT 4

THE EYE OF THE STORM

1 APPROACHING THE TOPIC

A. PREDICTING

Discuss these questions with a partner.

1. **Look at the picture. What does it show? What is happening here?**
2. **What do you think "the eye of the storm" means? What do you think the unit will be about?**

B. SHARING INFORMATION

Working in small groups, do the following activities.

1. According to the *World Disasters Report* of the Red Cross and Red Crescent Societies, floods and high winds are the most frequently occurring natural disasters. Have you ever experienced a flood, high winds, an earthquake, or another natural disaster? If not, do you know someone who has? Describe the experience to your group.

2. What natural disaster are you most afraid of? Why?

3. Look at the map of the world and the list of natural disasters. Draw a line from the name of each disaster to one or two areas of the world where you think it most frequently happens. Then discuss why you think it occurs in that part of the world. Check your answers in the Answer Key.

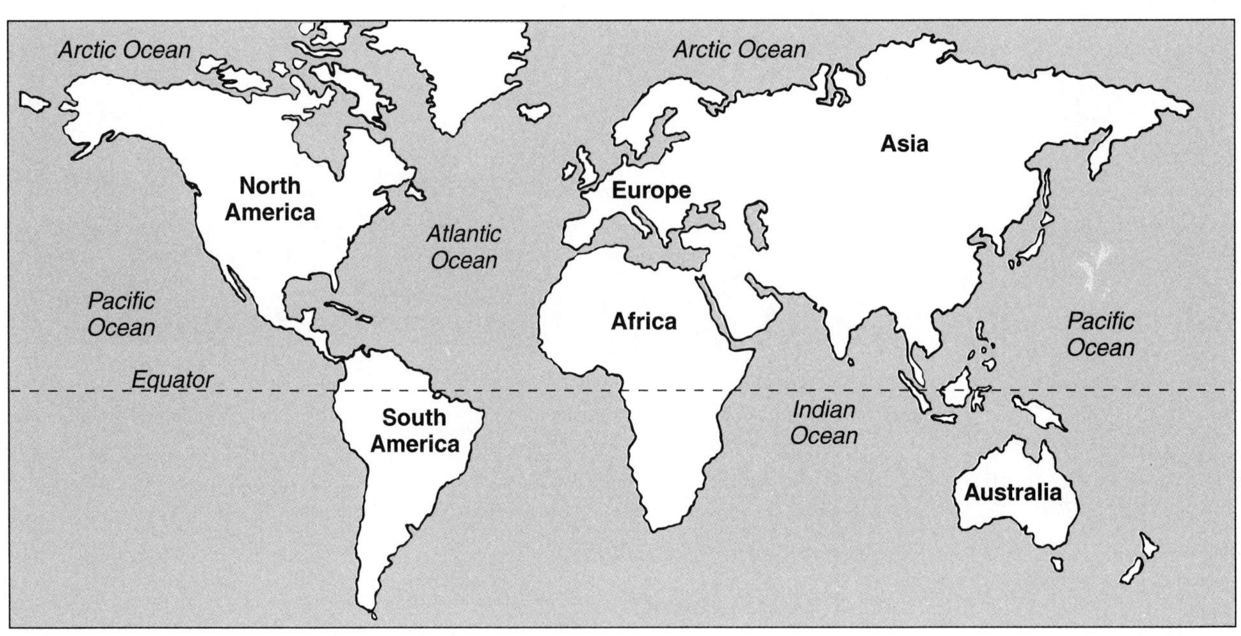

Blizzards Droughts Earthquakes Floods Hurricanes Tidal Waves Tornadoes Volcanoes

2

PREPARING TO LISTEN

A. BACKGROUND

❶ *In this unit, we will discuss hurricanes. How much do you know about this natural phenomenon? Take the quiz. Then compare your answers with those of a classmate. Check the Answer Key for the correct responses.*

WHAT DO YOU KNOW ABOUT HURRICANES?

1. Hurricanes are caused by ______.

   a. water vapor and heat energy **b.** lightning and wind **c.** earthquakes and high waves

2. In the northern hemisphere, hurricanes rotate ______.

   a. clockwise **b.** counterclockwise **c.** in both directions

3. Hurricanes are also known as ______.

   a. tsunamis **b.** tornadoes **c.** cyclones

4. In a hurricane, the most violent weather is ______.

   a. in the center, or "eye" **b.** just outside the eye **c.** in the area farthest away from the eye

5. A hurricane can be up to ______ miles wide.

   a. 20–50 **b.** 100–200 **c.** 400–600

6. When people die in a hurricane, it is usually because of ______.

   a. strong winds **b.** water **c.** electrocution

7. One of the deadliest hurricanes ever to hit the United States killed ______ people.

   a. 600 **b.** 6,000 **c.** 60,000

8. Hurricanes can cause damage ______.

   a. along the coast **b.** up to 10 miles inland **c.** over 100 miles inland

9. The most expensive hurricane in U.S. history, Hurricane Andrew, caused ______ dollars' worth of damage.

   a. 25 thousand b. 25 million c. 25 billion

10. As they move inland, hurricanes tend to ______.

   a. lose their strength b. become stronger c. increase in speed

❷ *Meteorologists (scientists who study the weather) are often able to predict a natural disaster. If they are sure that it will occur, they may urge residents in certain areas to evacuate immediately. Here is a list of some important items that you might take with you if you were told to leave your house. Working with a partner, discuss why the items might be needed. If you could only take three items, which ones would you choose? Circle them. Then discuss the reasons for your choices with the class.*

Item	**Reasons Why This Item Might Be Necessary**
flashlight	______________
battery-powered radio	______________
lamp	______________
matches	______________
plastic garbage bags	______________
fire extinguishers	______________
scissors	______________
change of clothes	______________
rain gear (coat, hat, boots)	______________
clock	______________
other (your own ideas)	______________

B. VOCABULARY FOR COMPREHENSION

Read the following story. Then match each underlined word with its definition in the list that follows each part.

The Hurricane of 1938

The great hurricane of September 1938 began in the Atlantic Ocean, southeast of Florida. Residents on the southern (1) coast, nervous at first, relaxed when the storm turned north and (2) inland, away from the shore. No one realized that the storm would soon pick up great speed and head toward the Northeast and New England. In 1938, meteorologists did not have the (3) sophisticated technology they do today. There were few (4) reconnaissance airplanes looking for storm systems, and there were no weather (5) satellites in space to send information back to Earth. (6) Radar was not yet being used to locate storm systems from the ground. Residents of the Northeast had no idea of the nightmare to come, but they soon learned just how (7) vulnerable they were.

The morning of the hurricane, the weather was (8) deceptively pleasant, though a bit windy, on Long Island, New York. Some beachside residents telephoned friends who lived inland and invited them to come and watch the huge waves that were beginning to roll in from the Atlantic. People sat on their porches and enjoyed the view. However, by mid-afternoon the sky had grown dark, and violent winds began to blow with such (9) intensity that light garden furniture sailed through the air and pieces of houses began to break off and fly away. People watched as a thick wall of clouds about forty feet high came toward shore. As it came closer, they realized it wasn't clouds at all; it was water!

(continued on page 74)

_____ information-gathering
_____ strength
_____ easily hurt
_____ radio waves to find the position of things
_____ seemingly, but not in fact
_____ the seashore; land next to the ocean
_____ complicated; highly developed
_____ away from the seashore
_____ objects that circle the Earth

Hurricane *(continued from page 73)*

Because there was little or no warning of the hurricane, people didn't (10) panic, but remained calm until disaster struck. When the hurricane hit the shore, some houses were suddenly under thirty feet of water. Some of the homes blew up; others flew into the air and crashed back into the water. In the city of Providence, Rhode Island, office workers later reported looking outside at the street, which was suddenly flooded. They saw desks, cars and toys (11) floating down the street, and they watched helplessly as people floated by, too.

The storm knocked over telephone and electricity poles, creating a power (12) outage that cut off communication. Many of the people had not received warnings to (13) evacuate, so they stayed in their homes until it was too late. Even those who had prepared for emergencies by (14) stocking up on food, water, and other (15) provisions couldn't save their homes or, in some cases, their lives. By the time its terrible work was finished, the hurricane of 1938 had left 600 people dead and 60,000 more (16) dislocated.

_____ move from a dangerous place

_____ saving or buying extra amounts for later use

_____ moved from one's normal place or home

_____ supplies

_____ feel a sudden fear or anxiety

_____ staying on the surface of water

_____ failure (usually electrical)

3 LISTENING ONE: Preparing for a Hurricane

A. INTRODUCING THE TOPIC

You will hear a radio report about preparing for a hurricane in southern Florida. Listen to the first part of the report. The radio's reception is poor, so you can't hear the end of the sentences. Read and listen to the beginning of the sentences. Then guess how to complete them. Write the end of the sentences in the blanks.

1. The sky is clear blue, and the ocean is deceptively calm here in Pitsea Beach in southern Florida. It's the kind of day when you would expect

____

____

2. But the beaches are ____

____

3. Traveling inland, though, you'll find a totally different mood. Parking spaces ____

____

4. . . . and there are long lines at ____

____

5. You see, despite the calm weather now, the citizens of Pitsea Beach are

____

____

B. LISTENING FOR MAIN IDEAS

Read the list of topics. Listen to the radio report. Number the topics in the order you hear them. The first one has been done for you.

____ a resident who almost lost her house

____ a resident who is not evacuating

____ a tourist who is scared

____ advice for tourists

____ how hurricane forecasts are made

____ supplies that people should buy

__1__ the mood in Pitsea Beach, Florida

____ the weather report

C. LISTENING FOR DETAILS

Read the sentences. Listen to the report again. As you listen, circle the answer that best completes each sentence. Compare your answers with those of another student.

1. The beaches are ______.
   a. packed with tourists b. closed to the public c. silent and empty
2. Inland, it is hard to find ______.
   a. a parking space b. supplies c. food and water
3. The hurricane has already caused damage in ______.
   a. Mexico b. Florida c. the Caribbean
4. The radio stations are stressing that people should ______.
   a. use their judgment b. leave town immediately c. follow official advice
5. Sophisticated equipment helps hurricane forecasters to predict ______.
   a. the potential damage b. the hurricane's possible path c. unexpected changes in temperature
6. Hurricanes often change ______.
   a. direction or intensity b. into rainstorms c. size
7. People should take a couple of gallons of water (approximately 7 liters) per ______.
   a. day b. family c. person
8. When returning home after a hurricane hits an area, residents should ______.
   a. wear boots b bring fresh water c. take medication
9. According to the reporter, what animals might have entered the house?
   a. rats b. snakes c. fish

10. Tourists going to a coastal spot should ______.

 a. ask for their money back if there's a hurricane
 b. plan for a possible hurricane
 c. choose another place for a vacation

11. Tourists may need access to ______.

 a. extra money
 b. a reliable car
 c. alternative hotels

12. The basic advice authorities are giving the tourists is to ______.

 a. make a plan and stick to it
 b. be prepared to change plans
 c. make plans with relatives or neighbors

D. LISTENING BETWEEN THE LINES

Step 1 *Work with a partner. Listen to the excerpts from Listening One. In the left-hand column on page 78, take notes on the advice the meteorologist gives about hurricanes. Write short sentences in the spaces provided. The first one has been done for you.*

Residents return to their homes near Kissimmee, Florida, after a severe tornado passed through the area.

Step 2 *Now imagine that the meteorologist is giving advice about two other types of natural disasters: an earthquake, and one of your own choice. Would his advice be the same or different? First choose a disaster you and your partner would like to discuss from the following list:*

blizzard

tidal wave (tsunami)

flood

forest fire

drought

tornado

volcanic eruption

mudslide

other: ____________________

Fill in the third column with your choice. Look at the statements you wrote in the first column, and circle ***Same*** *or* ***Different*** *after each statement. Then, discuss why planning for a hurricane is similar to or different from planning for the other two types of disasters.*

Excerpt One: What to do if a natural disaster is forecast

Hurricane	Earthquake	______ (Your choice)
1. Listen to the authorities.	Same/Different Why?	Same/Different Why?
2. ______	Same/Different Why?	Same/Different Why?

Excerpt Two: What to do after a natural disaster

Hurricane	Earthquake	______ (Your choice)
1. ______	Same/Different Why?	Same/Different Why?
2. ______	Same/Different Why?	Same/Different Why?
3. ______	Same/Different Why?	Same/Different Why?

Excerpt Three: What to do if visiting when a natural disaster occurs

Hurricane	Earthquake	______ (Your choice)
1. ______	Same/Different Why?	Same/Different Why?
2. ______	Same/Different Why?	Same/Different Why?

LISTENING TWO: Hurricane Hunters

A. EXPANDING THE TOPIC

You will hear a report by David Chang for a Florida radio station. With the Hurricane Hunters, Chang flew into the eye of Hurricane Haley.

Read the questions. Listen to the report and take notes as you listen. Then discuss your answers with a partner.

1. What do the Hurricane Hunters do? Why?

____

____

2. What are weather conditions like on the trip?

____

____

3. What can humans do that computers cannot?

____

____

4. Why would anyone want to be a Hurricane Hunter?

____

____

B. LINKING LISTENINGS ONE AND TWO

❶ *Work in pairs. Imagine that a hurricane is two days away from the coast of Florida. It seems to be gaining in intensity, and the Hurricane Hunters have flown into the area to investigate. They will relay the information to local authorities, who will then decide how best to advise the public about safety and possible evacuation.*

Step 1

Fill in the chart with some questions the two groups might ask each other.

HURRICANE HUNTERS	LOCAL AUTHORITIES (MAYOR, POLICE, FIREFIGHTERS)
What questions might you ask the local authorities?	What questions might you ask the Hurricane Hunters?
________________	________________
________________	________________
________________	________________
________________	________________
________________	________________
________________	________________

Step 2

Student A: You are a Hurricane Hunter.

Student B: You are a local authority, for example, the mayor of a town that might be heavily hit by the hurricane.

Plan a short dialogue, asking each other questions and giving information. Then perform it for the class.

❷ *Discuss your answers to the following questions with your partner.*

1. If you had to choose, would you rather be a hurricane forecaster (working in an office) or a Hurricane Hunter (flying into hurricanes in an airplane)? What aspects of each job appeal to you, and what aspects would you dislike?

2. Have you made any plans to follow in case of an emergency, like the ones outlined in the listenings? If your home were threatened, would you evacuate or stay there to protect it? Compare your reactions to those of the people you heard in the listenings.

3. How do you react during a crisis? Do you panic or remain calm? Give examples.

5 REVIEWING LANGUAGE

A. EXPLORING LANGUAGE: Active and Passive Forms of Adjectives

Certain adjectives have both an ***active form*** and a ***passive form***. The active form, ending in ***-ing***, modifies the doer of the action. The passive form, ending in ***-ed***, modifies the receiver of the action.

Complete the sentences with the simpler active or passive form of the adjectives listed.

1. exciting, excited

a. A severe snowstorm can be an ________________ experience for someone from a warm climate.

b. My Mexican friend, who was visiting my family in Vermont one Christmas, was ________________ when he heard that a blizzard was forecast.

2. amazing, amazed

a. At first, he was ________________ that the snow could get so deep that we couldn't open the front door.

b. The speed with which the snow accumulated was ________________ to him.

3. frightening, frightened

a. Later, when the power outage made our lights go out, he started to feel ________________. I think he felt very vulnerable.

b. I admit, it was also a little ________________ when our electric heat went off and the temperature outside was below 0° Fahrenheit. However, we told my friend not to panic.

4. heartening, heartened

a. At about midnight, it was ________________ to hear the sounds of snowplows clearing the road and power company trucks repairing the electric lines.

b. We were also ________________ when the power came back on a few hours later.

5. comforting, comforted

a. Having lights and heat again was ________________. We all started to feel relieved.

b. Fortunately, we had stocked up on provisions. We were ________________ by hot coffee and a good breakfast. Then, we finally relaxed and began to enjoy the beauty of the snow.

6. surprising, surprised

a. All in all, my own reactions during that blizzard were ________________. We had all stayed in good spirits through most of the night.

b. I was ________________ when my Mexican friend said later that the blizzard had been the best experience of his U.S. visit.

B. WORKING WITH WORDS

❶ *Pronounce the words with your teacher, then match the words in the list with words in the box on page 83. The matching word may be either a* ***synonym*** *(a word with the same meaning) or an* ***antonym*** *(a word with the opposite meaning). Write the words in the appropriate column. The first two have been done for you.*

~~be depressed~~
complicated
disbelieve
dry
easily hurt
electrical
encouraging
extremely frightened
functioning
get rid of
~~honest~~
path
prediction
reassurance
stay calm
stay in your home
stoppage
supplies
unimportant

Vocabulary	Synonym	Antonym
1. be in good spirits		be depressed
2. deceptive		honest
3. evacuate		
4. flooded		
5. forecast (n.)		
6. heartening		
7. manual		
8. out of order		
9. outage		
10. panic (v.)		
11. provisions		
12. route (n.)		
13. scared stiff		
14. second-guess (v.)		
15. sophisticated		
16. stock up on		
17. vital		
18. vulnerable		
19. warning (n.)		

2 *Work in pairs. For Dialogue 1, Student A looks at page 84. Student B looks at Student Activities, page 231. For Dialogue 2, Student A looks at pages 85–86. Student B looks at Student Activities, page 232.*

DIALOGUE 1

Part One: *The dialogue on page 84 is between two people discussing the interview with the Hurricane Hunters.*

Student A: Begin the dialogue. Complete each statement with the correct word from the box. Read your statement to Student B, who will check your answer. Then listen to Student B's reply, using column 2 to check Student B's answer.

deceptive	out of order	sophisticated	vital	vulnerable

Student A: Statements to Complete	Student B: Answers
1. The people who fly into hurricanes are really brave. I would feel so _______________ in that plane.	1. panic
2. No matter how _______________ the technology on that plane is, I still think being a Hurricane Hunter is frightening work.	2. power outage
3. Wow, what a thought! If the plane's instruments were _______________, what could you do? Walk out?!	3. evacuate

Part Two: *Improvise and continue the dialogue using the words in the box. Student B starts the dialogue.*

be in good spirits	manual	second-guess
contaminated	panic	stock up on
deceptive	provisions	vital
flooded	route	warning
forecast	scared stiff	

DIALOGUE 2

Part One: *The dialogue below is between two friends who are on vacation together. They have learned that a severe storm is approaching, and they are preparing to wait out the storm in their small beach house.*

Student A: Begin the dialogue. Complete each statement with the correct word from the box. Read your statement to Student B. Then listen to Student B's reply, using column 2 to check Student B's answer.

flooded	forecast	in good spirits	provisions	route

Student A: Statements to Complete	Student B: Answers
1. OK. Let's see: I guess we have enough ______________ to last for a few days. We've got plenty of canned food. . . . Oh, what about a can opener? This electric one may not work if there's a power outage.	1. manual
2. Wow! It looks like the road is already ______________. That means the sewers might back up and contaminate the clean water supply.	2. stock up on
3. I guess we're in for quite an experience. As long as we keep our heads, we'll be fine. But I sure wish we had believed the weather ______________ when we first heard about this storm.	3. second-guess

Part Two: *Improvise and continue the dialogue using the words in the box. Student A starts the dialogue.*

contaminated	outage	sophisticated
deceptive	panic	vital
evacuate	route	vulnerable
out of order	scared stiff	warning

A. GRAMMAR: Adjective Clauses

❶ *Examine the sentences, and discuss the questions that follow with a partner.*

- The Hurricane Hunters gather vital information <u>that</u> is needed to predict the path of a hurricane.
- The eye wall, <u>which</u> is the thick layer of clouds around the hurricane's eye, can be several miles wide.

a. The underlined words refer to other words in the sentences. Which ones do they refer to?

b. What information is added to the sentences after the underlined words?

FOCUS ON GRAMMAR

See Adjective Clauses in *Focus on Grammar, High-Intermediate.*

Adjective Clauses

Adjective clauses (also called **relative clauses**) are used to identify or add information about nouns. Usually, the adjective clause directly follows the noun it refers to. These clauses are introduced by a relative pronoun, such as ***who, that, which, whose,*** or ***where.***

Use of Relative Pronouns in Adjective Clauses

Use ***who*** to refer to people. It can be used as a subject or object of the adjective clause. In spoken English, *who* is usually used instead of the more formal *whom,* even when it is the object of the adjective clause.	The people **who** live in Florida were worried about the forecast of a hurricane. The people **who** (or whom) I told you about were on vacation in Florida during the hurricane.
Use ***that*** and ***which*** to refer to places and things. They can be used as subject or object of the adjective clause.	Pitsea Beach is the town **that/which** was hit by the hurricane.
That cannot be used in a non-identifying adjective clause or after a preposition.	Pitsea Beach, **which** is in Florida, was hit by the hurricane.
Use ***whose*** to refer to possessions. It can be used as a subject or object of the adjective clause.	The residents **whose** houses were destroyed are staying at a temporary shelter.
Use ***where*** to refer to a place.	Pitsea Beach is the town **where** my friends live.

Identifying and Nonidentifying Adjective Clauses

An **identifying adjective clause** gives essential information about the noun it refers to.	Pitsea Beach is the town **where my friends live.**
In identifying adjective clauses, English speakers often delete the relative pronoun in speaking when it is the object of the verb.	He was the meteorologist (who) **the radio reporter interviewed.**
A **nonidentifying adjective clause** gives additional information about the noun it refers to. In writing, the nonidentifying adjective clause is separated from the rest of the sentence by commas.	I live in Florida, **which is often hit by hurricanes**.
In speaking, people often pause before the clause, or they use a lower tone of voice to say the words in the clause.	Pitsea Beach, **which is in Florida,** was hit by the hurricane.

❷ *Work in pairs. Read the following warning announcements to each other, filling in the blanks with relative pronouns* ***who, that, which, whose,*** *or* ***where.*** *Listen carefully to each other. Then check the answers in the Answer Key.*

WARNING 1

People (1) ________________ are in poor health or over sixty-five years of age are being advised to stay indoors as the weather reaches record temperatures. A temperature of 105°F, (2) ________________ is a record for this time of year, was reported in Chicago yesterday, and in some areas it climbed even higher. If the apartment (3) ________________ you live is not air-conditioned, you might consider staying for a few days with a neighbor (4) ________________ home is cooler. There are certain basic things (5) ________________ you can do to stay safe: drink plenty of liquids, and stay indoors!

WARNING 2

If you're one of the many people (6) _______________ car has been washed away or waterlogged by the recent flooding in the area, do not attempt to leave your house. Wait for the help of the official rescue teams, (7) _______________ will be circulating in the flooded areas in special vehicles. A special warning to children (8) _______________ might be tempted to play outside in the lakes and rivers that have formed in their streets: Don't! Water (9) _______________ has been contaminated by sewers and broken pipelines can make you sick! You are advised to stay inside. That is (10) _______________ you will be safest.

WARNING 3

The snowy conditions (11) _______________ exist throughout the Northeast have forced many people to stay indoors, and transportation is extremely limited. If you're one of the many (12) _______________ driveways and paths are under four feet of snow, relax and stay at home. Those (13) _______________ are in good health might be tempted to dig out their cars, but don't forget that people (14) _______________ are unfit can give themselves a heart attack if they do such heavy work without being physically prepared. Instead, take out the book (15) _______________ you have been planning to read lately, and don't do heavy work for (16) _______________ you are not prepared!

❸ ***Guessing Game.*** *Divide the class into two groups: A and B. Group B looks at the instructions in Student Activities, page 233.*

Step 1

Group A: Complete the adjective clauses in the sentences on page 90 and read them to Group B, one by one. Group B has ten seconds in which to identify the item you are referring to. If Group B does not understand, you should repeat the definition. After ten seconds, Group B gets a point. The team with the fewest points wins.

Example

Group A: They're the people <u>who</u> fly into the eye of a hurricane.

Group B: Hurricane Hunters.

Clues	Answers
1. It's the state ______________ the report takes place.	1. (Florida)
2. Give me the name of an item ______________ you need for an emergency.	2. (flashlight; radio)
3. It's the area ______________ includes countries like Cuba, Jamaica, and Haiti.	3. (the Caribbean)
4. They're the people ______________ are often unprepared for hurricanes because they don't live in the area.	4. (tourists)
5. They're the machines ______________ are usually out of order in a hurricane.	5. (cash machines)
6. Name a country ______________ there are many earthquakes.	6. (Japan)

Step 2

Group A: Listen to Group B. Name the item described. You have ten seconds in which to respond.

B. STYLE: Expressing Surprise and Shock

There are many ways of expressing surprise or shock. Word choice and also intonation affect how much surprise or shock you express. Here are some phrases that can be used:

Mild Surprise/Interest	Strong Surprise/Disbelief	Shock/Dismay
Really?	Wow, that's amazing!	Oh, no!
That's interesting.	That's unbelievable!	Oh, my gosh!
I didn't know that.	That's incredible!	That's terrible!
Huh!	You're joking!	That's awful!
Oh, yeah?	I can't believe it!	That's horrible!
Oh, come on!	You're pulling my leg!	

Work with a partner. Take turns reading the comments below. The other student will decide whether to respond with a comment of mild surprise, disbelief, or shock. Notice how your partner's tone of voice changes when he or she expresses disbelief or shock.

1. The summer population of coastal areas can be up to 100 times the size of the winter population.
2. After a recent hurricane, authorities found the handle of a broomstick sticking through the trunk of a tree.
3. A man in a town on the Gulf of Mexico was found clinging to a metal pipe after a hurricane. He was wearing shoes and socks, but his clothes had been torn off by the wind.
4. In April 1974, there were 148 tornadoes in the American Southwest within a period of 28 hours.
5. Near the eye of a hurricane, winds can reach up to 200 miles per hour.
6. There were 830,000 deaths from an earthquake in China in 1556, which is the highest earthquake death toll in history.
7. In 1958, a tsunami that was 1,720 feet high hit Alaska at 100 miles per hour.
8. A recent hurricane was so intense that high winds sent a plastic drinking straw through a metal street sign.
9. In a hurricane, coastal areas can get hit with waves over forty feet high.
10. Hurricane Hunters don't carry parachutes.
11. The Krakatoa Volcano eruption of 1883 was about 26 times as powerful as the largest hydrogen bomb test. It was also heard over 8% of the Earth's surface.
12. In the past, U.S. officials used only women's names for hurricanes, but now they use men's names, too.

7 ON YOUR OWN

A. SPEAKING TOPICS: A Disaster Warning Announcement

Imagine that you have just heard an emergency weather report on the radio and have been asked to make a public announcement in your school or workplace.

1. Work in pairs and create a short warning message. Choose a disaster you have read about, or another type of natural disaster you know about. Use the information and expressions you have learned in this unit. Add details of your own.

2. Deliver your announcement to the class in person, or make an audio tape and play it for the class. The announcement should tell your classmates what is happening and what they need to do.

3. Listen to the announcements of other class members. Take notes on what they say. Then discuss which announcements are the most effective, and say why.

B. FIELDWORK: Natural Disasters, Real and Imagined

WATCHING A DISASTER MOVIE

Watch a movie about a disaster, such as *Titanic* (disaster at sea), *Twister* (a tornado), or *The Towering Inferno* (a fire). Notice how people were warned, how they prepared, and how the movie made you feel. Discuss which parts of the film seemed realistic and which didn't. Discuss why disaster movies are so popular.

CONDUCTING AN INTERVIEW

If you know someone who has experienced a natural disaster, do an in-depth interview of that person. Ask what it was like before, during, and after the disaster. Take notes so you can tell the story to a small group.

UNIT 5

YOU WILL BE THIS LAND

1 APPROACHING THE TOPIC

A. PREDICTING

Look at the illustration. With a partner, discuss the following questions.

1. **This picture is a reprint of a postcard. It was first published by Co-op America, an organization that promotes a clean, healthy environment. What messages does the picture communicate?**
2. **Look at the title of the unit. What do you think the unit will be about?**

B. SHARING INFORMATION

In small groups, discuss your answers to the following questions.

1. There are many environmental problems today. The Earth and its environment are being mistreated. How are people harming the environment? Name some ways people are harming:

   a. rivers, lakes, and oceans
   b. the air
   c. forests and plants
   d. animals

2. What are some specific things that people can do to solve the environmental problems you've identified in question 1?

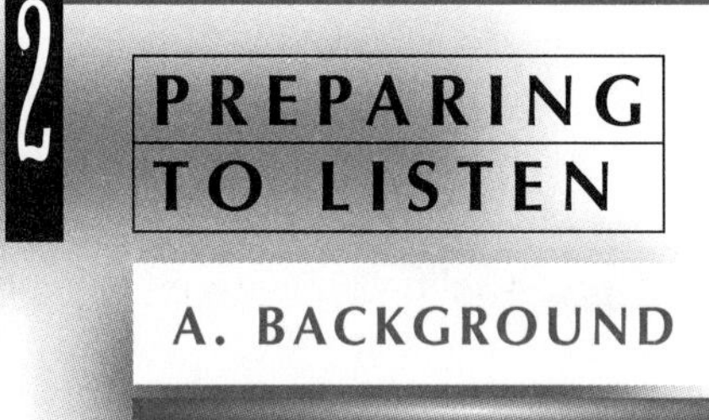

2 PREPARING TO LISTEN

A. BACKGROUND

The Bald Eagle

Read the information and discuss the questions that follow with a partner.

Native American Religion and the Environment

There are hundreds of Native American Indian tribes in North America today, each with its own religious beliefs. Yet most tribes share some beliefs and practices. For example, religious ceremonies about the relationship between people and the Earth are common. One of these is a ceremony performed before an animal is killed. People give thanks to the animal for giving its life so that people can be fed.

Because of their feeling for the Earth, many Native Americans are interested in conservation and ecology. They have both a religious and a practical interest in protecting the land. To many Native Americans, destruction of the environment means destruction of their religious values and of their way of life.

Eagles are a symbol of the Native American attitude toward nature. Eagles are large, soaring birds which are admired for their beauty and excellent hunting abilities. One type of eagle, the Bald Eagle, is a symbol of the United States which can be found on coins and postage stamps. Eagles were once common in the United States, but they have become endangered because of the effects of pollution and loss of their natural habitat. Many Americans respect the birds for their beauty and majesty. To Native Americans, however, eagles also have a religious meaning. The Pawnee Indians, for example, believe that the eagle exists to remind people of the lessons of the Creator. The Pawnee story "The Teachings of the Eagle" shows these beliefs:

> Look at the Eagle and you will see [the Creator's] teachings. Eagle has two wings and those wings are balanced in strength when it flies. In the same way, a man and a woman are balanced in strength and are two. . . .
>
> Look upon the Great Eagle's feathers. You will see that half of the feather is dark and half of it is white. Just so, we have day and night, winter and summer, sunshine and clouds. . . .
>
> As the Eagle flies, it looks in two directions. Just so, we human beings may look in two directions. We may look in the direction of good or we may look in the direction of that which is bad. We may see happiness or we may see sorrow.[1]

Thus, to the Pawnee, if people harm the eagle, they are harming a symbol sent by the Creator to teach them about life.

1. Based on what you have read, how do you think traditional Native Americans would feel about the following activities? Try to support your answer with information from the reading. How do you feel about these things?

- Raising animals for meat
- Hunting animals for meat
- Hunting animals for sport

2. What else do you know about the Native Americans of North America? Where did you learn this?

[1] Michael J. Caduto and Joseph Bruchac, *Keepers of the Animals: Native American Stories and Wildlife Activities for Children* (Colorado: Fulcrum Publishing, 1991), p. 54.

B. VOCABULARY FOR COMPREHENSION

Read the statements. Then, from the list that follows, find a word or expression that is similar in meaning to the underlined words. Write the appropriate letter in the blanks.

____ 1. As the human population grows, animals must compete with humans for land, water, and food. Unfortunately, people usually win the contest for natural resources.

____ 2. Many vegetarians don't eat meat because they don't want to take the life of an animal. They believe that killing animals is wrong.

____ 3. Each religion has sacred places where people go to worship. For example, the city of Jerusalem is sacred to Christians, Jews, and Moslems.

____ 4. Until recently, people gathered mushrooms in the wild. Now, instead of collecting wild mushrooms, people have discovered ways to grow them on farms.

____ 5. Ideally, political leaders should serve the interests of their people, but in reality they sometimes do things that do not benefit the people they represent.

____ 6. Some religions believe that a spirit occupies the body of a person until that person dies. Then the spirit is released from the body to travel to another place.

____ 7. Each person may not pollute very much, but the sum of all the pollution from all the people on Earth is a serious problem.

____ 8. Technology has added to the problem of pollution. For example, manual tasks, such as shoveling snow or washing dishes, are now performed by machines that use gas or electricity.

____ 9. When we throw garbage away, we think that it is gone forever. Actually, all our trash winds up in the environment. Our trash is buried in the earth, dumped in the water, or burned, with the smoke going into the air.

____ 10. Some farmers are trying to reduce the amount of pesticides, or poisons, they use to kill insects on their crops. They are trying organic methods to grow fruits and vegetables.

a. work for the benefit of
b. jobs done by hand
c. ends up; ends
d. harvested; collected
e. holy
f. kill
g. non-chemical ways
h. soul or mind
i. total amount
j. be rivals with

LISTENING ONE: Interview with a Medicine Priest

A. INTRODUCING THE TOPIC

You will hear an interview with David Winston, a Cherokee medicine priest, or spiritual leader. The Cherokee are a Native American tribe from the southeastern United States. David Winston talks about Cherokee beliefs regarding the environment and conservation.

Listen to an excerpt from the interview. Then discuss your answers to the questions with a partner.

David Winston refers to the Cherokee beliefs about how people should live in relation to nature. He talks about two Cherokee concepts: the Great Life and the three Laws of Nature.

1. What do you think the Great Life is?

2. What do you think could be one of the three Laws of Nature?

B. LISTENING FOR MAIN IDEAS

Listen to the entire interview. Write down the three Laws of Nature. Take notes on the examples David Winston gives to illustrate each of the three laws. Compare your answers with those of another student.

1. **First Law of Nature:** ____________________

   Example: ____________________

2. **Second Law of Nature:** ____________________

   Example: ____________________

3. **Third Law of Nature:** ____________________

   Example: ____________________

C. LISTENING FOR DETAILS

Read the statements. Then listen to the interview again. As you listen, circle the best answer for each statement. Compare your answers with those of another student.

1. The Cherokee people believe that people should try to ______ nature.
   a. understand b. live with c. compete with
2. The needs of people are ______ the needs of animals and plants.
   a. less important than b. just as important as c. more important than
3. The great Laws of Nature tell people how to live in relationship with ______.
   a. other people b. animals and plants c. everything in the world
4. Following the Second Law of Nature, one good reason for taking life is to ______.
   a. make money b. hunt for sport c. protect yourself
5. The Cherokee people believe that stones are ______.
   a. alive b. magical c. important
6. Taking the life of a plant is ______ taking the life of an animal.
   a. less important than b. the same as c. more serious than
7. One spirit fills ______.
   a. all things b. only people c. the planet Earth
8. People are affected by everything that happens ______.
   a. in their communities b. to the land c. in any part of the Great Life
9. David Winston wouldn't use an electric toothbrush because it ______.
   a. doesn't work well b. uses energy c. is made of plastic
10. "Don't pollute where we live" means don't pollute ______.
    a. our home b. our country c. the planet Earth

11. The three Laws of Nature ______.

a. are difficult to follow today **b.** don't apply to today's world **c.** are not important today

12. In applying the three Laws of Nature today, David Winston does *not* mention ______.

a. recycling **b.** never using plastic **c.** organic gardening

D. LISTENING BETWEEN THE LINES

Listen to three excerpts from the interview in which David Winston describes the three Laws of Nature. Look at the chart of actions. How acceptable would the actions be under the Laws of Nature? Rate their acceptability from 1 (very acceptable) to 4 (not acceptable) and circle your choices. Then discuss your answers with the class.

EXCERPT ONE: FIRST LAW	VERY ACCEPTABLE			NOT ACCEPTABLE
Hunt an animal for sport.	1	2	3	4
Pick flowers growing wild in the forest.	1	2	3	4
Pick tomatoes on a farm.	1	2	3	4

EXCERPT TWO: SECOND LAW	VERY ACCEPTABLE			NOT ACCEPTABLE
Clean up a polluted beach.	1	2	3	4
Put endangered animals in the zoo.	1	2	3	4
Cut down trees to build a house.	1	2	3	4

EXCERPT THREE: THIRD LAW	VERY ACCEPTABLE			NOT ACCEPTABLE
Dump garbage in the ocean.	1	2	3	4
Start a neighborhood recycling program.	1	2	3	4
Send garbage into outer space.	1	2	3	4

4 LISTENING TWO: Ndakinna—A Poem

A. EXPANDING THE TOPIC

You will hear the poem *Ndakinna* (Our Land) by poet and storyteller Joseph Bruchac of the Abnaki tribe from the northeastern United States.

❶ *In order to take care of the Earth, we have to understand it. Joseph Bruchac feels that we should understand the land in certain ways, but not in others. Listen to the poem. Decide whether Bruchac would agree or disagree with each statement below. Check* **Agree** *or* **Disagree***. Then compare your answers with those of another student.*

According to Bruchac, we should understand the land . . .

	Agree	Disagree
. . . with maps.	☐	☐
. . . with eyes like birds.	☐	☐
. . . by walking on roads.	☐	☐
. . . by walking where deer walk.	☐	☐
. . . by using all five senses.	☐	☐

❷ *Now read the poem. Fill in the words you remember. Then listen to the poem again. Fill in the missing words. Check your answers with those of your classmates.*

Ndakinna

You cannot understand
this land with ________________,
lines drawn as if earth
were an ________________ carcass[1]
cut into pieces, skinned,
though always ________________ ________________
than thrown away.

________________ this land instead
with a wind-eagle's eyes,
linked with ________________ and ________________
like sinews[2] through leather,
sewed strong to hold the ________________
to the ________________.

Do not try to know the land by ________________.
Let your ________________ instead
caress[3] the soil
in the way of deer,
whose trails ________________
the ways of least resistance.

When you feel this land
when you ________________ this land
when you hold this land as lungs hold breath
when your songs ________________ this land,
when your ears sing this land,
________________ ________________ ________________ this land.
________________ ________________ ________________ this land.

---

1 *Carcass:* dead body.
2 *Sinews:* threads made of leather.
3 *Caress:* to gently touch.

❸ *Read the statements below. Listen to the poem again. Decide whether Bruchac would agree or disagree with the statements. Write **A** for agree or **D** for disagree. Discuss your answers with a partner. Use statements from the poem to support your opinion.*

Would Bruchac agree or disagree with these statements?

____ **1.** The Earth is like a dead animal.

____ **2.** People are sometimes wasteful.

____ **3.** Rivers divide the Earth.

____ **4.** We should explore the land with all of our senses.

____ **5.** We can learn from other animals.

____ **6.** Human beings are a part of nature.

The Hudson River Valley, New York State. Many Native American tribes hunted and fished along the river's banks.

B. LINKING LISTENINGS ONE AND TWO

In a small group, discuss the following questions.

1. How do you think Joseph Bruchac would react to the Cherokee Laws of Nature that David Winston described? Give examples from the poem *Ndakinna* to support your opinion.

2. At the end of his interview, David Winston says, "The Great Life can live without us, but we can't live without the Great Life." What does the statement mean? Would Joseph Bruchac agree with it? Do you agree or disagree with it?

3. What lessons do you think we can take from the Native American beliefs about people and the environment? Which ideas do you agree or disagree with? Why?

5

REVIEWING LANGUAGE

A. EXPLORING LANGUAGE: *th* Sounds [θ] and [ð]

The English ***th*** sounds [θ] and [ð] are made by putting the tip of your tongue between your teeth. [ð] is made with the voice, as in *breathe*, while [θ] is voiceless, as in *breath*.

Be careful. Some students substitute /s/, /z/, /t/, or /d/ for the ***th*** sounds. All these substitutions are incorrect. Putting the tip of your tongue between your teeth is the key to pronouncing ***th*** correctly.

❶ *Listen to the words on the tape. You will hear only one word or term from each pair. Circle the words or term you hear. Then check your answers in the Answer Key.*

1.	three	tree	**8.**	though	dough
2.	say	they	**9.**	soothe	sued
3.	there	tear	**10.**	day	they
4.	sink	think	**11.**	bathe	bays
5.	though	so	**12.**	udder	other
6.	ladder	lather	**13.**	breeze	breathe
7.	worthy	wordy	**14.**	Zen	then

❷ *Pronounce the words on the same list with another student. Take turns checking each other for clear **th** sounds when appropriate.*

❸ *Work in pairs. First practice the words below. Then, Student B does not look at the clues. Student A reads the clues on page 104 to Student B. Student B guesses the word from the list and tells the word to Student A, using correct pronunciation. Then switch roles.*

Select from these words:

breath	theirs	this	three
Earth	there	those	throw
thanks	things	though	toothbrush
that	think	thread	within

Student A: Read the clues to your partner. Tell your partner if he or she guessed correctly. Listen for correct pronunciation, too. Answers are in parentheses.

Clues

Air in our lungs	(breath)
Not here	(there)
I believe	(think)
Nevertheless	(though)
Not that	(this)
Objects	(things)
Our planet	(Earth)
You're welcome	(thanks)

Student B: Read the clues to your partner. Tell your partner if he or she guessed correctly. Listen for correct pronunciation, too. Answers are in parentheses.

Clues

For your teeth	(toothbrush)
Opposite of catch	(throw)
Inside	(within)
Not ours	(theirs)
Two plus one	(three)
Not these	(those)
Used to sew	(thread)
Not this	(that)

4. *Listen to Bruchac's poem again while looking at the text on page 101. Underline all the words with **th** sounds. Then read the poem to another student. Pay careful attention to correct pronunciation of **th**.*

B. WORKING WITH WORDS: Word Forms

1. *Work in pairs. Each partner chooses five words from the box and looks up the missing forms in the dictionary. Share your information so both partners can complete the chart. An X means there is no common word form for this category.*

Noun	Verb	Adjective	Adverb
benefit			
1. competitor **2.**	compete		
		1. electric **2.** electrical	
		1. industrial **2.** industrialized	X
nature	X		
pollution			X
1. protection **2.**	protect	**1.** protective **2.**	
	recycle		X
spirit	X		
			wastefully

❷ *Read the paragraphs, and fill in the blanks with the appropriate form of the words from the box in Exercise 1. Each blank contains a different word form. Compare your answers with your partner's. Then circle whether you agree or disagree with the statements, and discuss the reasons why with your partner.*

1. benefit **Agree / Disagree**

In modern life, we generally think of nature as existing for the (**a**) ___benefit___ of people. However, the relationship is usually not (**b**) ___beneficial___ to nature. We (**c**) ________________ from the food, water, and air that nature offers us, without thinking about what we are giving back.

2. competition **Agree / Disagree**

Modern development forces us to have a (**a**) ________________ relationship with animals. We (**b**) ________________ for natural resources, such as clean water. Ultimately, this (**c**) ________________ is good for neither people nor animals.

3. **electricity** **Agree / Disagree**

Since the invention of (**a**) ________________, people have tried to (**b**) ________________ everything. These days, almost anything can be (**c**) ________________ run. This has greatly increased our demand for (**d**) ________________ power.

4. **industrialization** **Agree / Disagree**

With the growth of modern (**a**) ________________, pollution has increased. In addition, people in (**b**) ________________ societies don't feel connected to the Earth, so they don't see the impact of the pollution. As society continues to (**c**) ________________, the problem will get worse.

5. **nature** **Agree / Disagree**

People who live in cities don't have much connection with (**a**) ________________, and they lose their (**b**) ________________ connection to the Earth. People should try to live more (**c**) ________________ by moving out of the cities and giving up the technology of modern life.

6. **pollution** **Agree / Disagree**

Factories (**a**) ________________ the rivers by dumping their waste into the water. The (**b**) ________________ rivers run into the sea, contributing to the (**c**) ________________ in the ocean.

7. **protection** **Agree / Disagree**

We must do more to (**a**) ________________ endangered animals. We need more (**b**) ________________ laws to save animals' natural habitats. By (**c**) ________________ their environments, we will be able to save endangered animals.

8. **recycling** **Agree / Disagree**

(**a**) ________________ can be good for business, as well as for the environment. Companies can increase their profits when they (**b**) ________________. Many consumers want to buy products that are made from (**c**) ________________ materials.

9. spirit **Agree / Disagree**

Conservation is a topic that is (a) ________________ important to many Native Americans. They believe that people have a (b) ________________ connection to the Earth, and that animals, plants, rivers, and mountains all contain (c) ________________. They are right.

10. waste **Agree / Disagree**

It is easy to live less (a) ________________ in modern society. For example, don't buy things in (b) ________________ packaging. Then you don't have to throw away so much (c) ________________ each day.

6 SKILLS FOR EXPRESSION

A. GRAMMAR: Past Modals—Advisability in the Past

1 *Working with a partner, examine the excerpt from a pamphlet put out by an environmental group. Notice the underlined words, and discuss the questions that follow.*

"People have a responsibility to protect the Earth, but in the past we did not live up to that responsibility. We should have protected the Earth. We shouldn't have allowed the environment to become so polluted. We could have kept the water and air cleaner. If we had been more careful, we could've avoided a lot of the environmental problems that we have today."

a. Is the paragraph about actions in the past or present?

b. Do the sentences focus on things that were done, or on things that were not done?

c. What feeling is communicated in the paragraph?

FOCUS ON GRAMMAR

See Advisability and Obligation in the Past in *Focus on Grammar, High-Intermediate.*

Past Modals

To form a past modal, use the **modal** + ***have*** + **past participle.**	I **should have recycled** this can. **should've** (spoken form)
To express regret or blame and to talk about actions that were advisable or possible in the past, use: ***should have / (should've)*** ***could have / (could've)***	 We **should've protected** the river from pollution. (We didn't protect the river, and now we are sorry.) We **could've kept** the water cleaner. (It was possible for us to keep the water cleaner, but we did not do it.)
To make a negative statement or question, use: ***shouldn't have*** ***couldn't have*** **GRAMMAR TIP:** ***Couldn't have*** expresses past assumption, not blame or regret.	 **Shouldn't** the town **have closed** the factory? Yes, it should have. **It shouldn't have allowed** the factory to pollute the river. Town officials **couldn't have known** about the health risks. I just can't believe they knew.
In short answers, use the **modal** + ***have.*** With the verb *to be*, use the **modal** + ***have*** + ***been*** **GRAMMAR TIP:** In speech, the ***have*** in past modals is often pronounced like the word ***of:*** /shudəv/	**Should** the government **have passed** laws against pollution? Yes, it **should've.** Were you at the meeting? No, but I **should've been.**

❷ *Complete the sentences in this true story with a past form of the modals in parentheses. Then, working with a partner, read the story aloud using contractions and correct pronunciation.*

Love Canal is a small community in the state of New York. Over twenty years ago a manufacturing company disposed of its wastes in the normal way at the time: it poured chemicals into the ground.

1. At the time, the company officials ________________ (could/not/know) that the chemicals would have terrible effects many years later.

2. Workers at the company ________________ (should/not/pour) the chemicals into the ground, but they did.

Long after the company closed down, developers and the city bought the land and built new houses, despite the pollution. A school and playground were also constructed for the children in the area. The development resulted in disaster.

3. Developers ________________ (should/not/build) houses on a chemical dump, but they did.

4. City officials ________________ (should/be) very careful about selecting a place for the school and playground, but they weren't.

As time went by, the residents began to have serious illnesses more often than other people. Doctors and researchers became suspicious.

5. They felt the illnesses ________________ (could/be) related to chemicals in the environment.

6. They thought the chemicals in the ground ________________ (could/cause) the illnesses.

The town developed a strange chemical smell. The yards and gardens of some of the houses bubbled and produced strange liquids.

7. Finally, officials realized that chemical waste in the ground ________________ (could/stay) in the ground, even after twenty years. All the families of Love Canal had to leave their town and find new places to live.

❸ *Work in pairs to do the following activity.*

Step 1: *In his interview, David Winston suggested several things that people can do to take care of the Earth and live by the three Laws of Nature, even in industrialized societies. Discuss what you have done (or not done) recently to conserve energy and natural resources, and to reduce pollution.*

Step 2: *Think about your actions in the past month, and evaluate the effect they have had on the Earth. Look at the categories and the examples of things people can do, and give yourself a grade from A (excellent) to F (failed) for each category. Check* ***A*** *if you did a lot to protect the environment. Check* ***F*** *if you didn't do anything to protect the environment. Then discuss your grades. What do you feel proud of doing? What could you have done differently or better? Use the past modals* ***should've*** *and* ***could've.***

Example

A: How about conserving gasoline and oil? What grade did you give yourself?

B: I gave myself a D on this one. I've driven to school every day when I could've walked. I don't live far away. I shouldn't have been so lazy. But I could've done worse—I did walk to the grocery store!

A: I gave myself a B+. I couldn't have walked to school—I live too far away. I did use my car a few times, but maybe I should've taken the bus every day.

An Environmental Report Card

CATEGORY	YOUR GRADE				
Conserving Energy and Natural Resources	A	B	C	D	F
Gasoline and oil	☐	☐	☐	☐	☐
• avoid using car when possible • keep heat low in home					
Water	☐	☐	☐	☐	☐
• don't run faucet when brushing teeth or doing dishes • conserve water when showering					
Electricity	☐	☐	☐	☐	☐
• turn off lights when you're not in the room • run power appliances only when necessary					
Animal / plant life	☐	☐	☐	☐	☐
• avoid wasting food • avoid littering					

CATEGORY	YOUR GRADE				
Reducing Pollution	A	B	C	D	F
In the air	❑	❑	❑	❑	❑
• keep car in good condition					
On land	❑	❑	❑	❑	❑
• follow recycling rules					
• make efforts to buy recycled products					
In the water	❑	❑	❑	❑	❑
• don't pour chemicals and chlorine cleaners down the drains					

B. STYLE: Asking For and Giving Examples

When talking with David Winston, the interviewer asked him to give examples of the ideas he was explaining. It is often easier to understand a speaker's ideas when he or she gives examples to illustrate a point. Also, the listener can request examples to clarify an idea.

To ask for examples:	**To give examples:**
Could you explain in more detail?	For example,
Could you give me an example?	For instance,
Such as?	Such as
Could you tell me what you mean?	

Example

A: My government is getting more and more concerned about protecting the environment.

B: Could you tell me what you mean?

A: Well, there are a lot of new recycling programs.

B: Such as?

A: For example, a factory that recycles tires has just opened.

In this conversation, the first speaker makes a general statement, and the second speaker asks for examples to illustrate the first speaker's point.

Work in small groups. Tell each other about specific programs or policies that your government or community has initiated. As each student describes the program, the other students should ask for specific examples, using expressions from the box above.

Example

A: Peter, what about your national government? How much does it do to protect the environment?

B: Quite a bit, I think.

A: Can you give us an example?

B: Well, we have a national recycling program. There's publicity about it on TV, in schools, and in magazines, and most people cooperate.

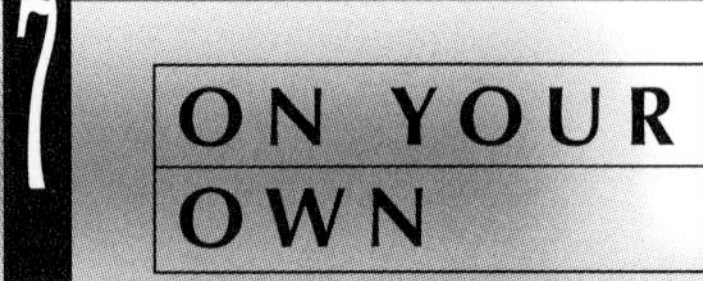

7 ON YOUR OWN

A. SPEAKING TOPICS: Role Playing and Reacting to Nature

1 *Read about the situation and the roles below. Then follow the procedure for the role play.*

SITUATION

The Acme Paper Company wants to build a paper-making factory on some Native American land in Washington state. However, the company does not have a good history with the Native Americans. In the past, the paper company built a similar factory near Native American land in another part of the country. The factory caused a lot of environmental problems. Trees were cut, and the river and land were polluted. The factory also harmed the culture of the Native American tribe. Sacred animals and plants were destroyed, so the tribe members could not follow their traditional religious practices. In addition, the company hired workers from other parts of the country to work in the factory, instead of hiring people from the tribe. The tribe members were unemployed, and many new people moved into the area and built houses and stores. In the end, many members of the tribe moved away from the area.

Role 1: Factory Representative

You believe this land is the best place to build the company's factory. It is close to the forest where the company will cut down the trees to make paper. It is also near a river which can provide water for the factory. However, this time the company does not want to repeat its mistakes. It wants to work with the tribe to build a factory that will not destroy the environment or harm the tribal culture.

Role 2: Medicine Priest

You are opposed to the factory. You don't trust the paper company. You feel that the land, trees, and river are sacred and should not be harmed. You feel that the factory representative doesn't understand your tribe's religious beliefs. You are also worried that some members of your tribe are forgetting their traditional ways and care more about earning money than protecting the Earth.

Role 3: Unemployed Tribe Member

You are in favor of the factory, but only if it is built in an environmentally safe way and if it employs tribal members. You feel that if the factory is not built, many people will move away because they don't have jobs. You think that the factory can be built in a way that will protect the environment.

TASK

The factory representative, the medicine priest, and the unemployed tribe member meet together. They discuss what was wrong with the way the factory was built before, and how the company and the tribe can compromise to build a new factory.

PROCEDURE

1. Choose one of the three roles to play. An equal number of students should choose each role.

2. Meet with the other students who will be playing the *same* role. Discuss the character. Brainstorm ideas about what you will say in the role play. Use information from the unit, and think of new ways to solve the problem.

3. Now, work in new groups of three, with each student playing one of the three roles. Role play a meeting to discuss the proposal for the paper factory. Each role (person) should discuss his or her point of view. Use past modals (see Section 6A) to discuss past mistakes made by the company. Use examples (see Section 6B) to make your points clearer. Try to reach a compromise that everyone can live with.

4. Meet as a class. Discuss how each person felt playing his or her role. Compare the different solutions each group came up with.

❷ *Find a special picture or photograph that shows the beauty of the Earth, or use the photograph "Hudson Valley Mythic" on page 102. Work with a partner.*

1. List the images you see in the picture.
2. Describe the way this picture makes you feel, or explain the memories it brings back to you.
3. Write a poem about the picture. If you wish, you can begin in the same way as Bruchac: "You cannot understand this land . . ." or "See this land . . .".
4. Read or recite your poem to the class, and show them the picture.

❸ *Find a short poem about nature. It could be by a Native American poet or by a poet from a different background. Read the poem and analyze it. Decide what message the author is giving about nature. Then recite the poem for the class, and explain the meaning.*

B. FIELDWORK: Environmental Issues and Indigenous Groups*

Like the Native Americans in North America, indigenous groups in other parts of the world have also become involved in the environmental movement. For example, the Maori (New Zealand), the Sami (Scandinavia), the Aleuts (Alaska), the Aborigine (Australia), and the Kayapó (Brazil) have become involved in environmental issues in their native lands.

With another student, choose an environmental problem that affects indigenous groups in different regions of the world. Go to the library, look on the Internet, or speak to a local representative of an indigenous environmental group. Find answers to the following questions:

- How does the environmental problem affect the indigenous group?
- What is the group doing to solve the problem?
- Is the group working with other environmental groups? In what way?

Present your findings to the class. Then discuss the similarities and differences in the ways indigenous people are affected by, and solve, environmental problems around the world.

---

* *Indigenous groups:* people who were first to live in a land; natives.

UNIT 6

It's Better to Give Than to Receive

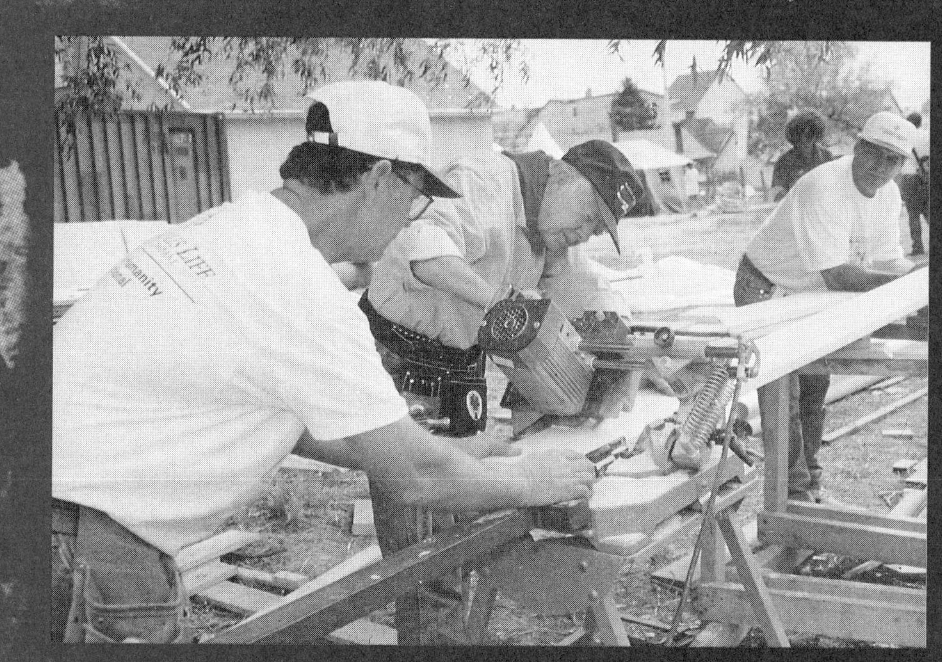

Former president Jimmy Carter (center) working for Habitat for Humanity, an organization that builds houses for poor people. Volunteers help build the houses for no pay, and local businesses donate the construction materials.

1 APPROACHING THE TOPIC

A. PREDICTING

Discuss these questions with a partner. Then share your ideas with the class.

1. Look at the photo and read the caption. Why do you think a former president of the United States does construction work to help build houses for poor people? Do you think this is an appropriate activity for a former president? Why or why not?
2. Read the title of the unit. What does it mean? Do you think it is better to give than to receive? Why or why not?

B. SHARING INFORMATION

Read the definition of ***philanthropy.*** *Then discuss your answers to the following questions in a small group.*

Philanthropy is a way of showing concern for people by giving money or time to help others. Some people and organizations give money to individuals or to charities (organizations that help people or do other good work), while other people volunteer (work without pay).

1. Do you know of any famous philanthropists? Do they give money, time, or another kind of aid? Describe their philanthropy.

2. Have you ever given money or volunteered your time to help other people? Why or why not? If you have, describe what you did and how you felt about it.

3. In 1996, Americans gave a total of $150.7 billion to charity. Look at the pie graph showing the percentage of money that was given to different types of organizations. Guess what percentage of donations went to each type of organization listed on page 117. Write the types of organizations in the blanks. Then check your answers in the Answer Key. Which answers surprised you? Why?

________________	46%
Educational	12%
________________	10%
________________	8%
Arts	7%
________________	5%
________________	3%
________________	1%
Other	8%

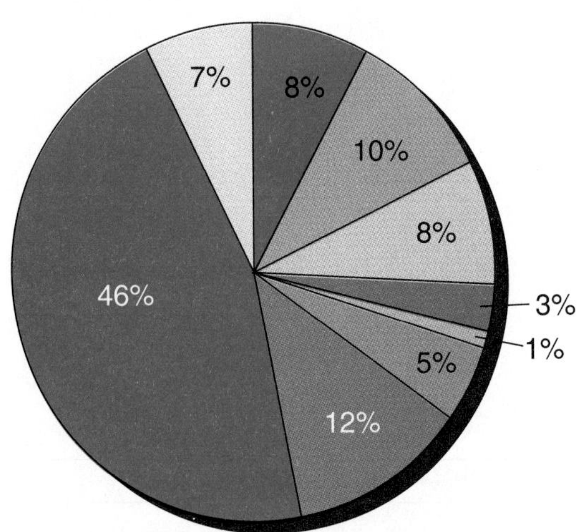

Where Americans Gave in 1996

Types of Organizations

Arts, humanities, and culture (museums, theaters, performing arts groups)

Educational (universities, colleges, schools)

Environmental / wildlife (pollution control, animal rescue)

Health related (hospitals)

Human services (homeless shelters, food banks)

International (organizations that promote cooperation among countries)

Public / social benefit (libraries, community centers, parks)

Religious (churches, synagogues, mosques, temples)

Other

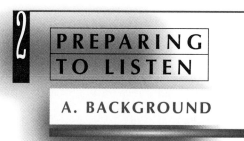

2 PREPARING TO LISTEN

A. BACKGROUND

Read the passage. Then do the activities that follow.

Philanthropy has always had an important role in American history and is an accepted American custom. In fact, 72 percent of Americans donate to charity, and 51 percent do volunteer work. About 2 million not-for-profit organizations and charities in the United States today receive this help. These not-for-profit organizations include universities, hospitals, religious groups and their charities, social service agencies, museums, and scientific research organizations.

There are three types of philanthropists: individuals, foundations, and private corporations. Individuals give money or volunteer their time to support causes that are important to them. On average, an American family donates about $1,000 dollars per year to not-for-profit organizations. Surprisingly, low-income people give twice as much of their income (3.6 percent) as high-income people (1.7 percent). Very wealthy individuals may give a large amount of money to start a foundation, an organization whose "business" is not to make a profit but to give money away to not-for-profits. Private corporations may also use a portion of their business profits to make donations, or they may give away their products free of charge. However, foundations and corporations are responsible for only 20 percent of charitable donations, while 80 percent comes from individuals.

Why do people and corporations give? One reason is *altruism,* the unselfish desire to help other people and make the world a better place. However, there are also selfish reasons for giving. Under U.S. tax law, an individual or business does not have to pay income tax on the money that is donated to a charity. For extremely wealthy individuals and corporations, this means millions of dollars less to pay in taxes to the government. In addition to tax benefits, donors (people and companies who give) often receive favorable publicity for making donations, and they have an opportunity to influence the world around them.

Work in a small group. Read the reasons for donating. Add some other reasons you think people give. Then read the newspaper clippings about some recent donations. Next to each clipping, write the number for the reasons you think the donors gave, and discuss your choices.

Some Reasons People Donate Money

1. so others can do something the donor felt fortunate to be able to do
2. so others can do something the donor never had a chance to do
3. so others will feel grateful to the donor
4. so the donor will feel good about himself/herself
5. so the donor can receive publicity for his/her company
6. because the donor feels guilty about having a lot of money
7. because the donor doesn't have anyone else to give the money to after he/she dies
8. to change society / to change the world
9. to say "thank you" for help in the past
10. to encourage others to give
11. to become famous
12. to pay less in income taxes
13. to satisfy religious beliefs
14. ______________________
15. ______________________
16. ______________________

_____ **G. J. Ford Donates $20 Million to Southern Methodist University**

As the chairman, CEO, and principal stockholder of a bank worth $30 billion, G. J. Ford says he owes his success to the education and preparation for life he received as a Southern Methodist University student in the 1960s. In return, he has made a $20 million payment on "his debt of gratitude" to SMU, to help the Dallas school build a 32,000-seat football stadium and all-sports facility.

_____ ***Foster Leaves $7.5 Million to Portland Animal Clinic***

The Dove Lewis Emergency Animal Hospital in Portland, Oregon, has received a $7.5 million donation from the estate of David Story Foster. The gift establishes the Lucky Dog Fund, which will provide an estimated $400,000 yearly to the hospital. Foster, who was unmarried and had no children, died in May 1996 at age 49. He had owned a number of dogs that received emergency treatment at the hospital. Said Foster's older brother, Thomas, "The animals were really important in his life. They were his real family."

_____ **Oracle Corporation Donates $100 Million**

Oracle Corporation and its chairman and CEO, Larry Ellison, will give $100 million in support of America's Promise — Alliance for Youth. The donation by the world's second-largest computer software company will go to Oracle's Promise, a nonprofit foundation with the goal of putting a computer on every student's desk. "We need a computer that is affordable and easy to use, so that every child can have [one]," said Ellison. "Today's personal computer is creating a society of haves and have-nots."

B. VOCABULARY FOR COMPREHENSION

Read the pamphlet on page 120 encouraging people to give money to a charity. Choose the best definition of the underlined words from the list that follows. Write the number next to the definition.

SOMEONE IN NEED . . .

- A (1) stunned family standing in front of their house after it was destroyed by fire.
- Children who go to school in dirty clothes because their house has no water and they have no place to do the (2) laundry.
- Parents who lost their jobs and had to spend their (3) nest egg, money that was (4) tucked away over many years, on food and shelter.

A HELPING HAND . . .

These are stories that (5) touch our hearts and make us feel like we want to help. Well, you can help. It's easy. Just fill out the enclosed card to (6) pledge a small amount of money to help people in need. The money will (7) fund programs to help people in need. We also have a special (8) scholarship to pay for needy children to go to college.

YOUR REWARD . . .

You won't (9) regret your decision to give because it will make you feel better about yourself. As a (10) benefactor, you will feel the rewards of helping people. The money you give will change someone's life! The (11) recipients of your gift will always remember that when life was at its worst, someone reached out to help them.

Thousands of generous people have already helped. Don't let them (12) show you up and make you look like you don't care.

_____ a. a person who helps someone by giving money

_____ b. cause you to seem less generous than someone else

_____ c. clothes that need to be washed

_____ d. feel sorry about

_____ e. make us feel an emotion

_____ f. money to pay for a student's study

_____ g. money saved for something special

_____ h. pay for

_____ i. people who receive something

_____ j. promise to give

_____ k. saved a little at a time

_____ l. very surprised; shocked

3 LISTENING ONE: Oseola McCarty—An Unusual Philanthropist

A. INTRODUCING THE TOPIC

Oseola McCarty

You will hear a report by television host Barbara Walters about Oseola McCarty, who was selected as one of the ten most fascinating people of the year.

Listen to an excerpt from the report. Then discuss your answers to the questions.

Who is Oseola McCarty? Where does she live? How old is she? What do you think she did that made her famous?

B. LISTENING FOR MAIN IDEAS

Listen to the entire report. Read the statements, and write **T** *for true and* **F** *for false. Correct the statements that are wrong.*

Oseola McCarty . . .

____ **1.** worked most of her life doing laundry.

____ **2.** saved almost $250.

____ **3.** has very little education.

____ **4.** pledged her money to start a scholarship at a university.

____ **5.** regrets giving away her money.

____ **6.** inspired local business people to contribute money.

C. LISTENING FOR DETAILS

Listen to the report again. As you listen, circle the best answers to complete the statements.

1. Ms. McCarty was ______ by many people before she gave away her money.
   a. well known b. visited c. not noticed

2. Ms. McCarty's scholarship is for promising ______ students.
   a. female b. black c. poor

3. Ms. McCarty has ______ children.
   a. no b. two c. four

4. Ms. McCarty left school to ______.
   a. work for a doctor b. get married c. take care of her grandmother

5. The president said if more people were like Ms. McCarty, there would be ______.
   a. more scholarships at universities b. very few problems in the United States c. few poor people

6. The trip to the White House was the first time Ms. McCarty had ______.
   a. left the South in fifty years b. traveled away from home c. been to Washington, D.C.

7. Stephanie Bullock is ______.
   a. a member of Ms. McCarty's family b. the first recipient of the Oseola McCarty scholarship c. a friend of Ms. McCarty's

8. Stephanie Bullock ______.
   a. hasn't started college yet b. is in college now c. has already graduated from college

9. Ms. McCarty ______.
   - a. has a new job
   - b. still does laundry for people
   - c. doesn't work anymore

10. Local business people ______.
    - a. are contributing to the Oseola McCarty scholarship fund
    - b. are starting a new scholarship fund
    - c. want Ms. McCarty to do their laundry

D. LISTENING BETWEEN THE LINES

Listen to three excerpts from the report. Write the reasons you think Oseola McCarty gave money to the university. Use some of the possible reasons from the list that follows, and think of other reasons. Then compare your answers with those of another student.

- change society
- make people admire her
- show other people up
- help people who can't afford to go to college
- help people do something she couldn't do
- get an income tax break
- be more powerful
- meet the president
- feel better about herself
- encourage local businesses to give money
- become famous
- get interviewed on TV
- show that giving is important
- (your own ideas)

Excerpt One

Reasons Ms. McCarty gave the money: ______________________________

____

Excerpt Two

Reasons Ms. McCarty gave the money: ______________________________

____

Excerpt Three

Reasons Ms. McCarty gave the money: ______________________________

____

4 LISTENING TWO: Please Donate or Volunteer—Public Service Announcements

A. EXPANDING THE TOPIC

Public service announcements (PSAs) are advertisements on television or radio that educate people about important issues or encourage people to do things for the good of society.

You will hear two public service announcements that encourage people to give money or volunteer to help others.

❶ *Listen to each announcement and write what it is asking people to do and why they should do it. Compare your answers with those of another student.*

	WHAT IS THE ANNOUNCEMENT ASKING PEOPLE TO DO?	ACCORDING TO THE ANNOUNCEMENT, WHY SHOULD PEOPLE DO IT?
PSA 1		
PSA 2		

❷ *Discuss the following questions in a small group and then with the class.*

1. Which PSA do you think is more effective? Why?

2. Which is less effective? Why?

B. LINKING LISTENINGS ONE AND TWO

Discuss the following questions with a partner and then with the class.

1. Oseola McCarty was selected as one of the ten most fascinating people of the year. Why is her story so interesting to people? Have you heard any stories similar to Ms. McCarty's?

2. Compare:
   - the reason Oseola McCarty gave money (Listening One)
   - the reasons people are encouraged to give money or volunteer time (Listening Two)

   How are the reasons similar or different?

3. You have heard several reasons why people in the United States give money to charity. Is giving money to charity common in your culture? Are the reasons for giving similar, or not?

4. If you had $20 million to give away, what types of organizations would you support? Why?

5 REVIEWING LANGUAGE

A. EXPLORING LANGUAGE: Consonant + Vowel Joining within Thought Groups

English speakers join words together within thought groups. To find which words should be joined together, follow these steps:

1. Make thought groups by taking logical and comfortable breaks after a thought. Do not pause between each word. Thought groups might look something like this.

   a. I always make donations to my favorite charities.

   b. Recently, I gave money to an animal rights group.

2. Inside the thought group, link words that end in a **consonant sound** with the following word that begins with a **vowel sound**.

   a. I've always volunteered my extra time for various organizations.

   b. I've even given money to a charity.

❶ *Listen to the tape as you read the story about Oseola McCarty.*

Part One

Pay special attention to how the speaker puts words into thought groups.

The story of Oseola McCarty, a washerwoman who gave away her life savings, has touched the hearts of everyone who has heard it. This frail old woman has become one of the most famous philanthropists in the nation. Year after year, for most of her life, Ms. McCarty worked for others, tucking away every penny she did not need for food and daily living expenses.

Part Two

Pay special attention to how the speaker links consonants and vowels within thought groups.

After many years, Oseola consulted a lawyer and made an announcement that stunned everyone: she had accumulated a nest egg of $250,000 and decided to give most of it away. The recipient was a fund to help worthy black students go to college. Businesses in the area followed Oseola's lead, and donations poured in.

❷ *Work in a small group and take turns reading the story of Oseola McCarty. First divide each sentence into thought groups. Then, within the thought group, link the consonant and vowel sounds.*

❸ *Read the dialogue. Mr. and Mrs. X. Treemly Rich want to donate $5 million to charity. They are discussing which organization should receive the money. Divide the sentences into thought groups. Then mark with linking symbols to join appropriate consonant and vowel sounds.*

MRS. RICH: Dear, let's talk about how we should donate our money.

MR. RICH: That's a good idea, sweetheart. Let's see . . . I admire the work of the Dinosaur Egg Association, don't you? They're trying to find out how to re-create dinosaurs from ancient DNA samples.

MRS. RICH: Well, that's interesting, yes, but I'm more impressed by Save the Rain Forests, or the Clean Ocean Fund. It helps clean up the oceans. I think we should encourage more ecological programs, don't you?

MR. RICH: Well . . . How about the Space Alien Research Institute? It would be great to make contact with some aliens from outer space, wouldn't it?

MRS. RICH: That's a silly way to spend our money. How about Options for Independence? It's an organization that helps elderly people live on their own.

MR. RICH: Sweetheart, I don't think we'll ever agree!

MRS. RICH: You know, honey, maybe we should split up the money and each give to different organizations.

MR. RICH: Terrific idea!

❹ *Work with a partner. Compare the way you both marked the dialogue for consonant-vowel joining. Then read the dialogue out loud, each student reading one part. When you have finished, switch roles and read it again.*

B. WORKING WITH WORDS

❶ *Pronounce the words below with your teacher. Then complete the newspaper article on page 128 with the correct words from the list that follows. Each word is marked as a noun (n), verb (v), or adjective (adj).*

benefactor (n)	regretted (v)
donation (n)	retired (adj)
fund (v)	stunned (adj)
nest egg (n)	touched someone's heart (v)
recipient (n)	tucked away (v)
	volunteer (n)

"Teddy Bear Lady" Surprises Hospital with Gift

Chicago's Children's Memorial Hospital is the lucky (**1**) _____________ of a surprise $18 million gift. Gladys Holm was a(n) (**2**) _____________ secretary who never earned more than $15,000 a year and never married. She lived alone in a tiny apartment in Evanston, Illinois, and worked as a(n) (**3**) _____________ at Children's Memorial Hospital in Chicago. She was called the "Teddy Bear Lady" because she brought stuffed animals to sick children on her regular visits. But Miss Holm, who died in 1996 at the age of 86, was also a longtime buyer of stocks. Over the years, she (**4**) _____________ money that grew into an impressive (**5**) _____________ of $18 million, which she left to Children's Memorial. It was the largest single (**6**) _____________ in the hospital's 115-year history. The hospital president, Jan Jennings, was (**7**) _____________ when she heard the news. "When [Miss Holm's attorney] called to tell me the amount, I asked him to repeat it, since I was certain I had misheard."

Why did Gladys Holm feel so strongly about Children's Memorial? Jennings says the hospital first (**8**) _____________ Miss Holm's _____________ nearly 50 years ago, when doctors there saved the life of her friend's daughter. She never forgot the relief she felt all those years ago.

Holm's gift will (**9**) _____________ heart disease research. People at the hospital said they (**10**) _____________ that they couldn't thank their (**11**) _____________ for the generous gift.

❷ *Work in pairs. Read the article that follows. Write a dialogue between two of the adult Burton children, as they discuss how best to use their father's money. Use at least ten of the words in the list in any form. Then practice the dialogue out loud and perform it for the class.*

Peter Burton Leaves $7 Billion to Charity

Peter Burton, former chairman of electronics giant Davis-Burton, died recently, leaving approximately $7 billion to his foundation. This gift makes the Peter and Leslie Burton Foundation one of the wealthiest foundations in the world. Burton established the foundation to "help people through the improvement of scientific knowledge, education, health, employment, and the environmental quality of life." Burton's four children must decide how the foundation will spend the money.

Terms to use in your dialogue:

benefactor (n)
charity (n)
donor (n)
donate (v)
feed the hungry (v)
foundation (n)
fund (n), (v)
nest egg (n)
philanthropy (n)
pledge (n), (v)
provide (v)
regret (n), (v)
retired (adj.)
scholarship (n)
show someone up (v)
stun (v), stunned (adj.)
touch someone's heart (v)
tuck away (v)
volunteer (n), (v)

A. GRAMMAR: Tag Questions

❶ *Read the following conversation. Pay special attention to the underlined words. Then discuss the questions that follow with a partner.*

A: You read that story about Oseola McCarty, <u>didn't you</u>?

B: No, what story was that?

A: She's a washerwoman who saved $250,000 and gave most of it to a university.

B: Wow. That's amazing!

A: Yes, it is, <u>isn't it</u>?

B: It sure is.

a. How are the underlined phrases similar?

b. How are they different?

Focus on Grammar

See Tag Questions in *Focus on Grammar, High-Intermediate.*

Tag Questions

In spoken English, people commonly use **tag questions.** Tag questions have two parts: a **statement** and a **tag,** an added question. If the verb in the statement is affirmative, the tag is negative. If the verb in the statement is negative, the tag is affirmative.

Tags always use a form of ***be,*** or the auxiliary verbs ***be, do, have,*** or ***will*** or a modal verb such as ***can, could, should,*** or ***would.***

There are two types of tag questions: the comment type and the question type.

Comment Type

Use a tag question to make a comment that is not really a question. An answer is not necessarily expected, but confirmation is. In this case, the tag question means "Isn't that true?" For comment-type tag questions, use falling intonation.

A: Oseola McCarty is a wonderful woman, **isn't she**?

B: Yes, she is.

A: Oseola McCarty gave a lot of her money away, **didn't she**?

B: Yes, she did.

Question Type

Use a tag question to get information. Use rising intonation to show that a question is being asked.

A: Oseola McCarty didn't have any education, **did she**?

B: Yes, she did. She finished sixth grade.

A: My appointment for the volunteer interview is at 6:00 P.M., **isn't it**?

B: No, it's at 7:30.

Answering Tag Questions

Answer tag questions the same way you answer yes/no questions. You can agree with a tag question (comment type), or you can answer a tag question (question type) with real information.

A: Gladys Holm was a very caring person, wasn't she? (comment type)

B: **Yes, she certainly was.**

A: Gladys Holm did volunteer work at the hospital, didn't she? (question type)

B: **Yes, she did. She visited sick children regularly.**

❷ *Work with a partner to do the following activity.*

Step 1: *Complete the conversation with the appropriate tags.*

A: You've heard about Oseola McCarty's gift to the university, (1) ___haven't you___?

B: Yes, I have. It's an amazing story, (2) ________________?

A: Uh, huh. Some people are more generous than others, (3) ________________?

B: That's the truth. Most people wouldn't give away all their money, (4) ________________?

A: Of course not. Even very wealthy people don't give a very high percentage of their money away, (5) ________________?

B: Right. I remember reading that low-income people give an average of 3.6 percent of their income and wealthy people only 1.6 percent. That's surprising, (6) ________________?

A: But it's not true for everyone. Look at media tycoon Ted Turner. He gave one billion dollars to the United Nations, (7) ________________.

B: That's right. It's hard to imagine having that much money to give, (8) ________________?

A: It sure is. But more wealthy people should give away more of their money, (9) ________________?

B: I agree, but I wonder how I'd feel if I were rich!

Step 2: *Now listen to the conversation on the tape. Mark the rising and falling intonation. Then compare your work with your partner's.*

Step 3: *Practice the dialogue with your partner. Be sure to use the correct intonation in the tag questions.*

❸ *Read the statements about Oseola McCarty on page 132. Underline the parts of the statements that are **not true.** The first one has been done for you. If you are not sure, check the tapescript at the back of the book.*

1. Oseola McCarty was a hardworking woman who spent her life cleaning houses.

2. After finishing high school, she began to invest her money.

3. She was careful about watching over her nest egg as it grew.

4. When her three children grew up and moved away, Oseola lived alone in her older years.

5. Then she decided to make a contribution to help college professors.

6. She donated $100,000 to a university.

7. The first recipient of her scholarship didn't accept the money because she felt sorry for Oseola.

8. When she got older, Oseola couldn't afford to stop working.

4 *Work in pairs. Take turns asking tag questions to check the information in the story in Exercise 3.*

Example

STUDENT A: Oseola McCarty didn't clean houses, did she?
STUDENT B: No. She washed clothes for a living.
STUDENT A: That's right.

Then write the correct information above the underlined parts of Exercise 3. Check your corrections with another pair of students.

B. STYLE: Prioritizing or Ranking Ideas

We often need to **prioritize, rank,** or **list** our different ideas. It is helpful to indicate which are the most important and the least important ideas when we explain something. Here are some expressions that are commonly used:

Highest Priority	Also a Priority	Lowest Priority
Our top priority is . . .	But also important is . . .	Least important is . . .
First and foremost, . . .	Another consideration is . . .	Of least concern is . . .
Above all, . . .	Aside from that, . . .	

Work in a small group.

Step 1: *Read the ads for volunteer jobs. Then read the list of personal qualities.*

Step 2: *Discuss the jobs one at a time. Prioritize the personal qualities for each job. Use expressions from the list on page 132 and personal qualities from the box. Add other qualities to the box if you like.*

Example

STUDENT A: *First and foremost*, a volunteer at the animal shelter must love animals.

STUDENT B: I agree. *But also important* is having good communication skills because the volunteer will have some contact with the public.

STUDENT A: You're right. *Aside from that*, the volunteer must have some office skills for the administrative work.

Personal Qualities

- ability to finish tasks
- ability to work long hours
- ability to work with many kinds of people
- attention to detail
- assertiveness
- cheerfulness
- cleanliness
- compassion
- emotional strength
- flexibility
- good communication skills
- good listening skills
- good office skills
- a love of animals
- patience
- public speaking experience
- sense of humor
- stylish appearance

WANTED

Person needed to work part time at neighborhood animal shelter. Help find homes for abandoned animals. Do something useful for your community, and bring the joy of a new pet into someone's life. Responsibilities include feeding, walking, and taking care of animals. Some contact with public and administrative work necessary. Volunteers needed at least 8 hours per week during these times: Daily 8 A.M. to 10 P.M.

POSITION

Volunteer fund-raiser for charitable organization. Responsibilites include helping to find new donors and helping to raise $1,000,000 for yearly budget. Be responsible for formal fund-raising dinner and celebrity baseball night. Handle correspondence and telephone fund-raising drive.

VOLUNTEER HELP NEEDED

Hospital worker. Volunteer needed to comfort ill patients. Read aloud to patients, take them for walks, offer a shoulder to lean on. Our motto: "A friend when you need one." Call 994-5863.

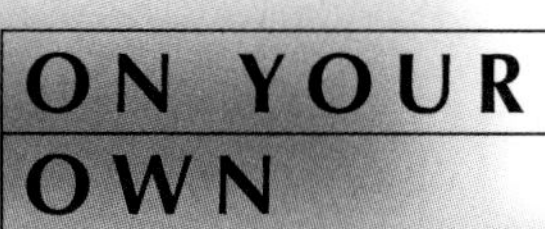

7 ON YOUR OWN

A. SPEAKING TOPIC: Creating a Public Service Announcement

Work in a small group and create a PSA.

1. Select a not-for-profit organization from the list. Give it a name. Decide on its purpose.

   - animal shelter
   - art museum
   - environmental group
   - homeless shelter
   - scholarship fund
   - scientific research organization
   - special hospital

2. Select a target audience. (For example, do you want teenagers to hear your PSA? If so, write it specifically for a music station that appeals to teens.)

3. Prepare a one-minute announcement for a radio station. Write it for several voices so that everyone in your group can have a part. Make your public service announcement interesting (to make people listen) and convincing (to make people donate or volunteer). For help, read the scripts for the public service announcements you heard in Listening Two.

   Your announcement should:

   - Describe what the organization does.
   - Tell why people should donate to or volunteer for the organization.

4. Record your PSA on an audiotape. Ask other groups to listen. The class will vote on which PSA is the most interesting and which is the most convincing. Try to use tag questions (Section 6A) to make comments and ask questions. Use the language from Section 6B on style to discuss priorities.

B. FIELDWORK: Philanthropy

RESEARCHING AN ORGANIZATION OR A PHILANTHROPIST

Select a not-for-profit organization or a philanthropist from the lists that follow, or think of another. Find out about the organization or person by doing Internet, library, or telephone research (for example, call the office of the organization). Use these questions to guide you in your research.

Questions to ask . . .

about a not-for-profit organization

1. When was it established?
2. Who established it? Why?
3. What are its goals?
4. How much money does it receive?
5. What are some of its accomplishments?
6. (Your own questions)

about a philanthropist

1. If the philanthropist is no longer alive, when did he or she live?
2. What is/was the person's life like? What does/did the philanthropist do?
3. Whom does/did the philanthropist help?
4. How were recipients selected?
5. (Your own questions)

Some Not-for-Profit Organizations

UNICEF
Nature Conservancy
Amnesty International
Save the Children
International Committee of the Red Cross
Salvation Army
Oxfam
Sierra Club

Some Philanthropists *

John D. and Catherine T. McArthur
Bill Gates
Brooke Astor
George Soros
John Kluge
Oveta Culp Hoby
Carol F. Sulzberger
Andrew W. Mellon
Charles F. Feeney
Andrew Carnegie
Warren E. Buffet
Robert Wood Johnson
John D. Rockefeller
Ted Turner

* You may need to look up the name as a foundation. For example: Robert Wood Johnson Foundation.

VISITING A VOLUNTEER ORGANIZATION

1. Visit a local organization that needs volunteers. Some examples are a hospital, a church or temple, an arts organization or museum, an AIDS organization, an organization that helps the elderly, a school, or an environmental organization.

   Use this list to ask questions during your visit:

   - number of volunteers
   - kind of work the volunteers do
   - reason the organization needs volunteers
   - job requirements for volunteers
   - satisfaction of the volunteers with their jobs

2. Report to the class about the organization you visited. Listen to each other's reports. Discuss which organization you would be most likely to volunteer for, and why.

UNIT 7

EMOTIONAL INTELLIGENCE

1 APPROACHING THE TOPIC

A. PREDICTING

Discuss the questions with another student. Then share your ideas with the class.

1. **Look at the cartoon. What is the man's profession? What is the cartoon saying about intelligence?**
2. **Read the title of the unit. What do you think the unit will be about?**

B. SHARING INFORMATION

❶ *What qualities or abilities make one person more intelligent than another? Look at the checklist. Decide whether each quality or ability is very important, somewhat important, or not at all important. Check (✓) the appropriate column. Add any other important qualities or abilities you think should be on the list. Then discuss your opinions in a small group.*

	Very Important	Somewhat Important	Not at All Important
1. Understanding math and science	☐	☐	☐
2. Thinking of new ideas	☐	☐	☐
3. Solving problems	☐	☐	☐
4. Learning quickly	☐	☐	☐
5. Understanding other people's feelings	☐	☐	☐
6. Having many years of schooling	☐	☐	☐
7. Understanding your own emotions	☐	☐	☐
8. Being hard-working	☐	☐	☐
9. ______________________	☐	☐	☐
10. ______________________	☐	☐	☐

❷ *Think of a very intelligent person you know. Describe the person to your classmates. Discuss your answers to the following questions in a small group.*

- In what ways is the person intelligent?
- How would you describe his or her personality?

2 PREPARING TO LISTEN

A. BACKGROUND

Read the information about intelligence testing and do the activity that follows on page 140.

Intelligence Testing

As early as the mid-1800s, people tried to measure intelligence with various types of tests. One common misperception was that by measuring the size and shape of a person's head, a person's intelligence could be determined. In 1905, the first modern intelligence test, known as the IQ (Intelligence Quotient) test, was developed by two French psychologists, Alfred Binet and Theodore Simon. The IQ test was used to predict how well children would do in school.

Since its development, the IQ test has been widely used in schools to evaluate students' abilities and predict their success. However, it has also been criticized for several reasons. One criticism is that the IQ test does not accurately predict a person's success in life. This criticism has been supported by research. In a study conducted near Boston, Massachusetts, 450 boys were given IQ tests. They were then followed throughout their lives to see how well they would do at work and in their personal lives. Researchers found that an IQ score did not predict whether a boy would have a happy, productive life. For example, they found that 7 percent of men with an IQ under 80 (below average intelligence) were unemployed for much of the time. But they also found that 7 percent of men with an IQ over 100 (above average intelligence) were unemployed. Clearly, these men needed more than intelligence, as defined by the IQ test, to be successful.

To address this problem, different theories of intelligence have been proposed. One of these is the theory of Emotional Intelligence, or EQ, which was popularized by American psychologist Daniel Goleman in his book *Emotional Intelligence*. Emotional Intelligence includes skills such as understanding one's own emotions and relating well to other people. Goleman believes that a person's EQ is as important as his or her IQ. He proposes that people be given more training in school and at work to develop their Emotional Intelligence.

Read the statements in the opinion survey. Decide if you agree or disagree with each one. Circle **1** *if you strongly agree and* **4** *if you strongly disagree. Then compare your answers in a small group. Explain your opinions using examples from your experience.*

Intelligence: An Opinion Survey

What Do You Believe About Intelligence?

	Strongly Agree			Strongly Disagree
1. Intelligence can be accurately measured.	1	2	3	4
2. Each person is born with a certain amount of intelligence, which stays the same throughout his or her life.	1	2	3	4
3. Scientists and mathematicians are more intelligent than artists and writers.	1	2	3	4
4. Very intelligent people do not have good "people skills" and are not good at relating to others.	1	2	3	4
5. Emotions do not help us think logically.	1	2	3	4
6. People who get good grades in school will also do well in their careers.	1	2	3	4

B. VOCABULARY FOR COMPREHENSION

Read the following sentences. Circle the word or expression that is closest in meaning to the underlined words. Then compare your answers with those of another student.

1. How do you <u>handle</u> your anger? One way is to do something physical, like going for a walk. By the time you get back, you won't feel angry anymore.

a. hide **b.** express **c.** understand

2. Some people do not <u>respond</u> in a positive way to criticism. They either become angry, or depressed and sad.

a. agree **b.** react **c.** listen

3. Some people feel that they must <u>make a big fuss</u> in order to get what they want. They become annoyed and complain until they get their way.

a. complain loudly **b.** become worried **c.** remain calm

4. We must all learn to deal with setbacks. When things go wrong, we must keep going and not let the problems stop us.

   a. choices b. surprises c. disappointments

5. I love the class I am taking now. I feel very enthusiastic about it.

   a. confused b. unhappy c. excited

6. You will get depressed if you always dwell on failures. You should think about the positive things in your life instead.

   a. think about b. forget about c. look for

7. Some people always seem to take life in stride. Difficulties don't seem to bother them, and they can keep living happily.

   a. balance the positive and the negative b. worry about everything c. exercise regularly

8. It's a bad idea to give up when you can't solve a problem. Instead, try looking at it in a new way, and eventually you will find a solution.

   a. feel sad b. stop trying c. ask for help

9. She's a very sharp manager. She's intelligent and perceptive about motivating her employees.

   a. smart b. reliable c. easygoing

10. It's common to feel resentful when other people succeed. But instead of feeling jealous, you can study them to find out what they did to succeed.

    a. strong and proud b. surprised and confused c. hurt and angry

11. When friends are upset, it's important to empathize with them. By recognizing their feelings, you will be able to help your friends feel better.

    a. understand b. ignore c. change

12. When you make a mistake, it's best to swallow your pride and admit that you did something wrong. Then you can try to correct the problem.

    a. taste your pride b. express your anger c. forget your pride

3 LISTENING ONE: Can You Learn EQ?

A. INTRODUCING THE TOPIC

You will hear a radio interview with hosts Claire Nolan and Bill Rodney about the Emotional Intelligence Quotient (EQ).

Listen to the beginning of the interview. Then discuss your answers to the questions with a partner.

1. The main focus of this discussion will be ______.

a. how to test a person's EQ
b. whether EQ can be learned
c. how to use EQ in the workplace

2. Bill Rodney will interview three people about their ideas on EQ. What do you think their opinions might be?

B. LISTENING FOR MAIN IDEAS

Listen to the entire interview. Complete the chart as you listen to each person discuss his or her opinions about EQ. Then compare your answers with those of another student.

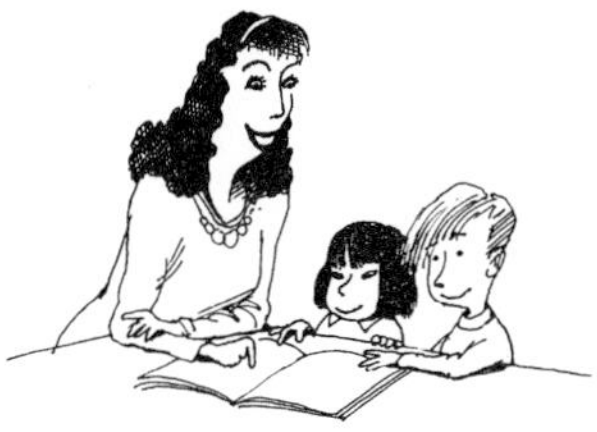

	WHAT IS THIS PERSON'S JOB?	HOW CAN A HIGH EQ HELP A PERSON?	CAN EQ BE LEARNED OR TAUGHT?
Betty Cortina			
Jim McDonald			
Jan Davis			

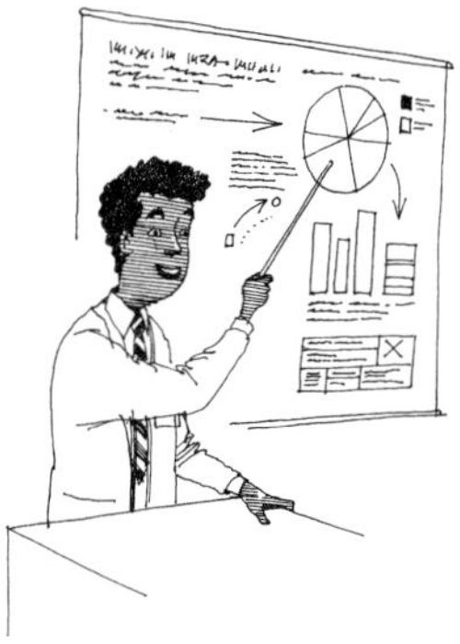

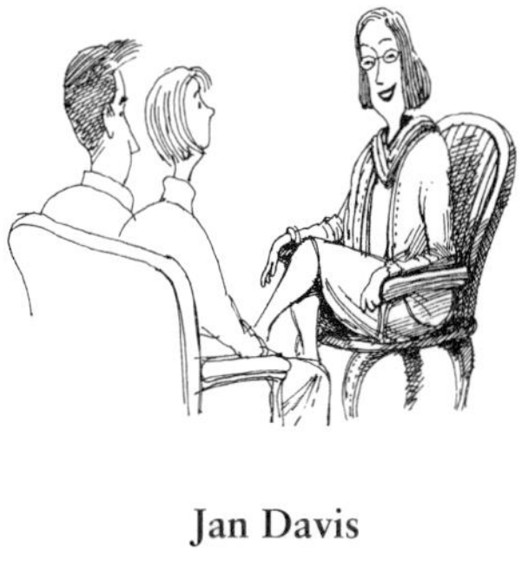

C. LISTENING FOR DETAILS

The people in the interview mention many qualities a person with a high EQ might possess. Read the list of qualities. Then listen to the entire interview again, one part at a time. Check the qualities you hear mentioned. Compare your answers with those of another student.

A person with a high EQ can . . .

PART ONE

____ 1. respond well to others
____ 2. talk openly about feelings
____ 3. be patient and easygoing
____ 4. control his/her emotions
____ 5. make a big fuss
____ 6. approach problems in different ways
____ 7. let negative feelings get in the way

PART TWO

____ 8. have a positive, enthusiastic attitude
____ 9. use time effectively
____ 10. respect others
____ 11. respond well to change
____ 12. have creative ideas
____ 13. see how his/her behavior affects others
____ 14. work well with other people

PART THREE

____ 15. convince people that he/she is correct
____ 16. empathize with others
____ 17. control his/her reactions when angry
____ 18. get promotions at work
____ 19. swallow his/her pride
____ 20. apologize effectively

D. LISTENING BETWEEN THE LINES

Emotional Intelligence includes qualities or skills such as understanding one's own emotions and relating well to other people. In his book, psychologist Daniel Goleman lists the five main skills of Emotional Intelligence.

Read the list of skills in the box. Then listen to the excerpts from the radio interview. You will hear about situations in which people did not possess one (or more) of the five main skills. Write the skill(s) each person needs to develop and why.

Five Skills of Emotional Intelligence

- Self-Awareness: Understanding your own emotions
- Self-Control: Managing your own emotions
- Self-Motivation: Using your emotions to get things done
- Empathy: Understanding other people's emotions
- People Skills: Relating well to people

Excerpt One

Skill(s) needed: ______________________________

Why? ______________________________

____

Excerpt Two

Skill(s) needed: ______________________________

Why? ______________________________

____

Excerpt Three

Skill(s) needed: ______________________________

Why? ______________________________

____

4 LISTENING TWO: Test Your EQ

A. EXPANDING THE TOPIC

In Listening Two you will hear the second part of the radio interview about EQ. Host Claire Nolan and psychologist Jan Davis discuss the answers to the Emotional Intelligence (EQ) test that follows.

Step 1

What's your EQ? Take this EQ test to find out. Read each situation and circle the letter of the answer that best describes how you would react.

Step 2

Listen to Claire Nolan and Jan Davis discuss the answers that show the highest EQ. Circle the letter of the High EQ answer, and write the reason(s) why it is the best answer.

EQ TEST[1]

1. Your four-year-old son is crying because some other children won't play with him. What do you do?
   - **a.** Don't do anything. Let the him solve the problem on his own.
   - **b.** Talk to him and help him figure out ways to get the other kids to play with him.
   - **c.** Tell him in a kind voice not to cry.

   High EQ answer: a b c

   Reason: ______________________________

2. You're a college student who had hoped to do well in a course, but you have just found out you failed the midterm exam. What do you do?
   - **a.** Make a specific plan for ways to improve your grade.
   - **b.** Promise yourself to do better in the future.
   - **c.** Drop the class and study something else.

   High EQ answer: a b c

   Reason: ______________________________

---

[1] Adapted from Daniel Goleman, "EQ: What's Your Emotional Intelligence Quotient?" *Utne Reader*, November–December 1995.

3. Your friend is driving. He is angry because a driver in another car almost hit him. You're trying to calm him down. What do you do?
   a. Put on one of his favorite tapes and try to distract him.
   b. Join him in insulting the other driver.
   c. Tell him about a time something like this happened to you and how you felt as angry as he does now.

   High EQ answer: a b c

   Reason: ______________________________

4. You are a manager in a company that has employees from different ethnic backgrounds. Your company is trying to encourage its employees to respect each other. You hear someone telling a joke about one ethnic group. What do you do?
   a. Ignore it. It's only a joke.
   b. Call the person into your office and tell him or her not to tell ethnic jokes.
   c. Say something to all the employees right away. Tell them that ethnic jokes are not acceptable in your organization.

   High EQ answer: a b c

   Reason: ______________________________

5. You've been assigned to lead a team of workers from different departments to solve a problem at work. You're having your first meeting to discuss the problem. What's the first thing you do?
   a. List what the group should do to make the best use of its time.
   b. Have people take the time to get to know each other better.
   c. Begin by asking each person for ideas about how to solve the problem.

   High EQ answer: a b c

   Reason: ______________________________

B. LINKING LISTENINGS ONE AND TWO

Work in a small group and discuss your answers to the questions.

1. What do you think of the theory of Emotional Intelligence? Do you think it is possible to improve your EQ? Use your own experiences to support your opinion.

2. Look at the five skills of Emotional Intelligence listed in Section 3D on page 145. Then look at the EQ Test in Section 4A on pages 146–147. Which skills are being tested in the situations described in the EQ Test?

3. Look at the Opinion Survey you took in Section 2A on page 140. How would the speakers in Listening One answer the questions? Do you still agree with your original answers?

4. The theory of Emotional Intelligence was developed in the United States. Do you think the theory applies in the same way in all cultures? Do some of the values stated in the theory seem particularly American? Analyze the situations in the listenings, and discuss whether any of the conclusions would be different in your culture. Explain why.

5 REVIEWING LANGUAGE

A. EXPLORING LANGUAGE: Unstressed Vowels

Words with two or more syllables usually have one syllable that is stressed, and one or more syllables that are unstressed.

success	suc-CESS	syllable	SYL-la-ble

In most words, the vowel sound in the unstressed syllables is reduced. The reduced vowel sound is pronounced "uh" (like the vowel sound in *but*), no matter how the word is spelled. This reduced vowel sound is called a *schwa*. The symbol for a schwa is [ə]. Sometimes the schwa sound is pronounced [i] as in *is*.

listen	LIS-t[ə]n	success	s[ə]c-CESS
syllable	SYL-l[ə]-ble	mistake	m[ə]s-TAKE

NOTE: Vowels with secondary stress are not reduced. For example, the vowel in the syllable *-back* in the compound noun *setback* is not reduced to a schwa.

❶ *Listen to the words from this unit. Put a slash between the syllables. Then listen again and draw a dot over the syllables with the strongest stress. Write [ə] over the vowel in the unstressed syllables.*

1. control (ə over "co", dot over "trol")	6. attitude	11. ability
2. adjust	7. negative	12. psychologist
3. success	8. resentful	13. intelligence
4. productively	9. empathize	14. relationship
5. people	10. personal	15. emotional

❷ *Listen to the words again and repeat them aloud. Make sure you pronounce the [ə] sound correctly.*

❸ *Work in pairs. Read the advertisement for a seminar about EQ. Mark the vowels in the syllables that are pronounced with a schwa sound. Use a dictionary to help you. Check your answers with another pair of students.*

Then practice reading the advertisement aloud to your partner. Your partner will listen for correct pronunciation of the schwa sound.

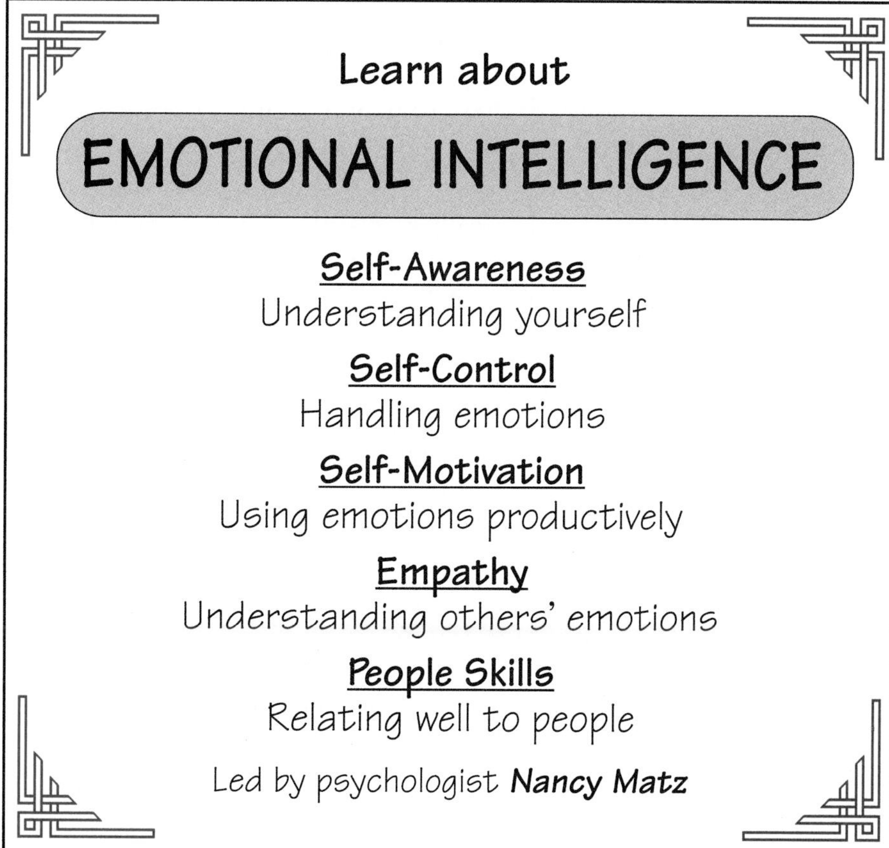

Learn about
EMOTIONAL INTELLIGENCE
Self-Awareness
Understanding yourself
Self-Control
Handling emotions
Self-Motivation
Using emotions productively
Empathy
Understanding others' emotions
People Skills
Relating well to people
Led by psychologist Nancy Matz

B. WORKING WITH WORDS

1 *Pronounce the adjectives and verb phrases with your teacher. Then, working with a partner, read aloud the opinions of people working in various occupations. They are discussing the qualities necessary to do their jobs well. Write in the best phrases to complete their statements.*

Adjectives	Verb Phrases	
easygoing	deal with setbacks	put yourself in someone else's shoes
enthusiastic	dwell on failure	respect others
patient	empathize with	respond well to change
perceptive	give up	swallow your pride
resentful	make a fuss	take life in stride
sharp	make allowances for	
spirited	put aside negative feelings	

1. "In the computer software industry, we work long hours, so you have to be someone who is (**a**) ______________ (enthusiastic about / resentful of) the work. You must (**b**) ______________ (dwell on failures / respond well to change) because in this field we are always facing something new."

2. "It's important for teachers to (**a**) ______________ (give up / be patient) when a student is having problems. A teacher should try to (**b**) ______________ (empathize with / be resentful of) the students who don't understand the work. Sometimes you have to help students (**c**) ______________ (respect others / swallow their pride) and admit they have a problem."

3. "As a trial lawyer, it's my job to fight for my client. A good trial lawyer is a/an (**a**) ______________ (spirited / easygoing) person. Winning is the most important thing. But you sometimes lose, so you must know how to (**b**) ______________ (dwell on failure / deal with setbacks)."

4. "A customer service representative talks to people who have problems with telephone service. You have to know how to respond when customers (**a**) ____________ (are spirited / make a fuss) because their telephones don't work. Sometimes the customers are very angry and yell at us, but you have to (**b**) ____________ (put aside your negative feelings / give up) and try to help them anyway."

5. "As a psychologist, I try to (**a**) ____________ (put myself in my clients' shoes / be easygoing with my clients) in order to really understand them. You have to be very (**b**) ____________ (enthusiastic / perceptive) in order to understand what a person is feeling."

6. "To be a good scientist, you have to be able to admit when you are wrong. You have to be able to accept criticism, (**a**) ____________ (swallow your pride / make a fuss), and continue your work. All in all, you need to be able to (**b**) ____________ (take life in stride / be resentful)."

❷ *How can EQ help people in other professions? Work in pairs. Use the vocabulary from the box in Exercise 1 to discuss the qualities needed in the jobs, careers, and roles listed below.*

artist	parent
athlete	police officer
doctor	salesperson
judge	waiter
manager	

6 SKILLS FOR EXPRESSION

A. GRAMMAR: Direct and Indirect Speech

❶ *Working with a partner, examine the sentences and discuss the questions that follow.*

- Betty Cortina said that some of her kids were more patient than others.
- Jim McDonald told the panel that it would be better for employees not to feel resentful.

a. In the examples, what were the speakers' exact words?

b. In the first example, why is the second verb in the past tense?

c. What tenses are used in the second example? Why?

FOCUS ON GRAMMAR

See Direct and Indirect Speech in *Focus on Grammar, High-Intermediate.*

Direct and Indirect Speech

When we use a speaker's exact words, we use **direct speech.** When we report what a person has said, we use **indirect** (reported) **speech.** In indirect structures, there is often a change in verb tense.

	Direct Speech	Indirect Speech
Use ***said*** or ***told*** to report speech. Use ***told*** if you want to mention the listener.	"An emotionally intelligent person knows when and how to apologize."	The psychology teacher **said** (that) an emotionally intelligent person knows when and how to apologize.
That is optional before the reported sentence.		The psychology teacher **told the students** (that) an emotionally intelligent person knows when and how to apologize.

	Direct Speech	Indirect Speech
Change **present tense** to **past tense:**	"**I'm** sorry **I'm** late."	The student said (that) she **was** sorry she **was** late.
Change **present progressive tense** to **past progressive tense.**	"**I'm having** a bad day."	She said (that) she **was having** a bad day.
Change **past tense** and **present perfect tense** to **past perfect tense.**	"The bus **broke** down."	The student said (that) the bus **had broken** down.
	"It **has** never **broken** down before."	She said (that) it **had** never **broken** down before.
The modals ***will, can,*** and ***may*** change form in indirect speech.	"I **won't** be late again."	She said (that) she **wouldn't** be late again.
	"I **can** take a taxi next time."	She said (that) she **could** take a taxi next time.
	"I **may** get a new car."	She said (that) she **might** get a new car.
Must changes to ***had to.***	"I **must** find a better way to get to work."	She said (that) she **had to** find a better way to get to work.
Do not change the modals ***should, could, might,*** or ***ought to.***	"I **should** get up earlier."	She said (that) she **should** get up earlier.
Change the pronouns, possessives, and time words to keep the original meaning.	"**I** can't drive **my** car because it broke down **yesterday**."	The student said (that) **she** couldn't drive **her** car because it had broken down **the day before**.

❷ *Work in a group of three. Each student should have a turn reading the statements and then using indirect speech. Switch roles after number 4.*

Student A: Read aloud the statements in column 1 one at a time.

Student B: After Student A reads each statement, ask Student C, "What did he/she say?" When Student C responds, check the answer in column 2. If Student C is correct, say, "That's right." If Student C is not correct, say, "I'm sorry, try again."

Student C: ***Close your book.*** *Use indirect speech to repeat Student A's statements. Student B will tell you if you are correct or not.*

Column 1	**Column 2**
1. I did very well on the EQ test.	1. ______________ said he/she had done very well on the EQ test.
2. I don't think the EQ theory will hold up.	2. ______________ said he/she didn't think the EQ theory would hold up.
3. I'm going to work on my EQ.	3. ______________ said he/she was going to work on his/her EQ.
4. I never learned about EQ in school.	4. ______________ said he/she had never learned about EQ in school.
	Now switch roles.
5. I am really busy.	5. ______________ said that he/she was really busy.
6. I can't talk to the boss right now.	6. ______________ said that he/she couldn't talk to the boss right now.
7. I haven't finished my work yet.	7. ______________ said that he/she hadn't finished his/her work yet.
8. I'll call the boss later.	8. ______________ said that he/she would call the boss later.

B. STYLE: Paraphrasing

When we **paraphrase,** we say the same thing in different words. Paraphrasing is useful to check your comprehension of someone's statement. In paraphrasing, it is important to explain the other person's ideas *in your own words.* Unlike direct and indirect speech, when you paraphrase you do not repeat the other person's exact words. Look at the following quotation and a possible paraphrase:

Quotation: "Love is the victory of imagination over intelligence."
—H. L. Mencken

Paraphrase: Mencken means that we don't think clearly when we are in love. Our feelings are stronger than our logical thoughts.

You can use phrases like this to begin a paraphrase:

- In other words . . .
- To put it another way . . .
- She means/meant that . . .
- He wants/wanted to say that . . .
- She is/was trying to say that . . .

Work as a class. Read the quotes about intelligence. Discuss the meanings of the quotes. Use your own words to paraphrase the ideas.

Example

"Love is the victory of imagination over intelligence."
—H. L. Mencken, U.S. journalist and author (1880–1956)

STUDENT A: I think he means that love is not very intelligent.

STUDENT B: What he's trying to say is that we don't think clearly when we are in love.

STUDENT C: I agree. In other words, when you love someone, you sometimes ignore reality and only see what you want to see.

1. "The height of intelligence is being able to hide it." [adapted]
—François, Duc de La Rochefoucauld, French writer (1613–1680)

2. "One of the problems of civilizations is that happiness and intelligence are so rarely found in the same person." —Anonymous

3. "Life is a comedy for those who think and a tragedy for those who feel." —Horace Walpole, 4th Earl of Oxford (1717–1797)

4. "Truly great madness cannot be achieved without significant intelligence." —Anonymous

5. "Artificial Intelligence [in computers] is not as great as natural stupidity [in people]." —Anonymous

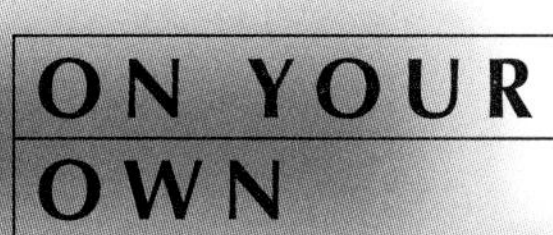

A. SPEAKING TOPICS: Role Play and an EQ Test

ROLE PLAY

❶ *Working in pairs, choose one of the situations. Decide whether you will illustrate high or low EQ. Review the five skills of EQ (page 145) to clarify your ideas. Practice the role play with your partner. Then perform your role play for the class.*

Situation 1: A Twenty-Year-Old and a Parent

Student A: You are twenty years old, and you live with your parents. Your mother/father is strict with you. She/he always asks where you're going, what you're doing, and who you're doing it with. You feel that she/he is treating you like a child, and it's driving you crazy.

Student B: Your child is only twenty but never wants to stay home. You can't understand why she/he has to go out so often or why she/he resents your asking where she/he is going or what she/he is going to do there. She/he's making you feel very frustrated.

Situation 2: A Boss and an Employee

Student A: You are extremely busy and have to give a report at an important meeting tomorrow. One of your employees just gave you information that you need for your report, but she/he didn't give you all the details you need. There is very little time, so now you will both have to work late tonight. You are quite annoyed.

Student B: At work, you have just completed a big report. You worked hard on it and are really satisfied with the results. However, your boss hardly looked at it but told you that it wasn't what she/he was expecting. You are very upset because you did exactly as you were told.

Situation 3: A Married Couple

Student A: You are tired. Your wife/husband begins to criticize you because you left your dirty dishes in the sink. You don't think you've done anything wrong. You think she/he is not being fair to you. You are very annoyed.

Student B: Your husband/wife has left dirty dishes in the sink again. You are tired and don't want to wash them. You think she/he is not being fair to you. You complain.

❷ *Watch as other pairs perform their role plays. As a class, discuss the role plays. Use indirect speech (Section 6A, pages 152–154) or paraphrasing (Section 6B, page 155) to discuss what people said. Answer these questions:*

- Were their responses appropriate?
- Did they show high EQ?
- How could they have handled the situation differently?

CREATE AN EQ TEST

1. Work in a small group. Create five multiple-choice EQ test questions. Write a question illustrating each of the five skills of Emotional Intelligence (see Section 3D, page 145). Write one "correct" answer that shows the high EQ, and write two incorrect answers that show low EQ. Look at the test questions in Section 4A (pages 146–147) for sample questions.

2. Share your EQ test questions with another group. Does the other group agree with the "correct" answers? Why or why not?

B. FIELDWORK: Interview

Choose a person you admire. Then interview him or her about Emotional Intelligence.

PREPARATION

You will need to explain the theory of Emotional Intelligence to the person you interview. (See Background, Section 2A, page 139, for a short explanation of Emotional Intelligence.)

Work in a small group. Think of examples for each skill of Emotional Intelligence. Use the examples when you explain the theory.

Self-Awareness: Understanding your own emotions.

Example: ____

Self-Control: Managing your own emotions.

Example: ______________________________

Self-Motivation: Using your emotions to get things done.

Example: ______________________________

Empathy: Understanding other people's emotions.

Example: ______________________________

People Skills: Relating well to people.

Example: ______________________________

THE INTERVIEW

Conduct the interview. Briefly explain EQ, and then ask the questions that follow. Take notes so you can report your findings to the class. Use indirect speech (Section 6A) and paraphrasing (Section 6B) to report on your interview.

Name: ______________________________

Occupation: ______________________________

Employer: ______________________________

1. Is Emotional Intelligence important in your profession? If so, which skills are the most important? (Ask for specific examples.)

2. How can an employer evaluate the Emotional Intelligence of someone applying for a job?

3. How can a person improve his or her Emotional Intelligence?

4. Should schools teach students the skills of Emotional Intelligence? Why or why not? If so, what can schools do to help students improve their EQ?

5. Should employers teach their employees the skills of Emotional Intelligence? Why or why not? If so, what can employers do to help their employees improve their EQ?

UNIT 8

JOURNEY TO THE RED PLANET

1 APPROACHING THE TOPIC

A. PREDICTING

Working with a partner, do the following activities.

1. **The planets in our solar system are Earth, Saturn, Mercury, Pluto, Mars, Neptune, Jupiter, Uranus, and Venus. Mercury is the planet closest to the sun. You can remember their order by referring to a memory device: "My Very Educated Mother Just Served Us Nine Pizzas." Look at the diagram, and use this device to label the planets.**
2. **Why do you think Mars is called the *Red Planet?* Do you think humans will ever live on Mars? Why or why not? Discuss your answers to the questions with your partner and the class.**

B. SHARING INFORMATION

Are we alone in the universe, or are there any other life forms out there? This question has always fascinated human beings. In fact, space and space travel have inspired some of our best and worst science fiction literature, television series, and films, including:

E.T.
Independence Day
Invaders from Mars
Mars Attacks
Star Trek
The Twilight Zone
The War of the Worlds
The X-Files

Work in a small group. Choose a movie or book about space travel or aliens from the list, or choose a different one that you have seen or read. Describe it to your group. Include the following information:

1. A summary of what happens in the story.
2. A description of the alien life forms, or extraterrestrials. Draw a picture.
3. An evaluation of the book or movie. Did you like it? Why or why not?

2 PREPARING TO LISTEN

A. BACKGROUND

How much do you know about the "Red Planet"? Take this quiz about Mars. Read each statement and decide if it is **true** *or* **false.** *Mark the appropriate box. Then check your answers in the Answer Key. Give yourself one point for each correct answer.*

What Do You Know about Mars?

		TRUE	FALSE
1.	There are water and energy sources on Mars.	☐	☐
2.	For life to exist, it must have water. However, this water could be in liquid, frozen, or gas form.	☐	☐
3.	Mars is about the same size as Earth.	☐	☐
4.	The temperature on Mars is higher than it is on Earth.	☐	☐
5.	The atmosphere of Mars is made up mostly of CO_2 (carbon dioxide).	☐	☐
6.	A day on Mars is much longer than a day on Earth.	☐	☐
7.	A meteorite from Mars hit the Earth in the Stone Age.	☐	☐
8.	Mars is called the "Red Planet" because it is boiling hot.	☐	☐
9.	Scientists have photographs of the Martian landscape.	☐	☐
10.	There are fierce dust storms on Mars.	☐	☐
11.	The gravity on Mars is so strong that it would be impossible for a human being to walk there.	☐	☐
12.	Unmanned equipment has already landed on Mars.	☐	☐
13.	Primitive life forms, such as bacteria, probably exist on Mars.	☐	☐
14.	In the 1970s, the United States sent a spacecraft to search for life on Mars.	☐	☐
15.	If we managed to get people to Mars, they could make building materials from the Martian soil.	☐	☐
16.	The U.S. agency that sends spacecraft to Mars is called NASA (National Aeronautics and Space Administration).	☐	☐

YOUR TOTAL SCORE: ____________

RATINGS: 16–14: You are a Mars expert.
9–13: You know a lot about Mars.
below 9: You have more to learn about Mars.

B. VOCABULARY FOR COMPREHENSION

Read the following sentences. Look at the possible meanings for the underlined expression. Two are similar to the underlined expression. One is not. Cross out the choice that seems ***least*** *similar in meaning. The first one has been done for you.*

1. Although some people believe that it is human destiny to explore the universe, others think it is a waste of money.

   a. future　　b. ~~choice~~　　c. fate

2. Many people support space exploration for romantic reasons: they imagine that we will find other intelligent life forms.

   a. practical　　b. idealistic　　c. imaginary

3. Although there have been several manned missions into space, most space exploration has been done by unmanned spacecraft that carry robots and computers to carry out scientific experiments.

   a. controlled from Earth　　b. carrying people　　c. transporting astronauts

4. A good scientist keeps an eye on new discoveries in order to stay up to date in her field.

   a. learns about　　b. pays attention to　　c. makes

5. Some people believe that exploring other worlds is not relevant to solving the problems we face here on Earth.

   a. different from　　b. useful for　　c. related to

6. One day, people may leave the Earth to live in colonies on other planets.

   a. groups　　b. houses　　c. settlements

7. When a robot is pitted against a human, the robot may work faster, but the human will be more creative.

   a. works with　　b. competes against　　c. challenges

8. Right now, there are ideas <u>on the drawing board</u> for inexpensive ways to travel to Mars. So far, however, these plans have not been put into effect.

   a. being discussed **b.** being considered **c.** being rejected

9. So far, there have been several <u>missions</u> to Mars without astronauts, and scientists will send more spacecraft in the near future.

   a. trips **b.** voyages **c.** plans

10. Just as the Moon revolves around the Earth, the planets in our solar system travel in <u>an orbit</u> around the Sun.

    a. a ring **b.** a location **c.** a circle

11. After <u>scooping up</u> soil samples, scientists can analyze their mineral content.

    a. collecting **b.** creating **c.** gathering

12. Rockets need a lot of power to exit a planet's <u>atmosphere</u> and enter into space.

    a. surface **b.** gas **c.** air

13. If you have a good idea and can get other people <u>behind</u> it, your dream may become reality.

    a. questioning **b.** financing **c.** supporting

14. <u>Innovative</u> ideas have led to important inventions that we use every day, such as the lightbulb, the telephone, and the automobile.

    a. creative **b.** expensive **c.** new

15. To solve difficult problems, scientists sometimes get together and <u>brainstorm</u>, talking about even the wildest possibilities before selecting the best one.

    a. imagine and discuss **b.** argue and debate **c.** relax and have fun

16. Scientists believe that other planets have underground <u>thermal</u> systems, like the hot springs we find on Earth.

    a. heated **b.** water **c.** high-temperature

3 LISTENING ONE: Journey to the Red Planet

A. INTRODUCING THE TOPIC

You will hear David Alpern, host of *Newsweek on Air,* interview Sharon Begley, science editor for *Newsweek* magazine. She discusses exploration on the planet Mars.

❶ *Sharon Begley discusses a group called the Mars Underground. Who do you think they are? What do you do? Write down your ideas, and discuss your answer with the class.*

____

❷ *With a partner, listen to excerpts of Sharon Begley's answers to questions in the interview. Then guess what question she is being asked. Write the question in the space. Discuss your questions with the class.*

Excerpt One

Q: ____?

A: As one scientist said, "Look, I'll pit my ten-year-old kid, who's great at Easter-egg finding, against your robot, and I guarantee that my ten-year-old kid is going to find something that the robot's not."

Excerpt Two

Q: ____?

A: Another approach—that first one is being done by NASA's Jet Propulsion Laboratory in California, which is in charge of robotic missions. Another approach is done by Johnson Space Center, which controls all the manned missions . . .

Excerpt Three

Q: ____?

A: There are a lot of interesting places. Most of them have to do with water and energy . . .

B. LISTENING FOR MAIN IDEAS

Read the following questions. Then listen to the interview and write short answers to the questions. Compare your answers with those of another student.

1. What is the Mars Underground?

2. What are members of the Mars Underground doing?

3. Why should we send humans instead of robots to Mars?

4. What is the "right stuff" approach to a manned Mars mission?

5. What is another approach to a manned Mars mission?

6. What is the benefit of the second approach?

7. Where will scientists focus their search for life on Mars?

The Sojourner Mars Rover takes pictures and measures the moisture of the soil.

C. LISTENING FOR DETAILS

Listen to the interview again. As you listen, read the sentences, and write **T** *(true) or* **F** *(false) in each blank. The first one has been done for you. Then discuss your answers with the class.*

1. Members of the Mars Underground . . .

__F__ **a.** are astronauts.
____ **b.** believe it is human destiny to go to Mars.
____ **c.** have been sending manned missions to Mars.
____ **d.** want to set up colonies on Mars.

2. Robots . . .

____ **a.** are waiting on the surface of Mars.
____ **b.** are not good at digging underground.
____ **c.** are better at finding things than a ten-year-old boy is.
____ **d.** will be sent to Mars in the next decade.

3. The "right stuff" approach for a manned mission to Mars . . .

____ **a.** is similar to the moon missions.
____ **b.** will send a spacecraft which orbits the planet.
____ **c.** will send down a lander to scoop up the astronauts.
____ **d.** will bring Martian rocks back to Earth.

4. Another approach for a manned mission to Mars . . .

____ **a.** will send up a craft that doesn't have enough fuel to get home.
____ **b.** will make water out of the Martian atmosphere.
____ **c.** is cheaper because it won't carry tons of fuel.
____ **d.** is being considered by NASA because it is innovative and inexpensive.

5. The search for life on Mars will focus . . .

____ **a.** in only a few places.
____ **b.** in dry lake beds and dry rivers.
____ **c.** where there are yellow stones.
____ **d.** on finding fossils, but not on finding surviving life forms.

D. LISTENING BETWEEN THE LINES

Read the following questions. Then listen to each excerpt from the interview. Answer the questions and complete the statements. Discuss your answers with a partner, then with the class.

Excerpt One

1. What does the name "Mars Underground" tell you about the group?

____

____

2. Sharon Begley says that there are "romantic reasons" why members of the Mars Underground want to explore Mars. Does she approve of these romantic reasons? Explain.

____

____

3. Complete this statement as you think Begley would: "They want to go to Mars for romantic reasons, for example . . ."

____

____

Excerpt Two

4. How would you describe Begley's tone of voice? Who is she making fun of?

____

____

5. Complete these statements as you think Begley would:

   Life forms on Mars do not ______________________________

   They are not ______________________________

Excerpt Three

6. According to Begley, how useful are robots on Mars missions?

____

____

7. Why does she use the example of a ten-year-old child? Does she think that we should send children to Mars?

____

____

8. Complete this statement as you think Begley would: "Robots are not good at finding things because . . ."

____

____

Excerpt Four

9. How likely does Begley think it is that one day, scientists will try these "make-your-own-fuel" missions?

____

____

10. In Begley's opinion, how does the top brass at NASA feel about new, innovative ideas?

____

____

11. Complete this statement as you think Begley would: "When deciding on a Mars mission, the most important factors to NASA are . . ."

____

____

4 LISTENING TWO: Terraforming—How to Colonize Mars

A. EXPANDING THE TOPIC

You will hear the second part of the *Newsweek on Air* interview. Kim Stanley Robinson, an author of science fiction novels, is interviewed by host David Alpern. Robinson is speaking about "terraforming" on Mars.

Listen to the interview. Take notes on the interview, using the questions on the next page to guide you. Compare your notes with those of a partner.

1. What is "terraforming"?

____

2. What are the steps in terraforming?
   - heat: ______________________________
   - water: ______________________________
   - life: ______________________________

3. How long would terraforming take?
   - estimates: ______________________________
   - in Robinson's novels: ______________________________
   - realistically: ______________________________

4. What would be the benefits of terraforming?

____

B. LINKING LISTENINGS ONE AND TWO

Scientists in the Mars Underground predict that there will be manned missions to Mars in the next decade. Kim Stanley Robinson, a science fiction writer, predicts colonization of Mars in the next five hundred years. What do *you* think will happen in the next fifty years?

❶ *Read the statements. Circle* ***Likely*** *or* ***Unlikely.*** *Give a reason why you made your choice, or give a related example. Then explain your reasons to another student.*

1. Evidence of intelligent life will be found on planets other than Mars and Earth.

   Likely / Unlikely

   Reason or related example: ______________________________

2. Countries will work together peacefully to explore Mars.

   Likely / Unlikely

   Reason or related example: ______________________________

3. Mars will be mined for minerals.

   Likely / Unlikely

   Reason or related example: ______________________________

4. People will try to terraform Mars.

   Likely / Unlikely

   Reason or related example: ______________________________

5. Humans will colonize Mars.

   Likely / Unlikely

   Reason or related example: ______________________________

On July 20, 1969, American astronauts Neil Armstrong and "Buzz" Aldrin landed and walked on the moon. This event had a big effect on the way Americans thought about themselves and the universe. They generally felt a new confidence in science and technology. They also felt a sense of wonder and pride in this achievement.

❷ *In a small group, discuss these questions:*

1. How might colonization of another planet affect how we on Earth view ourselves?

2. How might the discovery of intelligent life elsewhere in the universe affect how we on Earth view ourselves?

REVIEWING LANGUAGE

A. EXPLORING LANGUAGE: The Stress-Changing Suffix *-tion*

❶ *Work with a partner. Listen for the stressed syllable as each verb is pronounced on the tape. Remember: the stressed syllable is the one the speaker holds longer than the others.*

Listen again. Mark the stressed syllable of each verb. The first one has been marked for you.

éstimate	recite
innovate	indicate
colonize	beautify
educate	motivate
adapt	evolve

❷ *Now listen for the stressed syllable as the noun form of each verb in Exercise 1 is pronounced on the tape.*

Listen again, and mark the stressed syllables. The first one has been done for you.

Then compare the words in Exercises 1 and 2. How does the stress change? On which syllable does the stress usually fall for nouns that end in ***-tion****? How is* ***-tion*** *pronounced?*

estimátion	recitation
innovation	indication
colonization	beautification
education	motivation
adaptation	evolution

❸ *Work with a partner. Take turns asking each other the questions. To answer, choose a term from the list that follows.*

a beautification program	indication
a colonization project	innovations
evolution	motivation

1. What do we call a program to beautify the environment?
2. What do we call a project to colonize a planet?
3. What's the noun form of <u>indicate</u>?
4. When life forms evolve, what's the process called?
5. When people are innovative, what do we call their ideas or inventions?
6. What's a word that means <u>reason for doing something</u>?

❹ *Work in a small group to do the following activity.*

Think about the history of inventions and explorations. New ideas and discoveries are not always welcomed. They are sometimes met with surprise, doubt, fear, or anger. The discoveries of the English naturalist Charles Darwin, the Italian astronomer Galileo Galilei, and the Spanish explorer Ferdinand Magellan met with unfavorable reactions in their day.

STEP 1

Read the information about Darwin in the following example. Then read the paragraph discussing how others reacted to his ideas and discoveries. Note how the words in the box are used in the reaction.

Example

Charles Darwin, English naturalist

- *Author: The Origin of Species,* 1859
- *Theory:* that all life evolved from lower life forms and that humans and monkeys had common ancestors millions of years ago.
- *Popular belief at the time:* humans have had the same form since the Creation.
- *Consequence:* some religious groups were outraged and demanded that evolution not be taught in public schools.

evolve
create
react
educate

Reaction

In 1859, the English naturalist Charles Darwin wrote *The Origin of Species.* He said that humans and monkeys had evolved from common ancestors. Many people thought that Darwin's ideas about evolution went against religious teachings. They felt that Darwin was saying that humans had not been created by God. They reacted very angrily and tried to get schools to stop teaching the science of evolution. They felt that children should not be educated to believe in evolutionism.

STEP 2

Now use the information about Galileo Galilei and Ferdinand Magellan to discuss how people might have reacted to their ideas, discoveries, or accomplishments. Try to use some of the words from the box directly to the right of the information, but feel free to select words from the other boxes as well. Remember to change the word forms if necessary.

1. Galileo Galilei, Italian astronomer, 1564–1642
   - *Theory:* that the planets travel around the Sun, not around the Earth.
   - *Popular belief at the time:* the Earth was the center of the universe.
   - *Consequence:* Galileo was forced to give up his theory or face death.

predict
propose
react
educate

2. Ferdinand Magellan, Spanish explorer, 1480–1521
   - *Accomplishment:* sailed around the world
   - *Popular belief at the time:* the Earth was flat.
   - *Consequence:* people were forced to change their perceptions of the Earth.

persistent
propose
react
indicate

3. Use your own example from history.

B. WORKING WITH WORDS: Synonyms

The words in Exercise 1 are ***synonyms,*** words that are very similar in meaning. They are different, however, in that the words in column 2 have additional meanings, or *nuances*. For example, the noun *future* means time that is to come or something that will exist or happen in time to come. One of its synonyms, *destiny,* however, means something that must happen to a person or something that is unavoidable, someone's fate or fortune.

❶ *Draw a line to match the synonyms.*

Column 1	**Column 2**
certain	destiny
change	evolve
develop	hospitable
future	inevitable
impractical	innovative
livable	romantic
new	transform

❷ *Complete the sentences by writing one of the words from column 2 in the blank. The first one has been done for you.*

1. ____Destiny____ is something that must happen in the future.

2. An ________________ idea is completely new and unlike any idea that came before.

3. A ________________ person may imagine the adventure and beauty of space travel without focusing on the practical details of a space voyage.

4. To ________________ is to change to be completely different from before.

5. Something ________________ is certain to happen and can't be prevented.

6. To ________________ is to slowly develop and become different over a long period of time.

7. A ________________ environment is not just livable, but also welcoming.

❸ *Read the sentences. In some sentences, either synonym can be used. In other sentences, only one of the words is appropriate. Underline the words that can be used. The first one has been done for you.*

1. a. Terraforming would (<u>change</u>/<u>transform</u>) Mars into a completely different planet. *(Either word could be used.)*

   b. Bad weather may (<u>change</u>/transform) the plans to launch a new spacecraft today.

2. a. NASA built a(n) (new/innovative) space shuttle because the old one broke down.

   b. NASA built a(n) (new/innovative) space shuttle that had many new technological advances not found in any other spacecraft.

3. a. Manned missions to Mars are still far in our (future/destiny).

   b. Because humans continue to be curious about new places, it is our (future/destiny) to keep exploring farther and farther into the universe.

4. a. Some people have (impractical/romantic) ideas about meeting intelligent life forms from other planets. These ideas often come from watching too many television shows and movies.

   b. With the current level of technology, it is a(n) (impractical/romantic) idea to send large numbers of people into space.

5. a. I think it is (certain/inevitable) that people will travel to Mars someday.

   b. A mission to Mars is (certain/inevitable) to cost billions of dollars.

6. a. It took millions of years for life to (develop/evolve) on Earth.
   b. Before going into space, astronauts must (develop/evolve) skills to help them deal with living in a small place.

7. a. So far, spacecraft are (livable/hospitable), but they are not very comfortable.
   b. After terraforming Mars, it is hoped that the planet would provide a (livable/hospitable) environment, which would be attractive for all kinds of life.

6 SKILLS FOR EXPRESSION

A. GRAMMAR: Phrasal Verbs

❶ *Working with a partner, examine the statements and discuss the questions that follow.*

- In the "right stuff" approach to the Mars missions, a lander would collect some Martian rocks. A special arm would <u>scoop them up</u> and take them back to Earth.
- There are many competing ideas on the drawing board. Scientists from NASA have <u>teamed up</u> to find the best approach. So far, they haven't <u>come up with it</u> yet.

a. What is a one-word synonym for scoop up? What are synonyms for <u>team up</u> and <u>come up with</u>?

b. What do the pronouns <u>them</u> and <u>it</u> refer to in the underlined phrases?

Focus on Grammar

See Phrasal Verbs in *Focus on Grammar, High-Intermediate.*

Phrasal Verbs

Phrasal verbs consist of a verb and a particle (an adverb or preposition). The meaning of a phrasal verb may be very different from the meaning of the verb and particle alone.

Verb +	Particle	Meaning
scoop	***up***	lift; collect
come	***up with***	imagine; invent
team	***up***	begin working together

Phrasal verbs can be transitive or intransitive.

Transitive phrasal verbs take a direct object.	The robot **scooped up** some soil. The scientist **came up with** an idea.
Some transitive phrasal verbs are **separable.** The direct object can come between the verb and particle, or after the particle.	The robot **scooped** some soil **up.** OR The robot **scooped up** some soil.
If the direct object is a pronoun, it always comes between the verb and particle.	The robot **scooped** it **up.** NOT The robot **scooped** ~~**up** it~~.
If the direct object is a long phrase, it always comes after the particle.	The robot **scooped up** some soil, which the scientists later analyzed in the laboratory. NOT The robot **scooped** ~~some soil~~, ~~which the scientists later analyzed in the laboratory **up.**~~
Other transitive phrasal verbs are **inseparable.** The direct object always comes after the particle.	The scientist **came up with** an idea. NOT The scientists **came** ~~it **up with.**~~
Intransitive phrasal verbs do not take a direct object.	The scientists **teamed up** to complete the project.

❷ *Match the phrasal verbs with their meanings. The ones with an asterisk (*) are inseparable phrasal verbs. The first one has been done for you.*

Phrasal Verb	**Meaning**
__f__ 1. scoop up	a. choose
____ 2. come up with*	b. destroy
____ 3. get rid of*	c. establish; start
____ 4. hint at*	d. go as fast as
____ 5. keep down	e. invent
____ 6. keep up with*	f. lift; collect
____ 7. pick out	g. not have enough of
____ 8. run out of*	h. prevent from increasing
____ 9. set up	i. pursue; follow
____ 10. stick with*	j. reject
____ 11. think back on*	k. remember
____ 12. turn down	l. say indirectly

❸ *Complete the sentences with the phrasal verbs and objects in parentheses. Place the object between the verb and the particle whenever possible, and change the tense if necessary. Read the sentences aloud to a partner to check your answers. Sentences 1 and 2 have been done for you.*

1. The lander will collect Martian soil. An arm on the lander will __scoop it up__ (scoop up / it) and then go back up to the orbiter and come home.

2. We needed an innovative idea to reduce the cost of Mars missions, and scientists have __come up with it__ (come up with / it): making rocket fuel from the Martian atmosphere.

3. Life is pretty persistent—it's very hard to ________ (get rid of / it).

4. You ________ (hint at / it) earlier—that if there is life on Mars, it's not, you know, standing on the runway waiting to say: "Here we are!"

5. The cost of space technology is enormous. Governments will look for ways to ________ (keep down / it).

6. If you pit a ten-year-old kid against a robot, the kid won't be able to ________________ (keep up with / it). The kid will be slower, but he'll be better able to find things.

7. We need to identify the sites on Mars where we might find life. Robots can't ________________ (pick out / them), so we will have to send astronauts someday.

8. A lot of fuel is needed for the return trip from Mars to Earth. It's important not to ________________ (run out of / it).

9. Members of the Mars Underground believe that it is human destiny to have colonies on Mars. They hope to ________________ (set up / them) in the near future.

10. Scientist haven't figured out yet how to make Mars missions truly affordable. But they will ________________ (stick with / it) until the problem is solved.

11. The history of space travel is not long, but when you ________________ (think back on / it), there have been a lot of amazing advances.

12. If you had the opportunity to go to Mars, would you ________________ (turn down / it)?

❹ *Work in pairs.*

Student A: Read each question in the left-hand column to Student B.

Student B: Cover the left-hand side of the page and listen as Student A reads each question. Then complete the answer using an appropriate phrasal verb and pronoun. Refer to the list of phrasal verbs on page 177.

Student A: You have the answers. Correct Student B, if necessary.

Student A

1. When a spacecraft comes back to Earth, do the astronauts destroy the extra fuel? *(get rid of it)*
2. Kim Stanley Robinson doesn't say directly that he supports the colonization of Mars, does he? *(hints at it)*
3. Do you think human colonies will be established on Mars someday? *(set them up)*
4. How can a robot collect Martian soil? *(scoops it up)*
5. Space missions are very expensive. Can't we limit the costs? *(keep them down)*
6. Do you think people should keep trying to get to Mars? *(stick with it)*

Student B

1. Yes, I think they ________________.
2. No, but he ________________.
3. Yes, I think someone will ________________ eventually.
4. It just ________________.
5. No, it will be very difficult to ________________.
6. Yes, if we ________________, eventually the dream will become a reality.

Now switch roles.

Student B

7. Of all the space flights you remember during your lifetime, which one do you remember the best? *(think back on it)*
8. Who first had the idea of terraforming Mars? *(came up with it)*
9. Could a robot move as fast as an astronaut on the surface of Mars? *(keep up with him/her)*
10. How will scientists choose places to look for life on Mars? *(pick them out)*
11. Do you think governments will reject the idea of terraforming Mars? *(turn it down)*
12. What will happen if people don't take enough water to Mars? *(run out of it)*

Student A

7. When I ________________, I remember (your answer) the best.
8. I don't know who ________________.
9. No, I don't think a robot could ________________.
10. They will ________________ by looking for places where there used to be water.
11. They may ________________ because it will be very expensive.
12. If they ________________, they might be able to get some from underground sources.

B. STYLE: Supporting an Argument

When you give an opinion about something, you may need to add **support** to strengthen your argument.

Here are some expressions people often use before making the next point that strengthens their argument.

Formal	Informal
Furthermore, In addition, Moreover, Not only that, but also . . . To give you some idea, What's more,	And . . . And another thing, Besides, Plus,

Work with a partner. Take turns asking and answering the questions. As you answer, use the expressions in the box to add support to your response. Take a few minutes to prepare before you begin the exercise.

Student A

1. Why do people want to go to Mars?

Student B

1. Well, there is a political reason.

   Example: *In addition,* humans have a natural curiosity.

Student A

2. What are some problems with going to Mars?

Student B

2. It would be dangerous.

   Besides, . . .

Student A

3. I don't think the most powerful countries should decide what happens on Mars.

Student B

3. No, that's not fair to less powerful countries.

   (Introduce support, then continue the statement.)

Student A

4. Why do some people think it is wrong to travel to other planets?

Student B

4. There are enough problems to solve right here on Earth.

   (Introduce support, then continue the statement.)

Student A

5. Do you agree or disagree that we should be spending money on space travel? Why?

Student B

5. (Your own idea.)

Now switch roles.

Student B

6. Why are there so many science fiction books about space travel?

Student A

6. It's fun to imagine going far from home.

   Not only that, but also . . .

Student B

7. Why do some people believe that intelligent life exists only on Earth?

Student A

7. Maybe they think God put life only on Earth.

   Moreover, . . .

Student B

8. How could a mission to Mars help us solve problems here on Earth?

Student A

8. Humans have a great desire for knowledge.

   (Introduce support, then continue the statement.)

Student B

9. Are there really any benefits to space travel?

Student A

9. Well, for one thing, much of our everyday technology developed from space technology.

   (Introduce support, then continue the statement.)

Student B

10. Would you like to be an astronaut? Why, or why not?

Student A

10. (Your own idea.)

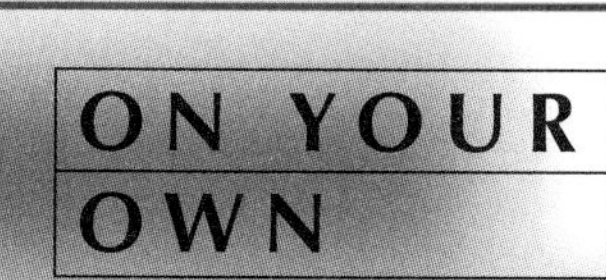

A. SPEAKING TOPIC: Planning a Mission to Mars

It's the year 3020, and a mission to Mars is about to be launched. You and your group are on the committee to select who and what will be taken aboard the terraforming spacecraft to begin a new colony on Mars.

❶ *As a class, decide what the purpose of the colony will be and who should establish a colony on Mars.*

❷ *Select ten people for the mission to Mars. You may choose from the professions listed below, or add more of your own. Fill in the details about the people's age, sex, nationality, marital status, and reason why he or she would be a good candidate for a new colony on Mars.*

PROFESSION	AGE	SEX	NATIONALITY	MARITAL STATUS	REASON FOR SENDING THIS PERSON TO MARS
Biologist					
Medical doctor					
Writer					
Artist					
Nutritionist					
Postal worker					
Homemaker					
Engineer					
Social worker					
Psychologist					
Child					
Other					

3 *Role play a group interview of the ten candidates for the mission to Mars. One-half the class will be candidates. The other half will be interviewers who will ask the candidates why they feel they would qualify for the mission and what skills they can contribute.*

4 *When you have finished the role play, present your group's mission proposal to the rest of the class. Justify your choices.*

B. FIELDWORK: The Role of Water in Space Exploration

How the Lunar Prospector finds water ice on the surface of the Moon: A neutron spectrometer skims the Moon's crust and measures the speed and heat of dislodged neutrons. Areas that are moist give off cool and slow neutrons, and areas that have little or no water give off hot and faster neutrons.

PREPARATION

Water has been discovered on the moon—frozen in moon craters. Look at the photo of the Lunar Prospector, which found water ice on the Moon's surface. Think about what you have read in this unit about CO_2 on Mars and the possibilities for converting it to fuel and water. If there were plenty of water on the moon, how might this affect future exploration and/or colonization there? Discuss the possibilities with the class.

RESEARCH ACTIVITY

Go to the library or search the Internet to learn more about the scientific implications of finding water on the moon. NASA has a Web site. The address is:

www.jsc.nasa.gov

Use these questions to help with your research:

1. What do scientists say about the significance of water on the moon?
2. What are the possible consequences of further exploration and colonization on the moon?
3. How might further moon exploration and colonization affect travel to and settlements on Mars and other planets?

SHARING YOUR FINDINGS

Present your findings to the class. Ask who in the class would like to be part of a mission to settle on the moon. Discuss the pros and cons of such an adventure.

UNIT 9

Finding a Niche: Experiences of Young Immigrants

1 APPROACHING THE TOPIC

A. PREDICTING

Work with a partner and answer these questions. Then discuss your responses with the class.

1. **Look at the photo and the title of the unit. What do you think *finding a niche* means? Predict what this unit will be about.**
2. **Have you or has anyone in your family ever lived in another country? Describe the experience.**
   - **How long did you live in another country?**
   - **What was the purpose of your stay?**
   - **What difficulties did you face?**
   - **What did you learn about living in another country?**
3. **How are the experiences of visiting another country and immigrating to another country similar? How are they different?**

B. SHARING INFORMATION

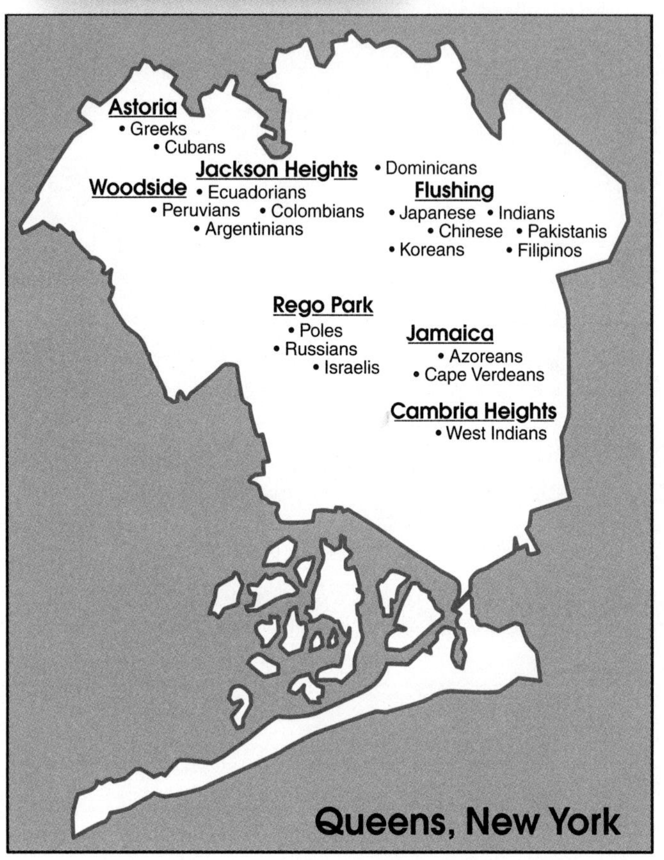

This map shows some of the immigrant groups of Queens, one of the five parts of New York City. Queens is one of the most ethnically diverse areas in the United States.

Work in a small group. Look at the map. In the chart, write the names of the countries and the languages the people probably speak. Then discuss your list with the class.

COUNTRIES/LANGUAGES	COUNTRIES/LANGUAGES
Colombia/Spanish	

2 PREPARING TO LISTEN

A. BACKGROUND

Read the information and do the activity that follows.

The United States has always attracted immigrants from around the world. Today, thousands of immigrants flood into large urban areas each year. Many are teenagers who have not yet completed their schooling. Unfamiliar with the language and the culture, they face the enormous task of learning to adapt to their new realities. Due to the diverse backgrounds and needs of these new immigrants, school teachers and administrators also face very complex tasks.

New York City is the destination for many immigrants. Within the New York City public school system, a number of programs have been established to address this situation. One such innovative program is the International High School in Queens. Its mission is to help new immigrant students develop not only academic skills, but also the cultural skills that are necessary for success in high school, college, and beyond. Only students who have been in the United States for less than four years are eligible for admission.

Some schools have no special programs for new immigrants, while others have bilingual or ESL programs. The International High School exemplifies a different approach: a multilingual program. Since it was established in 1985, the school has received a great deal of recognition for its success in teaching young people.

What do you think? Read the following statements. Write **A** *(agree) or* **D** *(disagree) in the blank space. Then work in a small group. Compare your opinions with those of other students.*

_____ **1.** Teenage immigrants should learn math and science in their own languages.

_____ **2.** As immigrant teens learn the language that is spoken in their new country, they become less proficient in their first language.

_____ **3.** One of the main responsibilities of teachers is to make sure that students maintain their own language and culture, even if it means that the students learn English more slowly.

_____ **4.** It is important that young immigrants study the same subjects as students who speak English well. Otherwise, they will never completely adapt.

B. VOCABULARY FOR COMPREHENSION

❶ *Read the following sentences. Try to determine the meaning of the underlined words from the context of the sentences. Then write a definition or similar expression under the sentence.*

1. For many immigrants, New York is home. It is a place where many immigrant businesses have started and neighborhoods have grown. It's a city where immigrant communities not only survive, but <u>flourish</u>.

   ____

2. Young adults experience conflict between the need to learn English and the desire to maintain their <u>native tongue</u>.

   ____

3. It can be difficult for young immigrants who have been <u>uprooted</u> from their home environments to adjust to their new environment.

   ____

4. Many of these young people come from large families that are very <u>tight-knit</u>. Family members know each other very well and see each other often.

   ____

5. For adults, moving to a new country might be a bit strange and confusing. For young people who are just developing their self-confidence, however, it can be very <u>intimidating</u>.

   ____

6. Priscilla was nervous because she thought she would not be allowed to speak her native language in class. She was <u>relieved</u> when she learned that her native language was welcomed.

   ____

7. At home, immigrant teens can speak their own language or dialect freely, but at school this practice is often <u>suppressed</u>.

   ____

8. My mother is going to visit France. She wants to <u>bone up on</u> her French because she hasn't practiced it since high school.

   ____

9. Hiroko is unique because she is the only student in her class who was born in the United States.

____

10. American television reflects mostly mainstream American culture. It doesn't necessarily show the rich ethnic variety of the American population.

____

11. Excellent study habits help set great students apart from average ones.

____

12. In the United States, strong differences among ethnic groups become less evident as those groups are assimilated into mainstream culture.

____

2 *Match the words on the left with a definition or similar expression from the list on the right. Write the appropriate letter in the blank space. Then compare your answers with those of another student.*

____ 1. relieved
____ 2. bone up on
____ 3. assimilate
____ 4. flourish
____ 5. intimidating
____ 6. mainstream culture
____ 7. native tongue
____ 8. set . . . apart
____ 9. suppress
____ 10. tight-knit
____ 11. unique
____ 12. uprooted

a. special; individual
b. removed from; torn from
c. the common way of thinking or acting
d. not allow to be expressed
e. frightening
f. make someone or something different
g. grow and develop well
h. review; study again
i. adapt and adjust
j. happy that a bad situation has been avoided
k. first language
l. close; sharing concerns

3 LISTENING ONE: A World within a School

A. INTRODUCING THE TOPIC

You will hear a report by Richard Schiffman, with host Mary Ambrose, from the Public Radio International program *The World*. Schiffman interviews teachers and students at the International High School in Queens, New York.

Listen to the introduction. Then work with a partner to answer the questions. Compare your responses with those of other students.

1. What is the teaching method, or approach, used at the International High School?

2. Speaking about the International High School, Ambrose notes: ". . . it seems to work." Predict some reasons for its success.

B. LISTENING FOR MAIN IDEAS

Read the statements. Then listen to the radio report and check (✓) the statements that are true.

At the International High School . . .

____ 1. students speak their native languages.
____ 2. students work in groups.
____ 3. students are all immigrants to the United States.
____ 4. students help each other in their native language.
____ 5. teachers lecture a lot.
____ 6. teachers want students to feel comfortable.
____ 7. teachers feel that immigrant students are a problem.
____ 8. students improve their English *and* their native language.
____ 9. teachers think that speaking two languages is valuable.
____ 10. students try to be assimilated quickly into American culture.

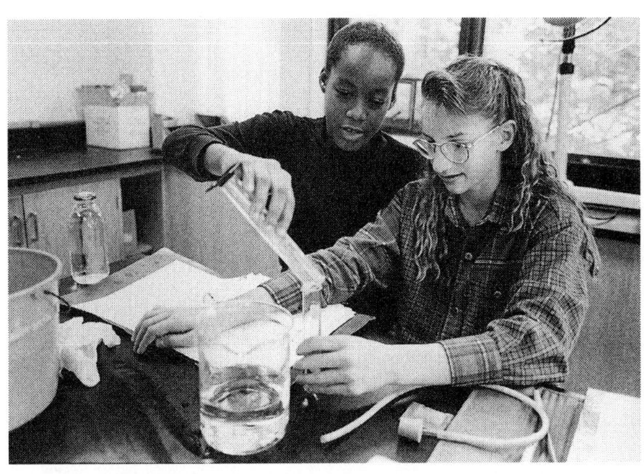

The two students are helping each other in science class as students do at the International High School.

C. LISTENING FOR DETAILS

Look at the list of people from the International High School. Listen to the report again. Check whether each person is a teacher or student. List what they like about the school, and summarize their comments. Check your answers with those of another student.

PERSON BEING INTERVIEWED	ROLE IN SCHOOL STUDENT / TEACHER		WHAT THIS PERSON LIKES ABOUT THE SCHOOL
Jennifer Shenke	☐	☐	
Priscilla Billarrel	☐	☐	
Aaron Listhaus	☐	☐	
Evelyna Namovich	☐	☐	
Kathy Rucker	☐	☐	

D. LISTENING BETWEEN THE LINES

Work with a partner. Listen to the four excerpts from the report on the International High School, and take notes. Read the statement in the middle column. Decide whether you agree or disagree. Then read the questions in the right-hand column, and discuss your opinion with your partner.

	AGREE OR DISAGREE	REACT AND DISCUSS
Excerpt One	This teacher probably feels that if students are allowed to speak their own languages in the classroom, she will have very little control over the students. agree/disagree	Is it good for students' academic progress if the teacher does not understand everything they say?
Excerpt Two	For this math teacher, how her students feel is more important than what they learn. agree/disagree	How important is it to feel comfortable when you are studying an academic subject? Should studying be difficult?
Excerpt Three	This teacher probably feels that her role is one of guide more than teacher. agree/disagree	How much can you learn from classmates? How important is a teacher in a classroom?
Excerpt Four	The students' similar experiences seem to help them overcome the differences in their cultural backgrounds. agree/disagree	How important is it to spend time with others who have similar problems? Is it better to spend more time with people who don't share your problems?

LISTENING TWO: Changing Trends of U.S. Immigration

A. EXPANDING THE TOPIC

❶ *Listen to the lecture about immigration to the United States. Look at the pie graphs below. The information in the statement on the left has been filled in for you. Work with a partner to fill in the statements on the right.*

U.S. IMMIGRANT POPULATION

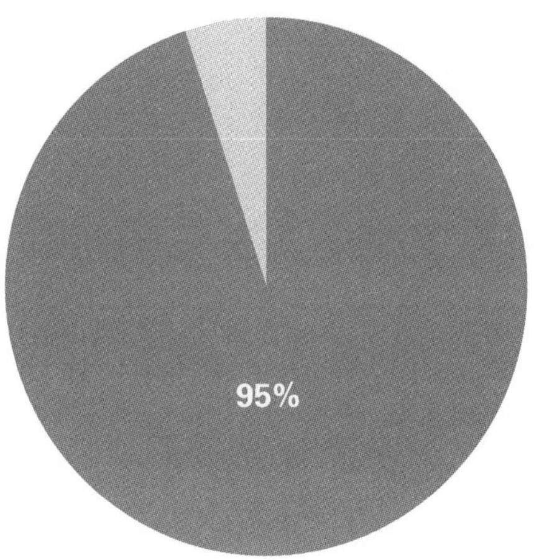

Early Part of the Century

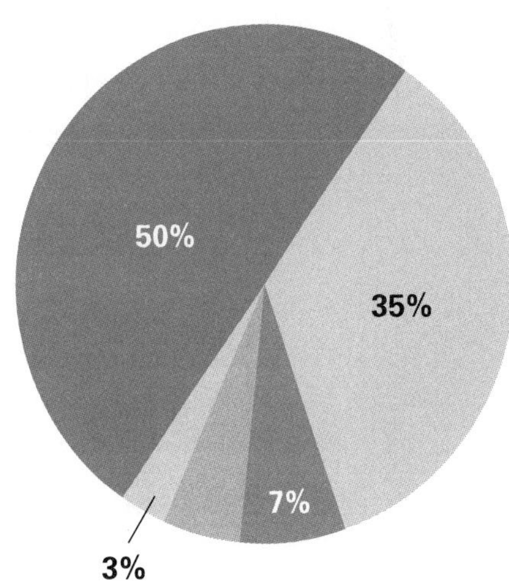

Latter Part of the Century

Early Part of the Century

95% came from <u>northern and western Europe</u>

Latter Part of the Century

50% came from ____________________

35% came from ____________________

3% came from ____________________

7% came from ____________________

❷ *Match the definitions with the models. Write the appropriate model name in the blank.*

- melting pot (assimilation)
- salad bowl (multiculturalism)

____________________	A term that refers to the blending of values, lifestyles, and institutions of immigrant groups with mainstream culture.
____________________	A term that describes a situation in which each immigrant group preserves its own unique characteristics.

B. LINKING LISTENINGS ONE AND TWO

In a small group, discuss the answers to the following questions.

1. The International High School is organized on a multicultural model: immigrant students are encouraged to maintain their native language and culture as they learn about others. What are the advantages and disadvantages of a "salad bowl" versus a "melting pot" approach?

2. What can a school do to help young immigrants "find a niche"? What problems might such students have? How might a school help students solve these problems?

5

REVIEWING LANGUAGE

A. EXPLORING LANGUAGE: Discriminating between Similar Sounds

The four sounds below are similar in some ways, but not in others. To pronounce these sounds clearly, notice the following differences:

voiceless	**voiced**
[ʃ] as in *she*	[ʒ] as in *pleasure*
[tʃ] as in *child*	[dʒ] as in *language, judge*

- To produce [ʃ] as in *she*:

  Force air out over your tongue and through your teeth. Do not use your voice. You use this sound to warn someone to be quiet.

- To produce [ʒ] as in *pleasure*:

  Pronounce this sound just as you pronounced [ʃ], but use your voice.

- To produce [tʃ] as in *child*:

  Press the tip of your tongue against your upper mouth, just behind your teeth. Then lower your tongue quickly, forcing the air out. Do not use your voice.

- To produce [dʒ] as in *language, judge*:

  Pronounce this sound just as you pronounced [tʃ], but use your voice. When this sound occurs at the end of a word, be careful not to release the sound too strongly or pronounce an extra syllable.

❶ *You will hear a list of words. Pay close attention to the focus sounds. For each word you hear, put a check (✓) in the column which describes the boldfaced sound. The first one has been done for you.*

	[ʃ] (**SH**E)	[ʒ] (PLEA**S**URE)	[tʃ] (**CH**ILD)	[dʒ] (J**UDGE**)
1. interna**ti**onal	☑	☐	☐	☐
2. langua**ge**	☐	☐	☐	☐
3. en**j**oy	☐	☐	☐	☐
4. a**dj**ust	☐	☐	☐	☐
5. mea**su**re	☐	☐	☐	☐
6. lec**tu**re	☐	☐	☐	☐
7. tradi**ti**onal	☐	☐	☐	☐
8. cul**tu**re	☐	☐	☐	☐
9. u**su**al	☐	☐	☐	☐
10. puni**sh**ment	☐	☐	☐	☐
11. spe**ci**al	☐	☐	☐	☐
12. sub**j**ect	☐	☐	☐	☐
13. **Ch**ile	☐	☐	☐	☐
14. televi**si**on	☐	☐	☐	☐
15. e**du**cators	☐	☐	☐	☐
16. occa**si**on	☐	☐	☐	☐
17. communica**ti**on	☐	☐	☐	☐
18. encoura**ge**	☐	☐	☐	☐
19. a. ni**che**	☐	☐	☐	☐
b. ni**che**	☐	☐	☐	☐
20. trea**su**re	☐	☐	☐	☐

❷ *Work with a partner and practice pronouncing* [ʃ], [ʒ], [tʃ], *and* [dʒ].

Student A: Read the comments or questions.

Student B: Use the words in parentheses to help you with your answers. Pay attention to your pronunciation of these sounds. Switch roles after item 7.

Student A	**Student B**
1. The United States attracts people from all over the world.	1. (That's right . . . salad bowl) **Example:** "That's right, it's a real salad bowl."
2. Do the students seem to like the International High School?	2. (Yes . . . enjoy it)
3. Is it typical for immigrants to feel uncomfortable at first?	3. (Yes . . . usually the case)
4. Immigrants have to learn to adjust in many ways.	4. (Yes . . . find their niche)
5. The high school we heard about seems unique.	5. (Yes . . . special)
6. Do the teachers at that school often lecture?	6. (No . . . only occasionally)
7. Ms. Shenke uses an unusual approach.	7. (Right . . . doesn't lecture)

Now switch roles.

Student B	**Student A**
8. The report said that the school was multilingual.	8. (That's right . . . different languages)
9. Was there a country in South America mentioned?	9. (Yes . . . Chile)
10. The teachers at this school don't seem to believe in discipline through fear, do they?	10. (No, they don't. Instead . . . encouragement)
11. Is it hard to tell how successful a new approach is at first?	11. (Yes . . . takes time to measure results)
12. Can you think of another word for instructor?	12. (Yes . . . educator)
13. Talking to others when you have a problem is important, don't you think?	13. (Yes . . . communication . . .)
14. The teachers seem to like seeing their students help one another.	14. (Yes . . . take pleasure in watching them)

B. WORKING WITH WORDS

❶ *Read the story. Match each underlined word with a similar expression from the list that follows the reading. Write the appropriate number in the blank. Then compare your answers with those of another student.*

CULTURE SHOCK: THE PROBLEM IS NOT JUST LANGUAGE

In his own country, Jun was an active, outgoing young man. He was optimistic, full of life, and had many friends. Jun was also an excellent student. When Jun was sixteen, his father was transferred to the United States. The family moved, but Jun felt (**1**) uprooted from his home. At school, he met American kids who were friendly to him, but he couldn't seem to (**2**) blend in.

Instead of feeling excited by his new classes, he felt (**3**) intimidated. His teachers tried to (**4**) encourage him. They suggested that he join clubs in order to meet other students. Jun appreciated their (**5**) support, but his feeling of being a foreigner (**6**) set him apart from the others. Sometimes he had difficulty communicating with his classmates, and there was no one who spoke his language and could (**7**) interpret for him. He felt that no one would ever listen to him or (**8**) value his opinion.

____ **a.** appreciate	____ **e.** mix well with others
____ **b.** fearful and shy	____ **f.** separated him
____ **c.** help	____ **g.** removed suddenly and roughly
____ **d.** help to become confident	____ **h.** translate

His unhappiness (**9**) extended to his family life, too. Although Jun's family was very (**10**) tight-knit, he did not want to talk about his problems. Instead, he (**11**) suppressed his sad feelings so his parents wouldn't worry about him. He thought that if only he knew more English, he wouldn't have such problems. Jun felt unable to (**12**) deal with even the smallest day-to-day tasks. Sometimes he disliked the United States and English.

Although Jun thought most of his problems were a result of his poor English, social scientists and psychologists know better. Jun was experiencing culture shock without knowing it. His insecurities and confusion were a temporary, but normal stage in the (**13**) adaptation process. His beliefs were suddenly being (**14**) challenged by a new set of values in his new country. All this was happening without his awareness. Jun's reaction was natural.

Gradually, Jun began to feel more comfortable in the United States, enjoying his school life and his new friends. He (**15**) was relieved after some months when he realized that he was no longer unhappy. Though he would always love his native country first, he had found his (**16**) niche in his new home and was able to enjoy his life once again.

_____ **i.** adjustment

_____ **j.** close and intimate

_____ **k.** felt better

_____ **l.** hid

_____ **m.** manage

_____ **n.** proper place

_____ **o.** questioned or threatened

_____ **p.** reached

SKILLS FOR EXPRESSION

A. GRAMMAR: Present and Past—Contrasting Verb Tenses

1 *Working with a partner, read the statements below. Carefully examine the underlined verbs. Then discuss the questions that follow.*

- When we're working in class, we help each other. We're all immigrants here, we all know what it feels like to be different, so we support one another.
- Sometimes it was so difficult because I didn't know what the subject was all about, what the teacher was speaking about.
- This project has been really successful. The students have learned a lot of math. They've been working together really well.

a. What time frame (past or present) is each speaker talking about?

b. Which verbs are in the progressive tense? Why did the speakers choose to use the progressive in each case?

FOCUS ON GRAMMAR

See Simple Present and Present Progressive and Simple Past and Past Progressive in *Focus on Grammar, High-Intermediate.*

Contrasting Verb Tenses

Simple Present and Present Progressive	
The **present progressive** is used to describe what is happening right now, an action that is in progress.	◆ The students in one group **are speaking** Polish.
The **simple present** is used to describe a general fact or habit.	◆ The students at the International High School **speak** many different languages.
The **present progressive** can be used with the **simple present** to describe a present action that is continuing while another present action takes place.	◆ While we**'re working** in class, we **help** each other.
The **simple present** is also used with non-action verbs to refer to actions taking place at the moment of speaking.	◆ The students **seem** to be enjoying the project they **are working** on right now.
Simple Past and Past Progressive	
The **past progressive** is used to describe an action that was in progress at a specific time in the past.	◆ The students **were designing** a temple during math class.
The **simple past** is used to describe an action that was completed in the past.	◆ The students **finished** building their temples by the end of class.
The **past progressive** can be used to describe two actions that happened at the same time.	◆ While the students **were working**, they **were speaking** their native languages.
The **past progressive** is used with the **simple past** to describe one action that was interrupted by another action.	◆ The teacher **was walking** around the room when a student **asked** a question.

The **simple past** is used to describe two actions that happened in a sequence, one after the other.	◆ Another student **stopped** working and **helped** her classmate with the answer.
Present Perfect and Present Perfect Progressive	
The **present perfect** and **present perfect progressive** are used to talk about things that started in the past, continue to the present, and may continue in the future.	◆ She **has lived** in the United States for several years. She **has been living** in the United States since her twenty-first birthday.
The **present perfect** is used to talk about things that happened at an unspecified time in the past.	◆ She **has taken** several tests.

❷ *Work with a partner. Read the essay about one woman's experience with immigration and language learning. Complete the sentences with the appropriate forms of the verbs provided.*

When my mother ______________ (1. was coming / came) to this country from Germany in the 1940s, she ______________ (2. is / was) eight years old. She ______________ (3. wasn't speaking / didn't speak) any English. When she ______________ (4. went / has gone) to school, there ______________ (5. weren't / haven't been) any special classes for immigrants. Immigrant students ______________ (6. have / had) to join the regular classes, even if they couldn't speak English. My mother said this ______________ (7. has been / was) very difficult for her at first. On the first day of school, she ______________ (8. doesn't understand / didn't understand) anything the teacher ______________ (9. was talking / has talked) about. But when my mother ______________ (10. was asking / asked) a friend to explain in German, the teacher ______________ (11. became / has become) angry and ______________ (12. was telling / told) her to speak only English.

My grandparents also ______________ (13. want / wanted) her to learn English quickly. They ______________ (14. have felt / felt) that it was important for her to blend into her new environment. They ______________ (15. have thought / thought) that learning English would help my mother succeed in their new country. Soon, my mother ______________ (16. feels / felt) the same way. In fact, today she ______________ (17. isn't speaking / doesn't speak) German very well at all, and she can't read or write it.

Since then, the world ______________ (18. changed / has changed) quite a bit. With all the new technology, it ______________ (19. is / was) much easier to travel and communicate with people all over the globe. We ______________ (20. are / were) truly part of a global economy, and many people's attitudes about language ______________ (21. were changing / have changed) as well. Today, many people feel that it ______________ (22. is / has been) an advantage to speak two or more languages.

You can see that change when you ______________ (23. look / looked) at my children. They ______________ (24. have spoken / speak) English at home all their lives, but today they ______________ (25. are attending / have attended) a "two-way" bilingual Chinese school, where English-speaking children ______________ (26. learn / learned) Chinese, and Chinese-speaking children learn English. My children ______________ (27. are loving / love) the school because all the students ______________ (28. became / have become) very good friends. They teach each other the new language: my children ______________ (29. were teaching / teach) their friends English, and their friends ______________ (30. help / helped) them learn Chinese. The immigrant Chinese students feel that their classmates ______________ (31. are valuing / value) their language and culture. I believe that in the future, knowing a second language will help my children get better jobs and find their niche in a multicultural society.

My mother's feelings ______________ (32. also changed / have also changed) since she ______________ (33. was / has been) a girl. Now she ______________ (34. is wishing / wishes) that she hadn't forgotten her native language. In fact, she ______________ (35. is taking / was taking) language lessons these days, trying to bone up on her German.

3 *Work with a partner.*

Student A: Ask Student B the questions about the reading. Be sure to use an appropriate verb tense. After Student B answers, ask follow-up questions to find out more about your partner's answers.

Student B: Answer Student A's questions. Be sure to use an appropriate verb tense. Some questions are not answered directly in the reading, so you must express your own opinion based on what you have read. Switch roles after question 7.

Student A	**Student B**
1. Where/be/the author's mother born? **Example:** "Where was the author's mother born?"	1. She was born in Germany.
2. How long/she/be/in the United States?	2.
3. How/she/feel/about speaking German when she was a girl?	3.
4. How/she/feel/about it now?	4.
5. Why/her feelings/change?	5.
6. What new technology/change/the way people learn other languages?	6.
7. How/you/feel/when people speak a language you don't understand?	7.

Now switch roles.

Student B	**Student A**
8. What/be/the author's native language?	8.
9. What/be/the benefits of a bilingual school?	9.
10. How/the bilingual school/help/the author's children?	10.
11. How/the bilingual school/help/the immigrant children?	11.
12. What types of jobs/require/a bilingual person?	12.
13. How/the author's views about language/differ/from her grandparents' views?	13.
14. In your opinion, what kind of school/be/better for immigrant children?	14.

B. STYLE: Hesitating in Response to a Question

When responding to a question or when asked for your opinion, you often need extra time to think about your answer and to find the right vocabulary. **To hesitate,** or buy time, you can say:

◆ I need a moment to think about that . . .	◆ Umm, that's a good question . . .
◆ I'm not sure . . .	◆ Well, er, . . .
◆ Let me think a minute . . .	◆ Well, let's see . . .

❶ *Study this short conversation. Underline what* **B** *says in order to hesitate.*

A: How long did it take you to adjust when you moved to this country?

B: Well, let's see . . . I'm not sure . . . about three years, I'd say.

A: That seems like a long time. Why do you think it was so difficult for you?

B: Umm, that's a good question. There was just so much to learn, and, well, you know, I had to get used to a different language and culture.

❷ *Work with a partner.*

Student A: Ask the first four questions.

Student B: Use an expression from the box to hesitate, or buy time, when you respond and give your reason or opinion. Switch roles after question 4.

Student A	**Student B**
1. Why do you think it's difficult for people to be assimilated into a new culture?	1. Let me think a minute . . .
2. Why do you think some schools try to suppress the students' use of their native tongues?	2.
3. Why do you think it might be intimidating for teenagers to study in a new language?	3.
4. Why do you think that immigrants sometimes feel so isolated from other people?	4.

Now switch roles.

Student B	**Student A**
5. When you are living in another country, what can you do to overcome loneliness?	5. I'm not sure . . .
6. In what ways is the International High School innovative?	6.
7. Do you think it's good for new immigrants to speak exclusively English in school?	7.
8. Why is it so hard for teenage immigrants to maintain their first languages?	8.

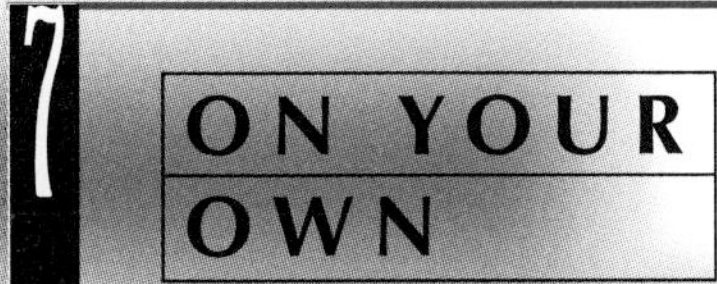

A. SPEAKING TOPICS: Designing a High School Education

In a small group, plan a new high school to educate immigrant students. It could be a school for immigrants in the United States, or it could be located in another country.

Step 1: Objectives

Decide on the objectives, or purpose, of your school. Read the suggested objectives below. If you think of another objective, write it in the space. Then decide how important each objective is. Write **VI** (very important), **SI** (somewhat important), or **NI** (not important) in the space after each objective.

Objective	**Importance**
◆ To keep native language and culture	________
◆ To be assimilated into the new culture	________
◆ To learn the new language	________
◆ To learn general subjects (math, history, etc.)	________
◆ Other: ______________________________	________

Step 2: Planning

Keeping your objectives in mind, plan the class schedule of your new school. Write down the name of the class, and then describe both the teaching style (lecture, group work, hands-on activities) of the class, and the language(s) that will be used. Make sure your choices support the objectives of the school that you agreed upon in Step 1.

DAILY SCHEDULE	CLASS	TEACHING STYLE(S)	LANGUAGE(S) USED
8 A.M.			
9 A.M.			
10 A.M.			
11 A.M.			
12 NOON	LUNCH	---	---
1 P.M.			
2 P.M.			
3 P.M.			

Step 3: Presentation

With your group, present your plan to the rest of the class. Explain:

- The objectives of your school.
- Why you chose those objectives.
- The daily schedule, including teaching methods and language(s).
- How the daily schedule will help to achieve the goals or objectives.

After all the groups have presented, discuss the similarities and differences among your plans.

B. FIELDWORK: Research on Immigration

Work in small groups. Choose a group that has immigrated to the United States or another country. You will find out how the group adjusted to the new culture.

Step 1

First, think of research questions about the immigrant group (the questions have been started for you in each topic area below). Use the appropriate verb tenses in your questions (see Section 6A).

Homeland & New Home

- Where did the immigrants come from? Why did they leave their homeland?
- Where did they go? Did they settle in specific areas?
- When did the majority of these immigrants arrive?
- ______________________________
- ______________________________
- ______________________________

Culture & Language

- How does the group keep its traditional culture and/or language?
- What traditions have changed since the immigrants left their homeland?
- ______________________________
- ______________________________
- ______________________________

Education & Work

- Do children receive any education in their native language (if there is a language difference for this group)? Why or why not?
- Have members of this group had any special difficulties or advantages in education or work?
- What are some common professions for immigrants in this group?
- ______________________________
- ______________________________
- ______________________________

Step 2

Assign the questions on one topic to different people in the group. Use the library or Internet to do your research. Look for special publications and organizations. For example, in the New York area, the Department of City Planning of New York has published a book on current immigration trends, *The Newest New Yorkers*, which may be available at your local library. Also in New York, an organization that does research on immigration is:

The Center for Migration Studies
209 Flagg Place,
Staten Island, New York 10304

Step 3

After completing the research, come back together as a group and share your results. Then present your results to the class. Compare what you learned, and discuss the similarities and differences among the experiences of the various immigrant groups.

UNIT 10

TECHNOLOGY: A BLESSING OR A CURSE?

David Sipress © 1998. From *The Cartoon Bank*. All rights reserved.

1 APPROACHING THE TOPIC

A. PREDICTING

Discuss the questions with another student. Then share your ideas with the class.

1. **Look at the title of this unit. What do you think the title means?**
2. **Look at the cartoon. Why do you think the man is hiding from his laptop computer and his cellular telephone?**

B. SHARING INFORMATION

❶ *Work with a partner. Fill in the chart with the ways you think the items listed have either improved or diminished the quality of our lives.*

ITEM	WAYS IT HAS IMPROVED OUR QUALITY OF LIFE	WAYS IT HAS DIMINISHED OUR QUALITY OF LIFE
1. personal computer		
2. cellular phone		
3. automatic teller machine (ATM)		
4. personal stereo equipment		
5. the Internet		
6. e-mail		
7. other (your idea)		

❷ *Share your views with the class. Explain the reasons for your opinions.*

2 PREPARING TO LISTEN

A. BACKGROUND

Technology might be a big part of modern life, but how much do you really know about the history of technological developments? What is your personal technology IQ? Take this test with a partner. Compare your answers. Then check your answers in the Answer Key.

Your Technology IQ

1. **Who invented the telephone in 1876?**
   a. Thomas Edison
   b. Martin van Buren
   c. Alexander Graham Bell
   d. Alfred Nobel

2. **Which of these inventions appeared in 1948?**
   a. Cable TV systems
   b. Color TV broadcasts
   c. FM radio broadcasts
   d. Fax machines

3. **Which of these electronic products was introduced after 1960?**
   a. Computer hard drive
   b. Computer mouse
   c. Videotape recorder
   d. Computer monitor

4. **Which of these products is the <u>most</u> common in the average U.S. household?**
   a. Telephone
   b. Television
   c. Camcorder (portable video camera)
   d. Cordless phone

5. **Which of these products was introduced first?**
   a. Compact disks
   b. Personal stereos
   c. Cellular telephones
   d. Camcorders

6. **When were TV sets first produced for the average U.S. consumer?**
   a. 1927
   b. 1931
   c. 1941
   d. 1946

7. **Which of these products or services is the *least* common in the average U.S. household?**
   a. On-line services
   b. Personal computers
   c. Cellular phones
   d. VCRs

8. **When was the World Wide Web developed?**
   a. 1980
   b. 1987
   c. 1991
   d. 1996

9. **Which of these events happened *most* recently?**
   a. Microsoft was founded.
   b. A commercial Internet service became available.
   c. The term "computer virus" began to be used.
   d. Governments started using the World Wide Web.

Your score: ______________

RATINGS:
7–9 You are a technology wiz!
5–6 You know a lot about technology. Keep it up!
Below 5 You don't know a lot about technology but will learn more in this unit.

B. VOCABULARY FOR COMPREHENSION

Read the sentences. Circle the item that has a similar meaning to that of the underlined word. The first one has been done for you.

1. To sleep well, you need to get some peace and quiet. However, in the city, noise can shatter the peace.

   a. increase b. annoy c. (ruin)

2. People who live near airports often complain about sonic pollution. They say that the air traffic disturbs their sleep and prevents them from living a normal life.

   a. noise b. strange c. solar

3. Some people believe that talking on cellular phones while driving is so dangerous that it should be banned.

   a. prohibited b. permitted c. requested

4. The use of the Internet at work has prompted companies to make new rules. For example, in some companies, employees can't use the Internet for personal business during business hours.

   a. reminded b. caused c. allowed

5. Many city noises are loud and sudden. They jolt people out of their sleep.

   a. ease b. coax c. shake

6. I haven't been sleeping well at night lately. As soon as I lie down, I get a nagging headache, and even though I take aspirin, it won't go away.

   a. constant b. slight c. feverish

7. At the end of the cowboy movie, the sheriff gathered a posse of men. He needed help to catch the gang of bad guys.

   a. a group b. a couple c. hundreds

8. When people feel that they have been hurt needlessly, they often get angry and sometimes take retaliatory steps. They do something to hurt the person who has hurt them.

   a. vengeful b. immediate c. official

9. Neighborhood vigilantes take the law into their own hands. Rather than call the police, they find a way to punish an offender themselves.

   a. heavily armed guards b. part-time police officers c. self-appointed representatives

10. When my alarm clock goes off in the morning, I never feel like getting out of bed. I'm always too tired.

    a. starts making noise b. stops making noise c. malfunctions

11. Last night, I heard a loud noise in my kitchen. I was so scared that I called 911. When the police came, it turned out that it was only the cat knocking down the recycling container.

    a. emergency services b. the operator c. directory assistance

12. Some neighborhood punks found an old car and mutilated it. The front was completely destroyed.

    a. damaged b. constructed c. criticized

13. If you park in a no-parking zone, the traffic police can tow away your car. You can't pick it up until you pay a fine.

    a. remove b. destroy c. park

14. I think a very heavy truck just went by. I could feel the vibrations shaking the whole house.

    a. sounds b. movements c. echoes

LISTENING ONE: Noise in the City

A. INTRODUCING THE TOPIC

You will hear a report from *Living on Earth* by Neal Rauch of National Public Radio. Rauch interviews several residents of a large city. Steve Curwood is the host of this news program that often reports on environmental issues.

Listen to a segment of the report, and think ahead. Work with a partner to answer the questions.

1. What could be causing the noise you heard?

 ____

2. How do you think people feel when they hear this noise?

 ____

3. What are some things they might do after hearing the noise?

 ____

4. Where do you think this report takes place?

 ____

B. LISTENING FOR MAIN IDEAS

Listen to the radio report. Read each statement and decide if it is true or false. Write T or F.

____ 1. New Yorkers agree about banning this form of sonic pollution.

____ 2. Car alarms disturb the sleep of many people in New York City.

____ 3. The police have formed a posse to reduce the amount of noise.

____ 4. When a car alarm goes off too often, some vigilante groups may do something to damage the car.

____ 5. Car alarms are very effective at preventing theft.

____ 6. Car alarms can seriously affect people's health and quality of life.

____ 7. There are no laws or penalties to punish drivers whose car alarms go off too often.

____ 8. Police can break into a car if the alarm goes off for too long.

C. LISTENING FOR DETAILS

Read the following questions. Then listen to the report again. As you listen, take notes on the opinions and comments expressed by the different people who are interviewed and by the interviewer himself. Then compare your answers with those of another student.

1. Judy Evans, scenic designer and artist
   - a. Why are car alarms such a problem at night?

     ____

     ____

     ____

   - b. What *usually* happens when a person makes a lot of noise in public?

     ____

     ____

     ____

2. The "egg man," a music producer and composer
   - a. What do he and his neighbors do when they hear a car alarm go off?

     ____

     ____

     ____

   - b. What do other vigilante groups sometimes do?

     ____

     ____

     ____

3. Lucille DiMaggio, a target of vigilante retribution
   - a. What happened to her car?

     ____

     ____

     ____

b. What happened when she set off her car alarm in the restaurant parking lot?

____

____

____

4. Judy Evans

a. What happened on a different night when she heard a car alarm going off?

____

____

____

5. New York State senator Catherine Abate

a. How does the noise from alarms affect people?

____

____

____

b. How can loud noise be particularly harmful to young people?

____

____

____

6. Neil Rauch, radio reporter

a. How have existing laws helped cut down on car alarm noise?

____

____

____

b. How will it be helpful if car alarm owners adjust their alarms to be less sensitive to vibrations?

____

____

____

D. LISTENING BETWEEN THE LINES

1. *Listen to the excerpts from the radio report. Listen carefully to each speaker's tone of voice and choice of words. Evaluate how serious or humorous the speaker sounds as he or she makes a complaint or gives an opinion, and check (✓) the appropriate column.*

	MOSTLY SERIOUS	SOMEWHAT SERIOUS	SOMEWHAT HUMOROUS	MOSTLY HUMOROUS
Excerpt One: Judy Evans				
Tone of voice	☐	☐	☐	☐
Choice of words	☐	☐	☐	☐
Excerpt Two: Lucille DiMaggio				
Tone of voice	☐	☐	☐	☐
Choice of words	☐	☐	☐	☐
Excerpt Three: Senator Abate				
Tone of voice	☐	☐	☐	☐
Choice of words	☐	☐	☐	☐
Excerpt Four: "Egg man"				
Tone of voice	☐	☐	☐	☐
Choice of words	☐	☐	☐	☐

2. *Discuss your reactions in a small group. Explain why you think each speaker sounds the way he or she does. Give specific examples to support your opinions.*

4 LISTENING TWO: Technology Talk

A. EXPANDING THE TOPIC

1 *Car alarms are not the only examples of technology that drive people crazy. Listen to the complaints of four people who phoned in to a radio show,* Technology Talk. *Write the type of technology each caller is talking about. Listen again and write the reasons the callers give for their annoyance or frustration. Then listen to the fifth caller's response to the complaints of the other callers. Take notes on her response. Compare your answers with those of a partner.*

Caller 1 Technology: ______________________________

Reason it drives the caller crazy: ______________________________

____

____

Caller 2 Technology: ______________________________

Reason the caller finds it frustrating: ______________________________

____

____

Caller 3 Technology: ______________________________

Reason they annoy the caller: ______________________________

____

____

Caller 4 Technology: ______________________________

Reason it frustrates the caller: ______________________________

____

____

Caller 5 Response to complaints of other callers: ______________________________

____

____

❷ *Read the cartoon title and captions. What is a "midlife crisis"? What is the humor or message of the cartoon?*

B. LINKING LISTENINGS ONE AND TWO

Working in small groups, discuss your answers to the following questions.

1. Modern life is full of noises, as the radio report said, and many of them are annoying. Close your eyes for one minute and sit quietly. Concentrate on the sounds around you. Then write down all the sounds you have heard. Are they pleasant or unpleasant?

2. What kind of noises surround you at home? In the workplace? Which ones do you like? Which ones bother you?

3. What do you think of vigilante groups that take action against something that bothers them in their neighborhood? Are these a good idea? Have you ever heard about other retaliatory steps?

4. List all the technologies or appliances that you use in your daily life. Sort them into the following categories, and discuss why you categorized them as you did.

TOO MUCH FUN TO GIVE UP	CAN'T LIVE WITHOUT	COULD LIVE WITHOUT OR REPLACE

5 REVIEWING LANGUAGE

A. EXPLORING LANGUAGE: Sound Words

❶ *Listen to some common noises. What do you think makes each noise? Write your response on the chart.*

NOISE	THIS NOISE IS PROBABLY MADE BY . . .	ADJECTIVES TO DESCRIBE THE NOISE
1. bang	a door slamming	jolting, loud
2. shatter		
3. ring		
4. rattle		
5. beep		
6. creak		
7. whistle		
8. tick		
9. screech		
10. honk		

❷ *Listen to the noises again. Choose one or two adjectives that describe each noise. Choose words from the list or other adjectives that you know. Write them on the chart in Exercise 1. Then compare your answers with those of another student.*

aggravating	faint	low	shrill
annoying	frightening	nagging	soft
awful	irritating	nasty	startling
comforting	jolting	piercing	sudden
constant	loud	rhythmic	surprising

B. WORKING WITH WORDS

Work with a partner. Student A looks at page 223. Student B looks at Student Activities, page 234.

Student A: Select the best word or phrase from the box to complete each sentence in the left-hand column. Read the sentence aloud. Then listen to Student B's response, checking the right-hand column to make sure Student B is using the correct word.

banned
defective
disturbing the peace
drive you crazy
fine
frazzled
frustrated
getting under my skin
go off
irritated
I've had it
jolts
offense
retaliatory steps

DIALOGUE 1

Student A

1. My new clock radio is really ________________. I wish I'd never bought it.

Student B

1. Why? Doesn't the alarm <u>go off</u> when it should?

Student A

2. Oh, sure it does. It goes off too often! And it makes a really loud noise. It ________________ me out of my sleep.

Student B

2. Maybe it's broken. Why don't you take it back? Most stores will give you your money back if a product is <u>defective</u>.

Student A

3. I can't. It's not broken. I just can't figure out how to set it. And the instructions are too complicated. I just get ________________ and give up whenever I try to read them.

Student B

3. Well, you sound really worn out. If you get too <u>frazzled</u>, you might get sick. You need to get some sleep.

DIALOGUE 2

Student A

4. Hi. What's up? You look really ________________.

Student B

4. I am. In fact, <u>I've had it</u> with the neighborhood kids and their boom boxes.

Student A

5. Yeah. They really play their music too loud. I guess it can ________________ if you hear it all day.

Student B

5. And all *night*. I've already called the police. They tried to calm me down and told me not to take <u>retaliatory steps</u>.

Student A

6. You're kidding! You called the police? Are those kids breaking the law? I mean, is it really a(n) ________________ to play loud music?

Student B

6. Actually, it is. Playing loud music is <u>disturbing the peace</u>, and that's against the law.

Student A

7. I guess those kids should pay a ________________ for breaking the law. Maybe then they would think twice about making so much noise next time.

Student B

7. You're right. I think boom boxes should be <u>banned</u> in public places.

SKILLS FOR EXPRESSION

A. GRAMMAR: Future Perfect and Future Progressive

1 *Working with a partner, examine the statements and discuss the questions that follow.*

- In fact, I have to call my wife at work right now. By the time I actually get through, she'll have already left.
- Well, Carol, we'll be getting some response to your strong stand on cell phones.

a. Notice that two different verb tenses are used. Read them aloud.

b. How are the two tenses different in form and meaning?

FOCUS ON GRAMMAR

See Future Progressive and Future Perfect in *Focus on Grammar, High-Intermediate.*

Future Perfect and Future Progressive

Both the **future perfect** and the **future progressive** are commonly used to speak about events in the future.

	Examples
Use the **future perfect** to talk about a future action that will already have been completed by a certain time in the future. The future perfect is often used with the simple present tense to show the relationship between two future events. The event that will take place first uses the future perfect. The event that will take place second uses the simple present tense.	By the time I **get through,** she**'ll have** already **left.**
To form the future perfect, active voice: Use ***will*** + ***have*** + **past participle**	By tomorrow evening, I **will have (will've) used** my computer about ten times.
To form the future perfect, passive voice: Use ***will*** + ***have been*** + **past participle**	By the end of the week, the computer **will have (will've) been used** twenty times.

Use the **future progressive** to talk about actions that will be in progress at a specific time in the future.	If the trend **continues**, and cellular phones **become** more and more popular, people **will be spending** most of their waking hours on the phone.
To form the future progressive: Use ***will*** + ***be*** + **present participle**	In the future, we**'ll be using** a lot of new technology.

❷ *Work with a partner. Play the "mystery item" game to practice using the future perfect.*

Student A follows the directions on this page. Student B turns to Student Activities, page 235.

Student A: Read the clues about technological items that are common today. Fill in the blanks with future perfect forms of the verbs in parentheses. Check whether an active or passive structure is needed. Then read the first two clues about the mystery item to Student B. If he or she cannot guess what the item is, give the third and fourth clues.

Mystery Item 1: Clues

1. By this time next year, you ________________ (replace) the battery in your mystery item.
2. About 80 million of them ________________ (make) by the end of this year, and almost everybody has at least one of these items.
3. This mystery item was invented in Germany around 1500.
4. Today it is the number one jewelry item in the world.

Mystery Item 2: Clues

1. You definitely use this item; in fact, you probably ________________ (use) it once or twice by the end of the day.

2. By the end of the day, these items ________________ (use) millions of gallons of water around the world.

3. The modern version of this item saves a lot more water than previous versions did.

4. It has greatly improved since it was first invented, and now you would probably find that it is very hard to live without this item.

Mystery Item 3: Clues

1. There is a good chance that someone in your family ________________ (turn on) your mystery item before nine o'clock tonight.

2. This mystery item will not go out of style. In fact, by the end of this century, this item ________________ (not / become) any less important than it is today.

3. Millions of people use the item every second.

4. This item was first available in black and white.

3 *What type of technology will people be using by the end of the next century? Look at the items below, and make predictions about what people will and won't be doing. Use the future progressive when you make your predictions.*

Example

By the end of this century, people will probably be taking trips to outer space.

- travel in outer space
- use video telephones
- live past the age of 100
- listen to music on CDs
- select their children's genetic characteristics
- clone themselves
- drive electric or solar-powered cars
- use robots to do housework
- use computers to learn English

B. STYLE: Expressing Frustration

In this unit, you have heard many people complain about their problems with different types of technology. Below are some phrases (preceded or followed by a noun or noun phrase) used to express frustration. Words such as *really, very,* or *extremely* are often added to intensify the meaning.

Example

I'm extremely frustrated with my new software program for doing my taxes. It's too complicated for me to set up! It's really driving me crazy!

I'm annoyed by . . .	. . . bothers me.
I'm irritated by . . .	. . . gets under my skin.
I'm frustrated with . . .	. . . drives me crazy.*
I'm getting fed up with . . .	. . . sends me over the edge.
I've had it with . . .	. . . drives me nuts.*
I'm sick and tired of . . .	

With another student, role play one of the following situations between neighbors, or create your own situation in which one of you complains. Practice using expressions of frustration in your dialogues. Then perform your role play for the class.

Situation 1

Neighbor One: Your next-door neighbor plays loud music during the evening. He doesn't turn it off until midnight. You don't like his taste in music, so it seems even louder to you. You have told him politely several times that you have to get up early in the morning. Each time, he gets the message and turns it down, only to do the same the following night.

Neighbor Two: When you get home from a long, tiring day at the office, you like to play a little soft music. Your neighbor is super-sensitive and sometimes asks you to turn it down. You always do. Tonight he was banging on the wall to get you to turn it down. You think that's really rude.

---

*very informal speech

Situation 2

Neighbor One: Your neighbor has an air conditioner that hums and clanks loudly all night. You can't sleep with the constant noise. You've mentioned it casually to your neighbor before, but your hint hasn't done any good. Your neighbor hasn't gotten the message. You've decided to be more direct to solve the problem.

Neighbor Two: Your neighbor mentioned your noisy air conditioner once before, but you can't do anything about it right now. You've explained that a new one is very expensive, and you don't want to buy one now. It's been hot lately, and you can't sleep without air conditioning. You thought that your neighbor understood your situation after you explained it. Everything seemed OK until today.

Situation 3

Neighbor One: Your neighbor's vacuum cleaner causes a power surge whenever she turns it on. Unfortunately, it causes your computer to shut down and you lose your work. This has happened several times. You've decided to do something about it.

Neighbor Two: You paid a lot a money for a powerful new vacuum cleaner. It uses a lot of electricity. When you turn it on, sometimes the power in the apartment fails. When that happens, you call the building superintendent, and he corrects the problem. You've noticed that when other people in the building are not home using electricity, there's no problem.

Situation 4

Neighbor One: Your neighbor has a loud car alarm. It's one of those modern versions that plays several musical tunes. It goes off all the time, even if no one is near the car. You can't stand it anymore. You are going to your neighbor's apartment to say something.

Neighbor Two: Your car alarm seems to be a little defective. Sometimes it goes off when it's not supposed to. You've taken it to be repaired, but it still seems to be a little too sensitive.

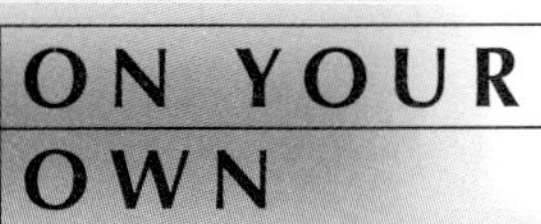

ON YOUR OWN

A. SPEAKING TOPICS: Gadgets

1 *Work in pairs. Look at ads in newspapers, specialized magazines, or catalogues for the most up-to-date gadgets you can find. Consider gadgets from the following categories:*

- Car gadgets
- Kitchen gadgets
- Camping gadgets
- Telephone technology
- Electronic gadgets
- Computer gadgets

1. Select one gadget to report on to the class. Answer the following questions:
   - What does this gadget do? How does it work?
   - What makes it useful or interesting?
   - How much does it cost?
   - What are the possible drawbacks?
   - Would you buy it or not, and why?
2. Take notes on each other's presentations. Ask questions about what you hear.

2 *Work in pairs. Think of a problem in modern life that could be solved by a new gadget. Then invent a gadget to solve the problem. Don't worry too much about practicality; just let your imagination run wild!*

1. After you have worked out your idea, draw a sketch of your invention. Design an ad for it. Use the expressions you have learned in this unit and some future progressive and future perfect structures to describe the gadget. Be sure to:
   - Describe the problem.
   - Explain your product.
   - Predict how your product will improve life in the future.
2. Present your ideas to the class. Evaluate the products other students have invented. Suggest ways to improve their products.

B. FIELDWORK: Technology Past and Present

❶ *Work in pairs. Choose Project A or Project B to research. Visit a library or do some Internet research.*

Project A

Find out about recent developments in one of the following areas:

- nano technology
- robotics
- electronics
- artificial intelligence
- cloning
- genetic engineering
- medical innovations
- your own idea

Project B

Today 98 percent of American households have telephones, 97 percent have televisions, 65 percent have stereo systems, 43 percent have computers, and 14 percent have automatic coffee makers. Take a trip back to the time (the 1940s and 1950s) when household appliances became widely available for the average American home. Find out what appliances people bought and how these appliances changed the lives of homemakers. Find out how this small revolution affected the average American family.

❷ *Present a summary of your findings to the class.*

STUDENT ACTIVITIES

UNIT 4 ◆ THE EYE OF THE STORM

5B. EXERCISE 2, pages 83–86

DIALOGUE 1

Part One: *This is a dialogue between two people discussing the interview with the Hurricane Hunters.*

Student B: Complete each statement with the correct words from the box. Then listen to Student A's statement, using column 1 to check Student A's answer. Then read your statement in response.

deceptive	evacuate	panic	power outage	vital

Student A's Answers	Student B: Statements to Complete
1. vulnerable	1. So would I. It would be hard not to _______________ if you saw yourself heading straight for the center of a dangerous storm—in an airplane!
2. sophisticated	2. I know what you mean. What if lightning caused a _______________ and the pilot couldn't work the controls?
3. out of order	3. I know the local authorities need that information to decide whether to _______________ the area, but I couldn't do that job!

Part Two: *Continue the dialogue using the words in the box. Student B starts the dialogue.*

be in good spirits	manual	second-guess
contaminated	panic	stock up on
deceptive	provisions	vital
flooded	route	warning
forecast	scared stiff	

DIALOGUE 2

Part One: *This is a dialogue between two friends who are on vacation together. They have learned that a severe storm is approaching, so they are preparing to wait out the storm in their small beach house.*

Student B: Complete each statement with the correct word from the box. Then listen to Student A's statement, using column 1 to check Student A's answer. Then read your statement in response.

in good spirits	manual	route	second-guess	stock up on

Student A's Answers	Student B: Statements to Complete
1. provisions	**1.** It's OK. There's a ______________ one in the drawer. Look! It's really raining hard!
2. flooded	**2.** You know, we're going to need clean water if that happens. We'd better ______________ drinking water.
3. forecast	**3.** Of course you're right. We acted as if nothing could stop our vacation. I'll never ______________ the weatherman again!

Part Two: *Continue the dialogue using the words in the box. Student A starts the dialogue.*

contaminated	outage	sophisticated
deceptive	panic	vital
evacuate	route	vulnerable
out of order	scared stiff	warning

UNIT 4 ◆ THE EYE OF THE STORM

6A. EXERCISE 3, pages 89–90

GUESSING GAME

Step 1

Group B: Listen to Group A read the definitions. You have ten seconds in which to guess the item they are referring to. If you do not understand, Group A will repeat the definition.

Step 2

Group B: Complete the adjective clauses in the sentences and read them to Group A, one by one. Group A has ten seconds in which to identify the item you are referring to. If Group A does not understand, you should repeat the definition. After ten seconds, Group A gets a point.

	Answers
1. It's a kind of equipment ______________ is used to track hurricanes.	1. satellite; radar
2. It's the name of the hurricane ______________ caused 25 million dollars' worth of damage.	2. Andrew
3. They're the people ______________ are most affected by hurricanes.	3. residents
4. What's the name of a scientist ______________ studies weather conditions?	4. meteorologist
5. It's the person ______________ flies an airplane.	5. pilot
6. It's the word ______________ means tidal wave.	6. tsunami

UNIT 10 ◆ TECHNOLOGY: A BLESSING OR A CURSE?

5B. Working with Words, pages 222–223

Student B: Silently read each sentence in the left-hand column and listen carefully to make sure that Student A is correctly using the underlined word. Then select the best word or phrase from the box to complete the response sentence in the right-hand column, and read it aloud.

banned	drive you crazy	frustrated	irritated	offense
defective	fine	getting under my skin	I've had it	retaliatory steps
disturbing the peace	frazzled	go off	jolts	

DIALOGUE 1

Student A

1. My new clock radio is really <u>getting under my skin</u>. I wish I had never bought it.

Student B

1. Why? Doesn't the alarm ______________ when it should?

Student A

2. Oh, sure it does. It goes off too often! And it makes a really loud noise. It <u>jolts</u> me out of my sleep.

Student B

2. Maybe it's broken. Why don't you take it back? Most stores will give you your money back if a product is ______________.

Student A

3. I can't. It's not broken. I just can't figure out how to set it. And the instructions are too complicated. I just get frustrated and give up whenever I try to read them.

Student B

3. Well, you sound really worn out. If you get too ______________, you might get sick. You need to get some sleep.

DIALOGUE 2

Student A

4. Hi. What's up? You look really ______________.

Student B

4. I am. In fact, <u>I've had it</u> with the neighborhood kids and their boom boxes.

Student A

5. Yeah. They really play their music too loudly. I guess it can ______________ if you hear it all day.

Student B

5. And all *night*. I've already called the police. They tried to calm me down and told me not to take <u>retaliatory steps</u>.

Student A

6. You're kidding! You called the police? Are those kids breaking the law? I mean, is it really an ______________ to play loud music?

Student B

6. Actually, it is. Playing loud music is <u>disturbing the peace</u>, and that's against the law.

Student A

7. I guess those kids should pay a ______________ for breaking the law. Maybe then they would think twice about making so much noise next time.

Student B

7. You're right. I think boom boxes should be <u>banned</u> in public places.

UNIT 10 ◆ TECHNOLOGY: A BLESSING OR A CURSE?

6A. EXERCISE 2, pages 225–226

Student B: Read the clues 4 to 6 about technological items that are common today. Fill in the blanks with future perfect and future progressive forms of verbs in parentheses. Check whether an active or passive structure is needed. Then read the first two clues about the mystery item to Student A. If he or she cannot guess what the item is, give the third and fourth clues.

Mystery Item 4: Clues

1. Most kids love these. It is likely that, your children ________________ (ask) you to buy them one of these items by the time they are five or six years old.
2. Now these items are made with eighteen or twenty-one gears. Maybe by the mid-twenty-first century, a new version with a hundred gears ________________ (invent).
3. A Scottish blacksmith first came up with the idea for this item. That is surprising, because there are so many hills in Scotland that these items are difficult to use there.
4. This mystery item usually has two wheels, and you ride it.

Mystery Item 5: Clues

1. Most likely, by the time you retire, you ________________ (have) to buy a pair.
2. At present, they are made mainly of glass, metal, and plastic, but it's likely that by the mid-twenty-first century, manufacturers ________________ (introduce) other materials. Despite the design changes, they will still probably look the same.
3. In the late Middle Ages, they were worn as ornaments for the face.
4. They first appeared in Italy, in the late thirteenth century, and were used in China around the same time.

Mystery Item 6: Clues

1. By 8 A.M. tomorrow, your mystery item ________________ (turn on).
2. By 8 A.M. tomorrow, millions of Americans ________________ (switch) one on for the news and weather.
3. You listen to this mystery item.
4. It usually gets both FM and AM frequencies.

TAPESCRIPT

UNIT 1 ◆ NO NEWS IS GOOD NEWS

3. LISTENING ONE: A New Approach to News

3A. *Introducing the Topic*

Alex Jones: A lot of people are pretty fed up with the news. It's not the quality so much that bothers them, but the content. It's just all bad news, or so it sometimes seems. So they tune it out. Fed up with reports of fires and floods? Tune it out. Too much tragedy and crime? Cancel your subscription to the paper. One person who couldn't take it anymore went a step further—or maybe I should say a quantum leap further. He founded his own newspaper . . .

3B. *Listening for Main Ideas*

Part One

Alex Jones: A lot of people are pretty fed up with the news. It's not the quality so much that bothers them, but the content. It's just all bad news, or so it sometimes seems. So they tune it out. Fed up with reports of fires and floods? Tune it out. Too much tragedy and crime? Cancel your subscription to the paper. One person who couldn't take it anymore went a step further—or maybe I should say a quantum leap further. He founded his own newspaper, and publishes only good news.

Now I want you to think about this for a minute if you will. Think about the old saying, "No news is good news." One way of interpreting that line is that real news is bad news. So if someone comes along with a newspaper that promises to deliver only good news, is that really news? And is that really a newspaper? I'm Alex Jones, and this hour, of *On The Media* we'll be looking into news—the good, the bad, and the ugly, to see—well, to see what it really is, and to see if the concept of news needs fixing; we'll also find out about a couple of different alternatives to the murder and mayhem that seem to surround us on TV, radio, and in print. . . . With me in the studio is David Christian Hamblin. He's the publisher of the *World Times*, a monthly paper dedicated, according to its marketing materials, to revealing to its readers that which leads to health, growth, liberation, and wholeness. David Hamblin, welcome. Glad to have you with us.

David Hamblin: Good afternoon.

Part Two

Alex Jones: I have to tell you right off the bat that I'm a little skeptical about a good news newspaper. Tell me something, first of all, what—what is the *World Times*, by your definition? What is a good news newspaper? What does it have in it? I mean, I've looked it over, but tell our listeners.

David Hamblin: Sure. Well I think what I wanted to do is to offer an alternative to people who read mainstream media, watch the evening news. I wanted to have an alternative that would bring hope into their homes, and from my own experience, of what happened to me in my life, I decided to take that experience and turn it around and come up with this idea of putting good news. And good news to me is not a superficial thing. What it is, is we're telling the whole truth of the stories that we report and so it's talking about some of the negativity that's out there; but what we're doing is, we're taking the positive and really forcing that issue. Putting the positive of any story . . . I'm saying that we're not the only paper that people should read; I'm not saying I'm the only media outlet that people should subscribe to; I'm saying I'm an alternative.

AJ: Well, give our listeners a sense of what they might find, what kind of articles and what kind of coverage they might find if they picked up the most recent issue of the *World Times*.

DH: Well, I think we have some political articles that are talking about solutions—I think that's what I would really like to get out there, is that our paper hopefully can be a paper of solutions: we have a lot of information on alternative medicine . . . just good news stories . . . about senior citizens who are out there doing incredible things.

3C. *Listening for Details*

(repeat Section 3B)

3D. *Listening between the Lines*

EXCERPT ONE

AJ: A lot of people are pretty fed up with the news. It's not the quality so much that bothers them, but the content. It's just all bad news, or so it sometimes seems. So they tune it out. Fed up with reports of fires and floods? Tune it out. Too much tragedy and crime? Cancel your subscription to the paper.

EXCERPT TWO

DH: And good news to me is not a superficial thing. What it is, is we're telling the whole truth of the stories that we report and so it's talking about some of the negativity that's out there; but what we're doing is, we're taking the positive and really forcing that issue. Putting the positive of any story.

EXCERPT THREE

DH: Well, I think we have some political articles that are talking about solutions—I think that's what I would really like to get out there, is that our paper hopefully can be a paper of solutions: we have a lot of information on alternative medicine . . . just good news stories . . . about senior citizens who are out there doing incredible things.

4. LISTENING TWO: Conversations about the News

4A. *Expanding the Topic*

CONVERSATION ONE

Tanya: Hi, Chen. What are you reading?

Chen: Hi, Tanya. This is a new newspaper, the *Community News*. It carries only good news.

Tanya: Oh, yeah. I think I've seen that.

Chen: Yeah, isn't it a great idea? I'm so fed up with all the bad news you read about all the time. It's about time someone came up with an innovative alternative to the mainstream newspapers.

Tanya: I don't know . . . the problem with it is, if it's only good news, how do you know you're getting the whole story, and not just some sugar-coated version of the truth? It doesn't sound like objective journalism—that both sides of a story and all facts are being reported.

Chen: Well, I think that we need alternative sources of the news. Mainstream papers don't always tell the whole story; in one sense there is no such thing as truly objective reporting. Every paper has to narrow down what to focus on. You know, I really believe that because of all the tabloid journalism these days, there's a tendency to go for the most sensational news, scandals, murder and mayhem. The positive stories are really being under-reported.

Tanya: But don't they have to leave out some news to make it all "good news"? I mean, if a bunch of people die in a fire, how can you make good news out of that? Do they cover that type of story?

Chen: Well, you're right. But so often these stories are so superficial, they don't tell us anything meaningful. They are so depressing. I'd rather read a positive story like how the fire department teaches people to protect themselves from fire. That would give me some useful information. It would make me feel better about life, instead of worse.

Tanya: Aren't you just lying to yourself, tuning out the negative news just to make yourself feel better?

Chen: Maybe. But I really think that the mainstream media is misleading us as well, by not telling the positive side of things.

Tanya: I'm not sure. Maybe you're right—I can't make up my mind. Maybe we need to read both kinds of papers.

CONVERSATION TWO

Rita: Look at this, Mark! Another movie star was caught cheating on his wife. And it's front page news!

Mark: Rita, what are you reading?

Rita: It's the *National Inquisitor*. I subscribe to it.

Mark: Isn't that a tabloid newspaper?

Rita: I guess so. It has a lot of great stories about celebrities. I like to know who's dating who, who's getting divorced, who's living where . . . all that stuff.

Mark: In my opinion, tabloid papers are a waste of time. They're so sensational! All they report about is people's personal lives. It's not really news—just gossip.

Rita: But I feel that it's so interesting! I love gossip.

Mark: I feel sorry for famous people. The reporters who cover them are so aggressive! They follow people around and take pictures of everything. I really think that celebrities should be able to have a private life, not to see everything they do on the front page of a newspaper. Famous people are victimized by the media.

Rita: Well, I'm sure that movie stars know that people are curious. It's natural. If they don't like it, it's too bad. Besides, I think a lot of them like all the attention.

Mark: But I really think there are more important things to read about in a newspaper, like what the government is doing to improve schools, or what shape the economy is in.

Rita: Oh, lighten up! It's fun. Why do you have to be so serious all the time?

UNIT 2 ◆ DO THE CRIME, SERVE THE TIME: Teen Boot Camps

3. LISTENING ONE: Do the Crime, Serve the Time

3A. *Introducing the Topic*

David Alpern: *Newsweek* Miami correspondent David González reported on correctional boot camps for this week's issue. He's on the line with us now, along with Dale Parent of Abt Associates in Cambridge, Mass., author of a new report on boot camps for the National Institute of Justice. Welcome to *Newsweek on Air.*

1. **David Alpern:** What do they do exactly, beyond the physical exertions and the discipline?
2. **David Alpern:** Any evidence that they're successful?
3. **David Alpern:** Indeed, isn't there a danger that . . . boot camps for young criminals will do just what boot camps for servicemen are supposed to do—make them tougher, more resourceful, and effective as criminals?

3B. *Listening for Main Ideas*

PART ONE

David Alpern: *Newsweek* Miami correspondent David González reported on correctional boot camps for this week's issue. He's on the line with us now, along with Dale Parent of Abt Associates in Cambridge, Mass., author of a new report on boot camps for the National Institute of Justice. Welcome to *Newsweek on*

Air. David, about how many states have these boot camp programs now?

David González: At this point we have about fifteen programs in nine states. There's a wide variation among them in terms of how much emphasis they put on the military routine.

DA: What do they do exactly, beyond the physical exertions and the discipline?

DG: OK, I visited the Florida program and I spent some time at the intake process with them. What they do is, they have basically four components to their program. One of them is military drill and ceremony, another one is obstacle courses—physical training, if you will. Another one is drug counseling and values clarification. It's basically aimed at getting them to change their ways of thought regarding crime and the responsibility to themselves and to the community they come from. . . .

DA: Any evidence that they're successful?

DG: It's, uh, it's difficult to come across it. There hasn't been anything that has been very systematic and analytical in its approach. You hear a lot of anecdotal evidence about its success. I talked with a couple of kids who went through it and said it did change their lives, but there's nothing hard. There's nothing that says this actually does, uh, reduce recidivism or, two, in the long run, wind up being less expensive.

DA: But it is a quicker way to set up a holding area for prisoners in a period when we're really running short of jail cells.

DG: That's part of it. That's part of the way it's sold—that it will reduce overcrowding; but again, unless there is solid evidence that it reduces recidivism, people may be fooling themselves. In the short run, one of the things that it does do, it appeals to people's instincts for a quick retribution among young offenders. People are tired of young punks terrorizing their communities, and when they see videotapes of these programs, it appeals to people on a very visceral level, seeing these young punks having to stand to attention, drop and do push-ups, say, "Yes, Sir, No, Sir," and march in double-time. That sells really well, and it sells especially well among politicians, who, in most cases, are the ones who initiate these programs. . . .

DA: Thank you.

DG: Correctional officials seem to be a little more reluctant about it.

Part Two

David Alpern: Thank you. For another view, we turn now to analyst Dale Parent, of Abt Associates in Cambridge. Thanks again for joining us on *Newsweek on Air.* How do you read the evidence on the effectiveness of boot camps?

Dale Parent: Well, it is strictly too soon to tell whether they have any special impact or not. There are evaluations under way in about five or six states of these programs that will in the next couple of years give us some hard evidence, but it appears now that on the basis of preliminary findings, there really is no difference in terms of effectiveness of these programs as compared to using straight prison or straight probation with similar kinds of offenders. But again, that's very preliminary evidence and it's by no means conclusive at this point. . . .

DA: Indeed, isn't there a danger that without other efforts at education, job training, and placement, boot camps for young criminals will do just what boot camps for servicemen are supposed to do—make them tougher, more resourceful, and effective as criminals?

DP: Well, I think that the idea of being able to deter people by a short period of extreme rigor or discipline is very questionable. I think if you're going to look for long-term changes in criminal behavior, you've got to deal with the basic problems that lead people to commit crimes, and those have to do with lack of education, lack of opportunity, to some extent. A large number of these people are heavily drug dependent, and so you have to deal with that problem as well. . . .

DA: Thank you. We've been talking about boot camp for young offenders with correctional analyst Dale Parent of Abt Associates in Cambridge, and correspondent David González in Miami.

3C. *Listening for Details*

(repeat Section 3B)

3D. *Listening Between the Lines*

EXCERPT ONE

David Alpern: Any evidence that they're successful?

David González: It's, uh, it's difficult to come across it. There hasn't been anything that has been very systematic and analytical in its approach. You hear a lot of anecdotal evidence about its success. I talked with a couple of kids who went through it and said it did change their lives, but there's nothing hard. There's nothing that says this actually does, uh, reduce recidivism or, two, in the long run, wind up being less expensive.

DA: But it is a quicker way to set up a holding area for prisoners in a period when we're really running short of jail cells.

DG: That's part of it. That's part of the way it's sold—that it will reduce overcrowding; but again, unless there is solid evidence that it reduces recidivism, people may be fooling themselves.

EXCERPT TWO

DG: . . . In the short run, one of the things that it does do, it appeals to people's instincts for a quick retribution among young offenders. People are tired of young punks terrorizing their communities, and when they see videotapes of these programs, it appeals to people on a very visceral level, seeing these young punks having to stand to attention, drop and do push-ups, say, "Yes, Sir, No, Sir," and march in double-time. That sells really well, and it sells especially well among politicians, who, in most cases, are the ones who initiate these programs. . . .

DA: Thank you.

DG: Correctional officials seem to be a little more reluctant about it.

EXCERPT THREE

DA: How do you read the evidence on the effectiveness of boot camps?

Dale Parent: Well, it is strictly too soon to tell whether they have any special impact or not. There are evaluations under way in about five or six states of these programs that will in the next couple of years give us some hard evidence, but it appears now that on the basis of preliminary findings, there really is no difference in terms of effectiveness of these programs as compared to using straight prison or straight probation with similar kinds of offenders. But again, that's very preliminary evidence and it's by no means conclusive at this point. . . .

4. LISTENING TWO: Are Boot Camps Effective?

4A. *Expanding the Topic*

Interviewer: Today, we have documentary filmmaker Thomas Adair with us. Mr. Adair has completed a number of projects on the justice system in the United States. Mr. Adair, thank you for talking to us.

Thomas Adair: Hi.

I: We've been hearing about boot camps as a form of punishment for young offenders. In your filmmaking, you've had a lot of experience with young people who break the law. What's your opinion of these camps?

TA: I think they're basically a good idea. They offer kids a form of discipline in their lives. They're a way of giving kids a second chance.

I: I understand what you're saying, but if young people commit the same crimes as adults, why should they be treated differently? Shouldn't they be punished like anybody else?

TA: Well, that's a popular view, but I disagree. There are repeat criminals who don't care about breaking the law again. It's going to take a lot of time and effort to change people like that. But I think with young people, first-time offenders especially, there's still a chance. I mean, don't get me wrong, I think that criminals should be punished. But we can't keep on throwing young people into prison. I mean, so often they just go to prison, get out in a few years, and wind up back in prison again. It's a revolving door. But if we can look at what's missing in a person's life and change his behavior, then that's what we should do.

I: In these boot camps, there's a lot of military routine. Stand at attention, do push-ups, say "Yes, Sir, No, Sir" . . . is that what appeals to you? Is that the kind of discipline you think kids need?

TA: Well, you know, I'm not usually a believer in harsh punishment, but I think in these cases . . . that kind of discipline . . . yes, it's needed.

I: Have you always felt this way?

TA: No. If you had asked me five years ago, I would have disagreed with the military aspect of boot camps for kids, but now, after spending time in boot camps and seeing how they work, I think that the problem with a lot of these kids is that they don't have structure in their lives, they don't have guidance.

I: And you think boot camps provide that?

TA: Well, some boot camps are more effective than others . . . but it's a form of punishment that gives kids the chance to think again about who they want to be.

I: Crime statistics keep going up, despite all the effort and money spent on criminal justice. Isn't it a little depressing?

TA: You have a point, yes, and I agree that there's an emergency in our society. But in my opinion, the biggest problem is not crime; it's a sense of hopelessness and pessimism, you know, negativity, about the future of these young people. As a group, they are poor and powerless in this society. And there just aren't that many of them. How can they be responsible for all of the problems in our society? But if you read the newspapers, that's the impression you get. It's ridiculous. We should be committed to helping them become decent adults.

I: Mmmm . . . So in your own work filming these kids, you've developed a different opinion from the one you started with?

TA: Absolutely. I've met some inspiring young people in prison . . . people who made mistakes, OK, but they still managed to turn over a new leaf. You know, I'm an optimist. From my own experience, things are not nearly as bad as they seem in the media. Most human beings want to have hope and optimism. These tough kids do, too. We can't just call them punks and slam the door in their faces after one or two mistakes. Boot camp may not be the whole answer, but it's a step in the right direction.

I: Well, we're out of time. Thank you, Thomas Adair.

TA: My pleasure.

UNIT 3 ◆ THE DOCTOR-PATIENT RELATIONSHIP

3. LISTENING ONE: Is Healing a Lost Art?

3A. *Introducing the Topic*

Christopher Lydon: You have earmarks, in your book, of trouble, Bernard Lown.

Bernard Lown: Yes.

CL: For example?

BL: If you come in and the doctor doesn't shake your hand, the doctor doesn't meet your eye, the doctor is looking at the clock, the telephone is ringing, and the secretary is coming in, this is not a doctor that you can have a healing relationship with. The patient also . . .

CL: Have you ever said, "Doctor, put that phone down; you're looking at me"?

BL: I have not chosen such doctors.

3B. *Listening for Main Ideas*

Christopher Lydon: From WBUR, Boston. I'm Christopher Lydon. This is *The Connection.* . . . You know the symptoms in what calls itself the best medical system in the world: the receptionist is more interested in your insurance than in your pain. . . . You can often feel that your examination, such as it is, is being conducted by that blinking machinery. What you're missing is the educated touch, the cocked head of a real doctor listening to your heartbeat, listening for your spirit. Without that human recognition, as one patient said, I am nothing but my illness.

We're in something like an intensive care unit this hour—talking about one of the critical relationships in life—a relationship which many people would say is beyond saving. We're talking about the doctor-patient relationship. . . . Can this thing be saved? . . . Is this the last requiem for a dying breed?

Or are you calling young doctors to a new standard? Can it be done?

Bernard Lown: The answer is categorically yes, because it must. Because otherwise you don't get medicine. Because medicine is not merely science, medicine is not only curing, but it's also healing. And healing requires the type of medicine that we are espousing. And if that is lost, medicine becomes a technology and is deprofessionalized; and that is what we're aiming to halt. . . . In part the crisis in medicine . . . began in my lifetime, really—it began, you know, with doctors distancing themselves from patients.

CL: To me, the most interesting thing about your book was the claim you made for taking the history. You said more, er, more people are cured or the more critical work of a doctor happens not from lab tests, not from anything that you can measure with a needle, or a number, er, but in the taking of the human history. Which is, of course, one of the patient's biggest—I mean, we're all longing for somebody to take our history and see it whole—mind, body, spirit—well or ill. I wish you'd tell some of those stories and make that point in your own words.

BL: Well, the point of it is, listening is the most important and most difficult single transaction . . .

. . . most difficult. And it takes time. There is no substitute. And the moment you start by not giving time, you cannot listen. And listening is not merely with the ears: listening is with your total being. And the fact of the matter is that in studies, carried out in Britain and other places, shows [sic] that 75% of all the valuable information that leads to correct diagnosis comes from the history. Another 10% comes from the physical examination, 5% comes from simple laboratory tests, and 5% comes from all the complex technology that you're launched against, and sometimes for, the patient. So listening is vital, because listening is not merely listening, but to establish a relationship.

CL: The question is . . . how do you explain to the insurance company, "No, no, no, this can't be done in fifteen minutes, and it won't be done in fifteen minutes"?

BL: Yeah, but from their point of view, it's inefficient. Because if you get all the information in this least costly way, immediately, you don't have to report to numerous specialists, you don't have to engage in complex and costly technologies, you don't launch drugs that create adverse reactions and require hospitalization and a whole array of consequentialities ensue.

So the doctor sees the patient for ten minutes, the doctor focuses on only one thing—the chief complaint. And the chief complaint may have nothing to do with what brings the patient to the doctor. This type of doctoring is essential, because 80% of all problems that come to doctors are trivial. . . .

Norman Cousins used to maintain, he says—"Americans think they're going to live forever until they get a cold, then they think they'll be dead within the next ten minutes." You know? The point of it, the point of it is, these are problems, er, largely from the rough and tumble of living. We live with our time. You don't have time, Chris . . . you are pressed by time, I'm pressed by time—we're constantly rushing. And these pressures, and tensions, create a whole array of problems. Our body revolts, in some ways—in olden times, with an extended family, you had a grandaunt, or a granddaddy, or somebody, who was able to pacify quietly, say if you take chicken soup, or whatever, you know, pineapple pulp, it'll solve your problems. But you see now that doesn't exist as such, and the doctor becomes an ombudsman for society in trying to allay the anxieties of an anxious age, and the doctor isn't there! The doctor isn't there, because the doctor doesn't want to listen. He's afraid to listen, he doesn't know how to listen, he hasn't been trained how to listen, there is no premium on listening, there's no reward for listening.

CL: And you say it can be saved?

BL: I'm an incorrigible . . .

CL: We've got work to do.

BL: I'm an incorrigible optimist. I'm an incorrigible optimist, because time and time again, the American people, if they begin to understand what good health is all about, what is good health? And good health begins first and foremost with caring. If you don't care for a patient, be somebody else, but don't be a doctor!

3C. *Listening for Details*

(repeat Section 3B)

3D. *Listening between the Lines*

EXCERPT ONE

We're in something like an intensive care unit this hour—talking about one of the critical relationships in life—a relationship which many people would say is beyond saving. We're talking about the doctor-patient relationship.

EXCERPT TWO

CL: You can often feel that your examination, such as it is, is being conducted by that blinking machinery. What you're missing is the educated touch, the cocked head of a real doctor listening to your heartbeat, listening for your spirit.

EXCERPT THREE

Bernard Lown: Norman Cousins used to maintain, he says—"Americans think they're going to live forever until they get a cold, then they think they'll be dead within the next ten minutes." You know? The point of it, the point of it is, these are problems, er, largely from the rough and tumble of living. We live with our time. You don't have time, Chris . . . you are pressed by time, I'm pressed by time—we're constantly rushing.

EXCERPT FOUR

BL: And these pressures, and tensions, create a whole array of problems. Our body revolts, in some ways—in olden times, with an extended family, you had a grandaunt, or a granddaddy, or somebody, who was able to pacify quietly, say if you take chicken soup, or whatever, you know, pineapple pulp, it'll solve your problems. But you see now that doesn't exist as such, and the doctor becomes an ombudsman for society in trying to allay the anxieties of an anxious age, and the doctor isn't there! The doctor isn't there, because the doctor doesn't want to listen. He's afraid to listen, he doesn't know how to listen, he hasn't been trained how to listen, there is no premium on listening, there's no reward for listening.

4. LISTENING TWO: *Body Talk*—A Call-In Show

4A. *Expanding the Topic*

Bill: Good morning, everyone. This is Bill and the show is *Body Talk*. Today's topic is problems with doctors. Now, who hasn't had a problem with a doctor? Call in and tell us yours. Our number is 1-800-555-BODY. That didn't take long . . . here's our first caller now.

Bill: Hello, this is Bill and you're on *Body Talk*!

Shelley: Morning, Bill. This is Shelley Travers, calling from New York City. Thanks for taking my call. I just want to say how important I think it really is for a doctor to listen to a patient.

Bill: Tell me about it! So, Shelley, what happened to you?

Shelley: Well, I was getting these really bad, shooting pains in my back. I couldn't sleep at night or anything. So I went to my doctor, and he examined me and had me do all these tests and things. And I even had to go into the hospital for some X-rays. But after all that—I mean, I took off a lot of time from work—they told me there was nothing wrong with me. I was thinking about trying alternative medicine and going to a chiropractor, when a co-worker . . . I'm a secretary . . . (voice trails off)

Bill: What was that, Shelley? I didn't catch all of what you said. You mean, you were in serious pain . . . the doctor's tests didn't show anything . . . you were going to go to a chiropractor . . .

Shelley: Well, yes, that's right. Awful, right? But a co-worker said, "You know, your desk chair is too hard. If you sat on a soft cushion, that might make your back feel better." Anyway, she was totally right. So then I felt really mad, because . . . I mean . . . I had taken all that time from work to see the doctor, but all I really needed was a cushion!

Bill: So . . . your doctor hadn't really listened and asked the right questions, right, Shelley?

Shelley: Yeah . . . that's right. He never asked me what kind of work I did, or how long I spent at the computer every day. If he had asked some questions, he probably wouldn't have sent me for all those tests!

Bill: Sure sounds like your doctor wasn't much help. . . . But, I'm glad the cushion worked. Thanks, Shelley. 'Bye, now.

Bill: Hi. Bill here. You're on *Body Talk*.

Linda: Hi there, Bill. My name is Linda Jenkins, and I'm calling from Atlanta, Georgia. I want to tell you what happened to me . . . it's kind of embarrassing though . . .

Bill: Ah, go ahead. Linda. Don't be embarrassed. . . . We're listening.

Linda: Well . . . ah . . . OK. I had this big wart on my foot. It got so bad that I could hardly . . .

Bill: Sorry to interrupt you, Linda. What did you say?

Linda: A wart, you know, a hard lump. Kids get them on their hands all the time, but I got one on the bottom of my left foot. So, my doctor said I'd probably need an operation to remove it. Burn it off, or something. He really scared me!

Bill: So, you were scared, . . . but did you take his advice?

Linda: No, actually, I didn't. But I was just desperate, because . . . you know . . . I could hardly walk. So, I decided to try acupuncture.

Bill: Wait a minute . . . I didn't catch that. What did you say?

Linda: I tried acupuncture—I went to an acupuncturist. And you know, she really listened to me and got me to change my diet and get more rest. She said the wart was probably a reaction to stress. . . . I had been working late a lot. Eventually, the wart cleared up. I really think that doctors have to be more careful before they recommend operations. Sometimes there's a much simpler treatment. I mean, if doctors put themselves in their patients' shoes, they might not be so quick to start cutting!

Bill: You know, Linda, you're absolutely right! I couldn't agree with you more! Thanks for sharing your story with us. Goodbye, and good luck!

Bill: Hello, you're on *Body Talk.*

Ray: Hello, Bill. Ray Ishwood calling from Eugene, Oregon.

Bill: How you doing, Ray?

Ray: Fine, Bill. . . . Ah, well . . . here's my story. For several years, I've had arthritis in my hands and wrists. This winter—it was so cold and rainy—the pain got really bad. My doctor gave me a series of injections, really painful, to my hands. He said that in a few weeks I would feel better.

Bill: Well, did you? Did those painful shots help?

Ray: Sorry, Bill, what was that?

Bill: I said, Ray, did they—the shots—help you? You said you had injections . . . did they help in any way?

Ray: Well . . . I don't really know . . . I mean, I'm feeling a lot better now, but I think it's because of the warmer weather. I tend to get worse when it's cold and rainy outside. So, I don't think that the shots were that much help. And they were very painful. I just don't want to continue with them if they don't really make much of a difference.

Bill: You're probably right, Ray. Well, I'm glad you're feeling better, and thanks for calling *Body Talk.*

5. REVIEWING LANGUAGE

5A. *Exploring Vocabulary: Pronouncing Elongated Stressed Syllables*

1. altérnative
2. ácupuncturist
3. inténsive
4. diagnósis
5. sýmptoms
6. médical
7. éducated
8. trívial
9. anxíeties
10. rémedies
11. chíropractor
12. ínteresting
13. spécialist
14. embárrassing
15. réaction
16. nátural
17. áilments
18. állergies
19. physícian
20. injéctions

UNIT 4 ◆ EYE OF THE STORM

3. LISTENING ONE: Preparing for a Hurricane

3A. *Introducing the Topic*

1. The sky is clear blue, and the ocean is deceptively calm here in Pitsea Beach in southern Florida. It's the kind of day when you would expect . . .
2. But the beaches are . . .
3. Traveling inland, though, you'll find a totally different mood. Parking spaces . . .
4. and there are long lines at . . .
5. You see, despite the calm weather now, the citizens of Pitsea Beach are . . .

3B. *Listening for Main Ideas*

Nora White: This is Nora White reporting for station KTFH in Florida.

The sky is clear blue, and the ocean is deceptively calm here in Pitsea Beach in Southern Florida. It's the kind of day when you would expect the beaches to be packed with tourists, enjoying the surf and sun. But the beaches are eerily silent, except for a few seagulls circling the waves. Traveling inland, though, you'll find a totally different mood. Parking spaces are hard to find, and there are long lines at every checkout counter as people stock up on batteries, water bottles, and flashlights.

You see, despite the calm weather now, the citizens of Pitsea Beach are getting ready for a hurricane, the first of this hurricane season.

With me today in Pitsea Beach is meteorologist Henry Anselma, who will tell us how to prepare for a hurricane. We'll also hear what local residents and tourists are doing to prepare for the storm. Henry, can you tell us what to expect?

Henry Anselma: Nora, Hurricane Haley is about 70 miles off the coast of Florida, with winds reported to be up to 100 miles per hour. Already, it has caused considerable damage to islands in the Caribbean. Notices warning residents and visitors to evacuate have been issued in several counties in southern Florida.

NW: So residents are being warned to evacuate. Let's ask a local resident what her plans are. Are you going to leave?

Resident 1: No, I'm not leaving, I'm staying here to protect my house. I think we'll be all right, though. In my experience, the hurricanes are not as bad as they usually predict. Everyone panics and gets ready, and then not much happens.

NW: But the radio stations are stressing that people should stay informed and NOT second-guess the authorities. Apparently, despite the sophisticated satellite, reconnaissance aircraft, and radar used by the National Weather Service, forecasting the path of a hurricane is not an easy task. Can you explain, Henry?

HA: We input a lot of data into the computer to get a forecast, but there's still an element of interpretation that needs to be done. Often the storm will change route or intensity unexpectedly, and folks must realize that they can be very, very vulnerable.

NW: Henry, what can people do in advance to be safe?

HA: Stock up on supplies. You should have plenty of water on hand, at least a couple of gallons per person, and more if possible. Don't forget that sewers back up, and water gets contaminated. You should have enough food to last you at least three days, more if you can do it; for your canned goods, make sure that you've got a can opener on hand—manual, not electric. You'll need a flashlight for a power outage, and a radio—battery-powered to keep informed. Don't forget any regular medication.

NW: Henry also says that a sturdy pair of work boots should be added to the list. Why is that, Henry?

HA: Yes, when you come back, if your place has been damaged, you don't want to be walking into dangerous things, including any snakes that might be floating around, dislocated by the hurricane like you've been.

NW: Thanks, Henry. . . . And now we'll find out what this gentleman is going to do.

Tourist: Well, I don't live here . . . um . . . I'm just a tourist. We came down here for a vacation, just to get away from it all, and it's turned out to be a nightmare! I'm from Minnesota, and we don't have hurricanes there. I have no idea what to expect. I'm scared stiff!

NW: Most tourists, ready for a carefree vacation, aren't prepared to face a hurricane. But if you're planning to visit a coastal spot during the summer months, you need to plan for the possibility of a hurricane before your trip. How can tourists do this, Henry?

HA: I think the main thing for tourists is to know what plans or provisions the hotel has and what they're going to do if the power's out, if the water's bad. You need to know where you're going if you have to leave early, because roads get flooded, and highways get backed up with traffic.

NW: Do you need extra money?

HA: Sure. If you're stuck longer, you'll need access to additional cash, and you should know how you're going to get it, even if the ATMs are out of order. Those money machines won't be working if the power's gone. You have to know, basically, how to change your plans fast.

NW: Thank you, Henry. . . . With me now is a woman who has lived in Pitsea Beach for over twenty-five years. Tell us, Mrs. O'Hara, are you going to stay or leave?

Resident 2 (Mrs. O'Hara): I'm not sure, Nora; I've been just glued to the TV—listening to weather reports. I want to be sure I'm ready for this. Hurricanes are really frightening. I almost lost my house during the last hurricane. I know that a really bad hurricane can hit shore when you least expect it. I just hope that it is not as big a hurricane as they predict.

NW: We all hope so. Thank you, Mrs. O'Hara.

Back in Pitsea Beach, all residents can do is watch, wait, and try not to panic. For Florida KTFH, this is Nora White.

3C. *Listening for Details*

(repeat Section 3B)

3D. *Listening Between the Lines*

EXCERPT ONE

Nora White: But the radio stations are stressing that people should stay informed and NOT second-guess the authorities. Apparently, despite the sophisticated satellite, reconnaissance aircraft, and radar used by the National Weather Service, forecasting the path of a hurricane is not an easy task. Can you explain, Henry?

Henry Anselma: We input a lot of data into the computer to get a forecast, but there's still an element of interpretation that needs to be done. Often the storm will change route or intensity unexpectedly, and folks must realize that they can be very, very vulnerable.

EXCERPT TWO

NW: Henry, what can people do in advance to be safe?

HA: Stock up on supplies. You should have plenty of water on hand, at least a couple of gallons per person, and more if possible. Don't forget that sewers back up, and water gets contaminated. You should have enough food to last you at least three days, more if you can do it; for your canned goods, make sure that you've got a can opener on hand—manual, not electric. You'll need a flashlight for a power outage, and a radio—battery-powered—to keep informed. Don't forget any regular medication.

NW: Henry also says that a sturdy pair of work boots should be added to the list. Why is that, Henry?

HA: Yes, when you come back, if your place has been damaged, you don't want to be walking into dangerous things, including any snakes that might be floating around, dislocated by the hurricane like you've been.

EXCERPT THREE

HA: I think the main thing for tourists is to know what plans or provisions the hotel has and what they're going to do if the power's out, if the water's bad. You need to know where you're going if you have to leave early, because roads get flooded, and highways get backed up with traffic.

NW: Do you need extra money?

HA: Sure. If you're stuck longer, you'll need access to additional cash, and you should know how you're going to get it even if the ATMs are out of order. Those money machines won't be working if the power's gone. You have to know, basically, how to change your plans fast.

4. LISTENING TWO: Hurricane Hunters

4A. *Expanding the Topic*

David Chang: This is David Chang for radio station KTFH reporting live from aboard a reconnaissance squadron, more commonly known as the Hurricane Hunters. The sun is shining in South Florida as the aircraft gets ready. It will carry its crew of six officers from the postcard-like weather here into the eye of Hurricane Haley, as the big storm turns northward through the eastern Caribbean. It will fly through the hurricane to relay vital information on wind speed, pressure, and organization of the storm back to the mainland.

Today, I get to go with them . . . into the eye of the storm. Two of the crew members, Andrea Davis and Miguel Ríos, are with me now.

As we fly toward the hurricane, the sky is blue and it's sunny, but in the distance, the storm clouds at the edge of the hurricane can be seen. Where are we headed now, Andrea?

Andrea Davis: See, on this flight we don't try and avoid the storm; we head right for it.

DC: That's amazing. So we're flying right into the eye? How big is it?

AD: I'd say it was about twelve miles wide.

DC: Really? Only twelve miles?

The interior of the plane becomes dark as we enter the eye wall, which is what we call the thick clouds around the center of the storm. The ends of the wings seem to disappear in the clouds and the rain. But as quickly as it becomes dark, it suddenly becomes so bright it's almost blinding, as the plane breaks through the eye wall and into the eye, which is always calm.

At this point, equipment is dropped from the plane to record data. Despite the danger, the crew still manages to stay in good spirits.

I don't understand why you just can't send a computer-guided plane through the storm. Aren't you frightened, Miguel? I mean, it must be dangerous to fly right into a hurricane.

Miguel Ríos: The thing is, machines still cannot replace an eyewitness account, which is what Hurricane Hunters provide. I mean, technology provides a very accurate position as to where the storm is located, but it's not as accurate as having people on board. For instance, humans can tell certain things about the speed and direction of the storm by looking down onto the ocean surface. When you're there, you can make judgments computers cannot make.

DC: Mmm, really?

MR: And you know, some people might ask why anyone would want to fly through a hurricane. But once I got started on this, I found that I really enjoyed it. It's actually very exciting.

DC: Really! Aren't you crew members under a lot of pressure?

AD: Well, it's a pretty intense experience, but it's a great feeling you get of really helping people. That's what we're doing here, and you know, that's a heartening thought. See, it looks beautiful from up here, but it's deceptive. This storm could kill anyone who gets in its way.

DC: Thank you both, Andrea and Miguel. Amazing work, and an amazing trip. For radio station KTFH, I'm David Chang.

UNIT 5 ◆ YOU WILL BE THIS LAND

3. LISTENING ONE: Interview with a Medicine Priest

3A. *Introducing the Topic*

Barbara Cassin: Hi, I'm here with David Winston, a Cherokee medicine priest. David, thank you for coming to talk to us today.

David Winston: Oh, you're very welcome.

BC: Would you tell us a little bit about the Cherokee beliefs regarding the environment and conservation?

DW: Yes, I'd be happy to. Uh, basically, Cherokee tradition tells us that we are part of nature and we depend on nature for our life, so we don't, uh, compete with it and we're not trying to tame it, we're trying to live with it.

BC: It's different from our contemporary view, I guess, that nature exists for the benefit of people.

DW: Well, yeah. We believe that we, as I said, we're a part of what we call the Great Life, and as part of the Great Life we are as important as everything else, but certainly no more important than anything else. And we feel that within the Great Life, there are what we call the Laws of Nature.

BC: The laws of nature . . . could you tell us more about that?

DW: Yeah, we believe that there are many laws of nature, but there are three great Laws of Nature, and those are the laws that tell us how we have to live in relationship to everything else.

3B. *Listening for Main Ideas*

BC: Hi, I'm here with David Winston, a Cherokee medicine priest. David, thank you for coming to talk to us today.

DW: Oh, you're very welcome.

BC: Would you tell us a little bit about the Cherokee beliefs regarding the environment and conservation?

DW: Yes, I'd be happy to. Uh, basically, Cherokee tradition tells us that we are part of nature and we depend on nature for our life, so we don't, uh, compete with it and we're not trying to tame it, we're trying to live with it.

BC: It's different from our contemporary view, I guess, that nature exists for the benefit of people.

DW: Well, yeah. We believe that we, as I said, we're a part of what we call the Great Life, and as part of the Great Life we are as important as everything else, but certainly no more important than anything else. And we feel that within the Great Life, there are what we call the Laws of Nature.

BC: The laws of nature . . . could you tell us more about that?

DW: Yeah, we believe that there are many laws of nature, but there are three great Laws of Nature, and those are the laws that tell us how we have to live in relationship to everything else. The First Law of Nature is that you don't take any life without a real reason. And a real reason would be for food, for medicine, for protection . . . uh, those would be the reasons for taking life. But basically, life is sacred.

BC: Uh huh. So you shouldn't kill needlessly. Would that include plants?

DW: Absolutely. We believe everything is alive. In fact, we believe stones are alive, trees are alive, plants are alive, animals are obviously alive, connected. And so to us, taking the life of a plant is just as grave a responsibility as taking the life of an animal. And all of those things should be done in a sacred way and in a good way. So for instance, when you go to gather a plant, you don't want to go and say, "Wow, here's a whole patch of plants," and gather them all. You gather a few, and then you gather a few from another spot, leaving the majority of the plants so that they can grow and, you know, continue to provide not only for themselves, but for us, and for our children, and for their children.

BC: Interesting. And what about the Second Law?

DW: The Second Law is that everything we do should serve the Great Life.

BC: Hmm. The Great Life. What exactly do you mean by that?

DW: Well, what we mean is . . . is that we believe that there's one spirit that fills all things, humans, plants, rocks, whatever. And the sum of all of that and more is what we call the Great Life. And so we all are part of this same Great Life. And everything we do affects the Great Life, and everything that happens within the Great Life affects us. So it's very, very important that within the Second Law of Nature, that what we do will not harm other parts of the Great Life.

BC: I . . . I wonder if you could give an example.

DW: Well, I could give a lot of examples. And on a very personal, simple level, an example could be for instance . . . uh, lots of people might go out and get an electric toothbrush. Uh, you know maybe it works a little bit better, it's certainly easier. The toothbrush does all the work for you. But I have a manual toothbrush and I've used one for my whole life, and it works just fine. To use the electricity necessary to power that electric toothbrush requires coal or nuclear power that harms the air, it harms the water, it harms the Great Life.

BC: I see, so we don't really need it. OK, so that's two. And what about the Third Law?

DW: The Third Law basically is . . . is that we don't pollute where we live. And, where we live is not just our home, it's not just our intimate small community, it's not just our country. It's this planet, this sacred altar we call the Earth. We don't pour chemical wastes down the drain because they all wind up in the water. So basically we don't pollute the Earth.

BC: I see. Well, they make sense, but it seems it's a little difficult to live by those three laws today. I mean, in this industrialized society, how could you apply the rules?

DW: Well, it's more challenging, certainly. The Cherokees didn't have a problem with . . . uh . . . plastic. We didn't have plastic. We didn't have a lot of the things that exist today. We still have a lot of options. There are small things that each one of us can do . . . things like recycling, things like choosing what we buy and buying things carefully. There are other things we can do—instead of using the car for every short trip to the store, save them up so we use the car as little as possible. We can do things like organic gardening. We can do things to create greater community within our communities. There are a lot of things that we can do to bring these laws into our lives. And ultimately, our lives really depend on these. The Great Life can live without us, but we can't live without the Great Life.

BC: Well, you've certainly given us a lot to think about today. Thanks, David Winston, for talking to us.

DW: You're welcome. Un dun Koh ha hee.

3C. *Listening for Details*

(repeat Section 3B)

3D. *Listening between the Lines*

EXCERPT ONE

BC: The laws of Nature, could you tell us more about that?

DW: Yeah, we believe that there are many laws of nature, but there are three great Laws of Nature, and those are the laws that tell us how we have to live in relationship to everything else. The First Law of Nature is that you don't take any life without a real reason. And a real reason would be for food, for medicine, for protection . . . uh, those would be the reasons for taking life. But basically, life is sacred.

EXCERPT TWO

DW: The Second Law is that everything we do should serve the Great Life.

BC: Hmm. The Great Life. What exactly do you mean by that?

DW: Well, what we mean is . . . is that we believe that there's one spirit that fills all things, humans, plants, rocks, whatever. And the sum of all that and more is what we call the Great Life. And so we all are part of this same Great Life. And everything we do affects the Great Life, and everything that happens within the Great Life affects us. So it's very, very important that within the Second Law of Nature, that what we do will not harm other parts of the Great Life.

EXCERPT THREE

BC: I see, so we don't really need it. OK, so that's two. And what about the Third Law?

DW: The Third Law basically is . . . is that we don't pollute where we live. And, where we live is not just our home, it's not just our intimate small community, it's not just our country. It's this planet, this sacred altar we call the Earth. We don't pour chemical wastes down the drain because they all wind up in the water. So basically we don't pollute the Earth.

4. LISTENING TWO: Ndakinna—A Poem

4A. *Expanding the Topic*

❶ **Narrator:** "Ndakinna" by Joseph Bruchac. "Ndakinna" means "Our Land" in Abnaki. Ndakinna. That's what we call America.

You cannot understand
this land with maps,
lines drawn as if earth
were an animal's carcass
cut into pieces, skinned,
though always less eaten
than thrown away.

See this land instead
with a wind-eagle's eyes,
linked with rivers and streams
like sinews through leather,
sewed strong to hold the people
to the earth.

Do not try to know the land by roads.
Let your feet instead
caress the soil
in the way of deer,
whose trails follow
the ways of least resistance.

When you feel this land
when you taste this land
when you hold this land as lungs hold breath
when your songs see this land,
when your ears sing this land,
you will be this land.
you will be this land.

(For Exercise 2, repeat Section 4A.)

(For Exercise 3, repeat Section 4A.)

5. REVIEWING LANGUAGE

5A. *Exploring Language:* th *Sound*

❶
1. three
2. they
3. there
4. think
5. so
6. ladder
7. worthy
8. dough
9. sued
10. they
11. bathe
12. other
13. breeze
14. Zen

(For Exercise 4, repeat Section 4A.)

UNIT 6 ◆ IT'S BETTER TO GIVE THAN TO RECEIVE

3. LISTENING ONE: Oseola McCarty—An Unusual Philanthropist

3A. *Introducing the Topic*

Barbara Walters: Deep in the heart of Mississippi, hidden behind wind-whipped sheets and sun-drenched linens, lives this year's most talked-about philanthropist. No one noticed the frail woman who spent most of her eighty-six years doing other people's laundry. Quietly, in between bundles of wash and ironing, Ms. Oseola McCarty tucked away $250,000.

3B. *Listening for Main Ideas*

Barbara Walters: Why would a poor washing woman give away her life savings? This story touched us the moment we first heard it, and the more we thought about it, the more we believed that Ms. Oseola McCarty had to be on our list.

Deep in the heart of Mississippi, hidden behind wind-whipped sheets and sun-drenched linens, lives this year's most talked-about philanthropist. No one noticed the frail woman who spent most of her eighty-six years doing other people's laundry. Quietly, in between bundles of wash and ironing, Ms. Oseola McCarty tucked away $250,000.

Oseola McCarty: I was surprised myself. I didn't know I had that much money.

BW: The woman who never went to high school, never went to college, stunned the academic world by pledging most of her life's savings to fund scholarships for promising black students at the university down the road.

OM: I didn't have no children. I didn't have nobody else to give it to.

BW: Ms. McCarty's own education was cut short. She left after sixth grade to care for her ailing grandmother. And she worked, taking in bundles of laundry from doctors, lawyers, and policemen, slowly building a nest egg of dollars and change at the bank downtown.

Announcer: The president of the United States.

BW: News of the gift has traveled far.

President: If this country had more people like you, we'd have very few problems, and we'd be even greater than we are.

OM: I didn't know I was so powerful until people began to tell me.

BW: The trip to the White House this September was her first time out of the South in fifty years.

These days, times are not so lonely at the frame house on Miller Street. There's a new visitor: she's Stephanie Bullock, the first recipient of the Oseola McCarty scholarship, and thanks to her benefactor, a college freshman.

Stephanie Bullock: I always knew that I was going to go to college. Didn't know how—but I was going to go. Ms. McCarty will be at my graduation, sitting right over there with my family.

OM: There's more in giving than it is to receive. And I tried it out.

BW: Her washing tools are retired now. Her hands are knarled by arthritis. But the years of crisp collars and pressed pleats now leave a legacy all their own.

OM: I don't regret it one minute. I just wished I had more to give.

BW: Ms. McCarty has started something big. Local business people around her town are now contributing to the Oseola McCarty scholarship fund.

She finds it all quite amusing, and told us that the locals weren't about to let some wash-and-iron woman show them all up. Good for you, Oseola.

3C. *Listening for Details*

(repeat Section 3B)

3D. *Listening between the Lines*

EXCERPT ONE

Barbara Walters: No one noticed the frail woman who spent most of her eighty-six years doing other people's laundry. Quietly, in between bundles of wash and ironing, Ms. Oseola McCarty tucked away $250,000.

Oseola McCarty: I was surprised myself. I didn't know I had that much money.

BW: The woman who never went to high school, never went to college, stunned the academic world by pledging most of her life's savings to fund scholarships for promising black students at the university down the road.

Excerpt Two

OM: I didn't have no children. I didn't have nobody else to give it to.

BW: Ms. McCarty's own education was cut short. She left after sixth grade to care for her ailing grandmother. And she worked, taking in bundles of laundry from doctors, lawyers, and policemen, slowly building a nest egg of dollars and change at the bank downtown.

Excerpt Three

OM: There's more in giving than it is to receive. And I tried it out.

BW: Her washing tools are retired now. Her hands are knarled by arthritis. But the years of crisp collars and pressed pleats now leave a legacy all their own.

OM: I don't regret it one minute. I just wished I had more to give.

4. LISTENING TWO: Please Donate or Volunteer—Public Service Announcements

4A. *Expanding the Topic*

PSA 1: Volunteering

In America, the Constitution doesn't require you to offer food to the hungry or shelter to the homeless. There is no ordinance forcing you to visit the lonely. Nothing says you have to provide clothing to the poor. In fact, one of the nicest things about living in America is that you really don't have to do anything for anybody. Yet, 80 million Americans volunteer their time and money anyway. Thank you for all you've given. Imagine what more could do. Call 1-800-55-GIVE-5. A public service message from the Independent Sector and the Ad Council.

PSA 2: Traffic

If you can drive a car, you can drive one for someone who can't. If you can pick up a few groceries, you can pick them up for someone who can't. To find out how easy it is to help, call the Points of Light Foundation, at 1-800-59-LIGHT. Do something good. Feel something real. A public service message from the Points of Light Foundation and the Ad Council.

5. REVIEWING LANGUAGE

5A. *Exploring Language: Consonant + Vowel Joining*

❶ Part One

The story of Oseola McCarty, a washer-woman who gave away her life savings, has touched the heart of everyone who has heard it. This frail old woman has now become one of the most famous philan-thropists in the nation. Year by year, for most of her life, Ms. McCarty worked for others, tucking away every penny she did not need for food and daily living expenses.

Part Two

After many years, Oseola consulted a lawyer and made an announcement that stunned everyone: she had accumulated a nest egg of $250,000 and decided to give most of it away. The recipient was a fund to help worthy black students go to college. Businesses in the area followed Oseola's lead, and donations poured in.

6. SKILLS FOR EXPRESSION

6A. *Grammar: Tag Questions*

❷ Step 2

1. **A:** You've heard about Oseola McCarty's gift to the university, haven't you?
2. **B:** Yes, I have. It's an amazing story, isn't it?
3. **A:** Uh, huh. Some people are more generous than others, aren't they?
4. **B:** That's the truth. Most people wouldn't give away all their money, would they?

5. **A:** Of course not. Even very wealthy people don't give a very high percentage of their money away, do they?

6. **B:** Right. I remember reading that low-income people give an average of 3.6 percent of their income and wealthy people only 1.6 percent. That's surprising, isn't it?

7. **A:** But it's not true for everyone. Look at Ted Turner. He gave one billion dollars to the United Nations, didn't he?

8. **B:** That's right. It's hard to imagine having that much money to give, isn't it?

9. **A:** It sure is. But more wealthy people should give away more of their money, shouldn't they?

   B: I agree, but I wonder how I'd feel if I were rich!

UNIT 7 ◆ EMOTIONAL INTELLIGENCE

3. LISTENING ONE: Can You Learn EQ?

3A. *Introducing the Topic*

Claire Nolan: Hi. This is Claire Nolan.

Bill Rodney: And I'm Bill Rodney, and this is "Psychology Wednesday." Today, we'll be discussing EQ—not IQ, EQ: emotional intelligence. We've been hearing a lot about EQ lately, and in fact you might have seen Daniel Goleman's best-selling book about it in the bookstore. Your emotional intelligence quotient seems to include both intra- and interpersonal relationships—in other words, how well you handle your own emotions, and how well you respond to others.

CN: Yes, but Bill, that's not exactly a new idea, is it? I mean—I know a lot of old proverbs about thinking before you act, and that kind of thing.

BR: That's true, but the term itself is a new one, and it shows that people have realized, the way you control your feelings is just as important as your education—maybe even more important. But what's really interesting, and the focus of today's session, is, can you learn EQ? We'll be talking to three people today—all educators, in their own way—to get their perspective on it. Don't go away!

3B. *Listening for Main Ideas*

PART ONE

Claire Nolan: Hi. This is Claire Nolan.

Bill Rodney: And I'm Bill Rodney, and this is "Psychology Wednesday." Today, we'll be discussing EQ—not IQ, EQ: emotional intelligence. We've been hearing a lot about EQ lately, and in fact you might have seen Daniel Goleman's best-selling book about it in the bookstore. Your emotional intelligence quotient seems to include both intra- and interpersonal relationships—in other words, how well you handle your own emotions, and how well you respond to others.

CN: Yes, but Bill, that's not exactly a new idea, is it? I mean—I know a lot of old proverbs about thinking before you act, and that kind of thing.

BR: That's true, but the term itself is a new one, and it shows that people have realized, the way you control your feelings is just as important as your education—maybe even more important. But what's really interesting, and the focus of today's session, is, can you learn EQ? We'll be talking to three people today—all educators, in their own way—to get their perspective on it. Don't go away!

BR: Welcome back to "Psychology Wednesday." Our first guest is Betty Cortina. Betty, you're an elementary school teacher. Do you really think that some kids have higher EQ's than others?

Betty Cortina: Oh sure! Even at five or six years old, some of the kids tend to be much more patient and easygoing than others. And then others are prone to shout and make a big fuss. I mean, I don't want to make it sound as if it's bad to be spirited, or anything, but if you can't control your emotions, even at that age, you can have a lot of problems.

BR: Like what?

BC: Well, if you can't deal with setbacks, you don't make progress, and if you're always impatient, your peers don't like you.

BR: Can you give us an example?

BC: Sure. One example is how kids deal with frustration. Imagine a child who is having trouble doing a math problem. She gets frustrated with the problem, throws her pencil down, yells angrily, "This is a stupid problem! I hate it!" Another child, with a higher EQ, might be able to handle the situation better. She might try different ways to approach the problem, or ask for help, and so on. And she will be more successful because she won't let her negative feelings get in the way of her task.

PART TWO

BR: I guess I can understand that, but my question is: Can you *learn* to have a higher EQ? Let's see, our next guest is Jim McDonald. Do you want to respond to that question?

Jim McDonald: Yes. Well, as you know, I run management training programs for a bank here in the city, and I agree, this EQ idea is definitely important. Let's face it, when the going gets tough, it's much better for an employee to have a positive, enthusiastic attitude than to dwell on failures. But what I find is that some people just take life in stride, and other people don't. I mean, of course you can point them in the right direction—that's what I try to do in my seminars—but some people never learn to improve their EQ.

BC: No, I disagree. Kids *can* be taught to have patience and not to give up when things go wrong. They *learn* to respond well to their emotions. They *learn* how to sit still and listen, and how to respect others. And I *don't* believe we are born with a high emotional intelligence quotient. I think we have to learn those skills.

JM: OK, so maybe you can teach children, but frankly, I don't see how adults can ever change. I mean, I work with a lot of managers, and the good ones are sharp, perceptive people who respond well to change. I don't think the others can learn that.

BR: Why not?

JM: Well, part of the problem is that people with a low EQ have a difficult time seeing how their behavior affects other people. They see no reason to change. Their behavior has negative effects—for themselves and for others—but they don't see it that way. They tend to blame other people for the problems they are having. People like this just don't work well with other people. I'd say they have a lower EQ and they'll probably never adjust their behavior.

PART THREE

BR: Thank you, Jim. Our third guest, Jan Davis, is a marriage counselor. Jan, from the perspective of a marriage counselor, can adults change their EQ's?

Jan Davis: Yes. I am a psychologist and I work with couples, married couples, who are having problems. From what I can see, some people, adults, I mean, *can* change their EQ's.

BR: How so?

JD: Well, I think that the key to keeping a relationship together is learning to empathize with your partner.

BR: Did you say empathize?

JD: Yes—it's crucial. Couples who have successful relationships try hard to understand each other's feelings. First, you have to put yourself in your partner's shoes. That makes it easier for you to make allowances for your partner's weaknesses. You have to learn to control your reactions even when you feel angry or resentful.

BR: So you're saying people *can* learn those things? Don't you think that, as Jim said, some people have it and some don't?

JD: No, I disagree strongly with what he said. I *do* see people change. (laughs) If I didn't think people could change, I'd be in a different line of work!

BR: I'm not quite sure I understand what you're saying. Tell us about someone you've seen acquire a higher EQ.

JD: Well, let me tell you about a case I saw recently. I had some clients, a husband and wife, a few months ago, and the wife had gotten a promotion at work. Now the husband was happy for her, of course, but he also felt a bit jealous. He felt like a failure because *he* hadn't gotten a promotion at *his* job.

BR: So what happened to them?

JD: Well, the husband had to learn to swallow his pride and put aside his own negative feelings. I told him to concentrate on the good thing that had happened to his wife instead of thinking about himself. With practice, he was able to see that her success was also his success, not his failure. I really think he raised his own EQ by doing that.

BR: Thank you, Jan. And I'll remember to keep EQ in mind. Maybe I can get a little better at it! And thank you, Betty and Jim, for joining us today.

3C. *Listening for Details*

(repeat Section 3B)

3D. *Listening between the Lines*

EXCERPT ONE

BC: Sure. One example is how kids deal with frustration. Imagine a child who is having trouble doing a math problem. She gets frustrated with the problem, throws her pencil down, yells angrily, "This is a stupid problem! I hate it!" Another child, with a higher EQ, might be able to handle the situation better. She might try different ways to approach the problem, or ask for help, and so on. And she will be more successful because she won't let her negative feelings get in the way of her task.

EXCERPT TWO

JM: Well, part of the problem is that people with a low EQ have a difficult time seeing how their behavior affects other people. They see no reason to change. Their behavior has negative effects—for themselves and for others—but they don't see it that way. They tend to blame other people for the problems they are having. People like this just don't work well with other people. I'd say they have a lower EQ and they'll probably never adjust their behavior.

EXCERPT THREE

JD: Well, let me tell you about a case I saw recently. I had some clients, a husband and wife, a few months ago, and the wife had gotten a promotion at work. Now the husband was happy for her, of course, but he also felt a bit jealous. He felt like a failure because *he* hadn't gotten a promotion at *his* job.

BR: So what happened to them?

JD: Well, the husband had to learn to swallow his pride and put aside his own negative feelings. I told him to concentrate on the good thing that had happened to his wife instead of thinking about himself. With practice, he was able to see that her success was also his success, not his failure. I really think he raised his own EQ by doing that.

4. LISTENING TWO: Test Your EQ

4A. *Expanding the Topic*

Claire Nolan: During the second portion of "Psychology Wednesday," Jan Davis will tell me how I scored on the EQ test I've just taken.

Jan Davis: Now that you've taken the test, it's time to find out the answers. Which answers show a high EQ? How did you score? Are you ready, Claire?

CN: I sure am.

JD: OK, number one, the situation with the crying child. The best answer is B: "Talk to him and help him figure out ways to get the other kids to play with him."

CN: Why is that?

JD: Emotionally intelligent parents use situations like this to teach their children about emotions—help their children understand what made them upset, what they are feeling, and what they can do to feel better.

CN: So the parents are actually teaching their child to have a higher EQ?

JD: Exactly. Now, moving on to number two, the college student who fails the exam. The answer is A: "Make a specific plan for ways to improve your grade." People with a high EQ are self-motivated and know how to overcome problems.

CN: Instead of dwelling on failure, the student thinks of specific ways to solve the problem.

JD: Right. Number three, about dealing with the angry driver. The answer is C: "Tell him about a time something like this happened to you and how you felt as angry as he does now." In this case, studies of anger have shown that the best way to calm an angry person is to empathize with him but also to suggest a different way of looking at the problem.

CN: So here, you have to be skillful at managing another person's emotions, to change their reaction.

JD: Number four, the ethnic joke. The answer is C: "Say something to all the employees right away. Tell them that ethnic jokes are not acceptable in your organization."

CN: Hmm. I put B.

JD: The reason why C is right is that the best way to create a feeling of openness and acceptance of different ethnic groups is to make rules about how people should behave. You can't always change how people *feel* about each other, but you can control how they *act* toward each other. And by acting with respect, people can often learn to put aside their negative feelings.

CN: Interesting!

JD: Finally, number five, solving the problem at work.

CN: Let me guess. The answer is B: "Have people take the time to get to know each other better."

JD: Yes, B is correct. Studies show that people are more creative and work better together if they feel comfortable and connected to each other, so you should spend time on that first.

CN: So now that we have the answers, what does this test mean? What does it show us about ourselves?

JD: Well, these questions can give you an idea of your strengths and weaknesses. It's a tool we can use to become more perceptive about our emotional skills, and hopefully improve our EQ.

5. REVIEWING LANGUAGE

5A. *Exploring Language: Unstressed Vowels*

1. control
2. adjust
3. success
4. productively
5. people
6. attitude
7. negative
8. resentful
9. empathize
10. personal
11. ability
12. psychologist
13. intelligence
14. relationship
15. emotional

(For Exercise 2, repeat Section 5A.)

UNIT 8 ◆ JOURNEY TO THE RED PLANET

3. LISTENING ONE: Journey to the Red Planet

3A. *Introducing the Topic*

EXCERPT ONE

Sharon Begley: As one scientist said, "Look, I'll pit my ten-year-old kid, who's great at Easter-egg finding, against your robot, and I guarantee that my ten-year-old kid is going to find something that the robot's not."

EXCERPT TWO

SB: Another approach—that first one is being done by NASA's Jet Propulsion Laboratory in California, which is in charge of robotic missions. Another approach is done by Johnson Space Center, which controls all the manned missions . . .

EXCERPT THREE

SB: There are a lot of interesting places, most of them have to do with water and energy . . .

3B. *Listening for Main Ideas*

David Alpern: . . . Tell us more about this "Mars Underground." Who are they, what have they been doing?

Sharon Begley: Well, they're several dozen scientists and engineers, some of them work at NASA, um, a lot of them work at universities, or some, em, em, space contractors, and these are people who just believe that it's humankind's destiny to go to Mars—er, a little bit for economic reasons, a little bit for political reasons, but really, for, you know, the same romantic reasons that sent us exploring in any other century—and they have been quietly—quietly, really, because no one has been interested—paying attention to some of the results from the unmanned missions that we have been sending to Mars for more than twenty years—and, keeping an eye on which discoveries might be relevant to getting humans to Mars, to letting them explore around there for a long time, and even, one day, setting up colonies there.

DA: So the $64 billion question is always what can humans do going to Mars that the machines we've already sent can't?

SB: Well, and that question has been raised by the, em, claim of life on Mars. And the answer is, as your tape hinted at earlier, if there is life on Mars, it's not, you know, standing on the tarmac waiting to say: here we are! Em, it's underground. And a robot is not good at digging underground, nor at looking at, er, what are the most promising sites. As one scientist said, "Look, I'll pit my ten-year-old kid, who's great at Easter-egg finding, against your robot, and I guarantee that my ten-year-old kid is going to find something that the robot's not." Em, so that's the current motivation for sending astronauts to Mars. You know, not next week, but sometime, um, in the next decade.

DA: Give us some idea of the competing approaches now on scientific drawing boards. One you call "the right stuff."

SB: That is similar to the moon missions. You send up a spacecraft, it parks in an orbit around Mars, it shoots out a lander, just as the moon landers carried an astronaut or two down to the moon, and then this lander would scoop up some Martian soil, or rocks, and then scoot back up to the orbiter, and come home. Another approach—that first one is being done by NASA's Jet Propulsion Laboratory in California, which is in charge of robotic missions. Another approach is done by Johnson Space Center, which controls all the manned missions, mission control for those—and that one differs by sending up a craft that doesn't have enough fuel to come home. But once it gets there, it makes rocket fuel out of the Martian atmosphere. It turns out that Mars's atmosphere is mostly carbon dioxide, and if you react that with some hydrogen, you get liquid oxygen fuel. And the benefit of that plan, is because you're not carrying up tons and tons of return trip fuel, your mission costs much less. It can be much smaller, and that's why you've saved a lot of money. Um, that is so different from anything the United States has done in space that the NASA brass is not exactly behind it, but it is so innovative, and has so much appeal for economic and other reasons, that they're at least going ahead brainstorming it.

DA: Last question for you—Where will scientists focus their search for life, past or present?

SB: There are a lot of interesting places. Most of them have to do with water and energy; again, if there was life, it needed liquid water, and it needed a source of energy. There are dry lake beds, there are dry river channels, there are places where there may be high, er, thermal systems, kind of like Yellowstone National Park, springs and fumeroles, and if there is or was life there, that's where you would look certainly for the fossils, and maybe even for some survivors.

DA: Sharon Begley, thanks a lot.

3C. *Listening for Details*

(repeat Section 3B)

3D. *Listening between the Lines*

EXCERPT ONE

. . . Well, they're several dozen scientists and engineers, some of them work at NASA, a lot of them work at universities, or some, em, em, space contractors, and these are people who just believe that it's humankind's destiny to go to Mars—er, a little bit for economic reasons, a little bit for political reasons, but really, for, you know, the same romantic reasons that sent us exploring in any other century —and they have been quietly—quietly, really, because no one has been interested—paying attention to some of the results from the unmanned missions that we have been sending to Mars for more than twenty years—and, keeping an eye on which discoveries might be relevant to getting humans to Mars, to letting them explore around there for a long time, and even, one day, setting up colonies there.

EXCERPT TWO

. . . if there is life on Mars, it's not, you know, standing on the tarmac waiting to say: here we are! Em, it's underground.

EXCERPT THREE

And a robot is not good at digging underground, nor at looking at, er, what are the most promising sites. As one scientist said, "Look, I'll pit my ten-year-old kid, who's great at Easter-egg finding, against your robot, and I guarantee that my ten-year-old kid is going to find something that the robot's not."

EXCERPT FOUR

It turns out that Mars's atmosphere is mostly carbon dioxide, and if you react that with some hydrogen, you get liquid oxygen fuel. And the benefit of that plan, is because you're not carrying up tons and tons of return trip fuel, your mission costs much less. It can be much smaller, and that's why you've saved a lot of money. Em, that is so different from anything the United States has done in space that the NASA brass is not exactly behind it, but it is so innovative, and has so much appeal for economic and other reasons, that they're at least going ahead brainstorming it.

4. LISTENING TWO: Terraforming—How to Colonize Mars

4A. *Expanding the Topic*

David Alpern: Next we turn to science fiction novelist Kim Stanley Robinson, author of the Mars trilogy, welcome to *Newsweek on Air*!

Interestingly, your notion is—you call it terraforming, it's not just building enclosures for man to live, it's really transforming the planet into a more Earth-like place, something between planting a garden, you say, and building a cathedral. What are some of the steps that would be required?

Kim Stanley Robinson: Well, the main step would be the application of more heat than it has now, and that would involve redirecting some of the sun's rays onto Mars that otherwise would have missed it with space-based mirrors, and perhaps releasing some of Mars's internal heat, although that's more difficult. And getting some of that frozen underground water onto the surface would be another really important step. Essentially, you'd have to create just a little bit more hospitable environment for life, and then introduce the life forms that we already have here on Earth, more or less in the sequence that they evolved here on Earth, and these life forms would be hitting empty ecological niches, and are likely to grow at great speed, especially the bacteria.

DA: Do you think this is inevitable?

KSR: Not at all inevitable, no. This is a matter of human choice.

DA: I think I saw something like it, though, in one of the *Star Trek* movies, and it took maybe twenty-three minutes, um, in film. How long would it take for it to see significant results? How long-term a project is this?

KSR: Well, it depends on the methods that we decide to use. I've seen estimates ranging from fifty years to a hundred thousand years. Which indicates to me that nobody really knows for sure, and it just depends on how intensively we try . . . we decided to pursue the project. My—er—in my novels, I've placed it at about three to five hundred years, and I think realistically, you could be thinking, say, in terms of five hundred to a thousand.

DA: And part of the payoff, you say, might be more living room than we yet imagine we'll ever need.

KSR: Well, the living room is, is, nice, but I think more important than that, is what we would learn from a project like this would enable us to keep Earth healthy, because we're essentially headed for an environmental crash, or, a, severe environmental problems here on Earth, because there are simply too many humans, and so in a way, although it's a beautiful project in its own right, it also becomes useful just as an education to us.

DA: Mr. Robinson, thank you.

KSR: Uh-huh.

DA: Kim Stanley Robinson is the award-winning author of *Red Mars, Green Mars,* and *Blue Mars,* speaking with us from the Sacramento area, where *Newsweek on Air* is heard on KFBK. We also heard from science editor Sharon Begley, at *Newsweek* in New York. Thanks again.

5. REVIEWING LANGUAGE

5A. *Exploring Language: The Stress-Changing Suffix* -tion

❶
estimate — recite
innovate — indicate
colonize — beautify
educate — motivate
adapt — evolve

❷
estimation — recitation
innovation — indication
colonization — beautification
education — motivation
adaptation — evolution

UNIT 9 ◆ FINDING A NICHE: EXPERIENCES OF YOUNG IMMIGRANTS

3. LISTENING ONE: A World within a School

3A. *Introducing the Topic*

Mary Ambrose: Students in cities like New York are used to hearing wide variations of English. In a town where immigrant communities flourish, many dialects and languages mix with standard English. In fact, there's an international high school that encourages immigrant students to use and develop their native tongues while learning English. It's a new approach, and as Richard Schiffman reports, it seems to work.

3B. *Listening for Main Ideas*

Mary Ambrose: Students in cities like New York are used to hearing wide variations of English. In a town where immigrant communities flourish, many dialects and languages mix with standard English. In fact, there's an international high school that encourages immigrant students to use and develop their native tongues while learning English. It's a new approach, and as Richard Schiffman reports, it seems to work.

Richard Schiffman: The philosophy of this school is that you learn by doing, and not by hearing the teacher lecture. In this math class, for example, six teams of young people are gathered around lab tables, building their own miniature temple out of cardboard. But to find out what really sets this school apart, you need to get up close.

The four teenage boys at this table are planning their temple in Polish. At the other tables, they're speaking Spanish, English, and Mandarin Chinese. This is not just a bilingual classroom, it's a multilingual one, and the pupils here are all recent immigrants to the United States. Their teacher, Jennifer Shenke, walks around the room, quietly helping out.

Jennifer Shenke: They love building things. This has been really successful, and they've learned a lot of math that they didn't have before, umm, just doing scale and proportion. And, and I feel pretty good about that because they, they didn't know that they were learning it until they had learned it.

RS: Shenke is happy that her pupils are learning math and enjoying themselves in the process, and she's especially pleased that they're teaching one another. She knows that many in her classroom wouldn't be able to follow her if she lectured. So she depends on the pupils who know more English and more math to help teach those who know less. That's what's happening now at the lab tables. They're helping each other out in their own languages . . .

Priscilla Billarrel: . . . I think what we share the most is a feeling of not fitting in.

RS: Priscilla Billarrel left Chile when she was fourteen years old. She says that although they come from all over the world, the students at the International High School understand each other very well.

PB: Since we all are immigrants [in] here, we all know what['s] to be different feels like, so we support one another. Whenever we have problems with pronunciation[s], or we're missing words or something, whatever we're saying, we correct one another kindly. We don't make fun of each other. That's what I really like about this school . . .

RS: . . . New York City can be an intimidating place, even for those who have spent their whole lives here. But for young people who have just been uprooted from tight-knit, extended families and traditional communities abroad, the city can seem positively unfriendly. Teacher Aaron Listhaus says that young immigrants don't just need a place to learn English and other subjects, they need, above all else, a place that feels completely safe and welcoming.

Aaron Listhaus: It's particularly important for these students to have a comfort level in a place called school and for that school to feel like home . . . to feel like their needs are going to get met, um, they're going to be listened to, they're going to be valued for who they are and the diverse backgrounds that they come from, and that those things are viewed as what makes them special rather than what makes them a problem.

RS: The fact that immigrant youngsters speak a language other than English, Listhaus says, is seen by most educators as a problem that needs to be corrected. The usual approach is to teach students exclusively in English, and to suppress the use of their native language. Evelyna Namovich, who came to the U.S. three years ago from Poland, remembers what it was like to find herself in a typical New York City school.

Evelyna Namovich: Sometimes it was so difficult because I didn't know [what was the subject all about, what was she speaking about], and I would need somebody to translate, even a little bit for me, you know. And we couldn't, because we would have to write something like . . . an essay, er, like punishment, if we spoke Polish.

RS: Evelyna says she was relieved when she transferred to the International High School, where she not only wasn't punished for speaking Polish, she was encouraged to bone up on her native language at the same time as she was learning English. Instructor Aaron Listhaus says that it's important that young immigrants don't lose their languages, as his own immigrant parents from Eastern Europe did.

AL: My parents have a hard time speaking in their native languages at this point. And to me there's something sad about that. Language is more than just the way that you communicate with the world; it's the way that you interpret the world in your own head. So to me, there's something more than just communication that's lost when you lose your native language.

RS: And teacher Kathy Rucker adds that speaking another language also has a practical economic value.

Kathy Rucker: People in the future are going to have to communicate in more than one language, it seems to me, because there's so much rapid travel, there's so much international business.

RS: . . . Today, as also in the past, immigrants to the U.S. often feel the need to assimilate as quickly as possible into mainstream American culture. But there is one place, at least, where new immigrants are being encouraged to keep what is unique to them.

From the International High School in New York, I'm Richard Schiffman, for *The World*.

3C. *Listening for Details*

(repeat Section 3B)

3D. *Listening between the Lines*

EXCERPT ONE

Richard Schiffman: This is not just a bilingual classroom; it's a multilingual one, and the pupils here are all recent immigrants. Their teacher walks around the room, quietly helping out.

EXCERPT TWO

Jennifer Shenke: They love building things. This has been really successful, and they've learned a lot of math that they didn't have before, umm, just doing scale and proportion. And, and I feel pretty good about that because they didn't know that they were learning it until they had learned it.

EXCERPT THREE

RS: . . . She's especially pleased that they're teaching one another. She knows that many in her classroom wouldn't be able to follow her if she lectured. So she depends on the pupils who know more English and more math to help teach those who know less. That's what's happening now at the lab tables. They're helping each other out in their own languages.

EXCERPT FOUR

Priscilla Billarrel: I think what we share the most is a feeling of not fitting in. . . . Since we all are immigrants [in] here, we all know what['s] to be different feels like, so we support one another. . . . we correct one another kindly. We don't make fun of each other.

4. LISTENING TWO: Changing Trends of U.S. Immigration

4A. *Expanding the Topic*

For many observers of U.S. life and culture, to say America is to say immigration. In fact, immigration is such an integral part of the history of the United States that in many ways it is impossible to study one without studying the other. Yet, as government policy has changed to accept more or fewer immigrants, the number of people arriving in the States has varied from year to year. In 1840, for example, less than two million people immigrated to this country. However, this number rose steadily, until in 1880, over 5 million immigrants arrived in the U.S. This figure climbed even higher around 1900, reaching a peak of 8.8 million immigrants. In the 1930s, partly as a result of restrictive laws, it dropped to half a million immigrants, but after World War Two, it began to rise once again, reaching 6.3 million in the 1980s. This trend will probably continue through the twenty-first century.

An interesting fact to consider is the composition of the immigrant population. If we look at the early part of the century, we see that 95% of all immigrants came from Northern and Western Europe. But in the latter part of the twentieth century, immigrants came from other places: close to 50% from Asia, 35% from Latin America, 3% from Northern Europe, and 7% from Southern and Eastern Europe, and the rest from North America and other places.

Of course, every one of these millions of immigrants has had to deal with the problem of adaptation—the task of finding their niche in the U.S. The traditional view of immigration was assimilation, or the "melting pot" approach. This means that the immigrant group adapts to the "core" or "mainstream" culture. There is a blending of values and lifestyles of immigrants with the mainstream.

Another, more recent model is multiculturalism. This describes a society in which many cultures live side by side, but do not mix. This model resembles a salad bowl, in which many ingredients are present, but distinct from each other, preserving their own flavor or identity.

Either way, the challenges society faces and the need to incorporate young immigrants into the country can only become more important in the twenty-first century.

5. REVIEWING LANGUAGE

5A. *Exploring Language: Discriminating between Similar Sounds*

❶

1. international	11. special
2. language	12. subject
3. enjoy	13. Chile
4. adjust	14. television
5. measure	15. educators
6. lecture	16. occasion
7. traditional	17. communication
8. culture	18. encourage
9. usual	19. niche
10. punishment	20. treasure

UNIT 10 ◆ TECHNOLOGY: A BLESSING OR A CURSE?

3. LISTENING ONE: Noise in the City

3A. *Introducing the Topic*

Neal Rauch: It's late. You're tired. Finally, after an exhausting day, you're ready to surrender to the world of dreams. Your head sinks into your pillow. Then . . .

3B. *Listening for Main Ideas*

Steve Curwood: Modern life is full of nasty noises, especially in the cities. Sirens can shatter serenity at any moment and jackhammers, loud music, and useless mufflers can all send us over the edge. For many people in New York City, there's one form of sonic pollution at the top of the list. They're calling for its banning, even though some nervous New

Yorkers savor the sound for security reasons. And as Neal Rauch reports, even as the controversy prompts loud debate, some aren't waiting for laws to be passed.

Neal Rauch: It's late. You're tired. Finally, after an exhausting day, you're ready to surrender to the world of dreams. Your head sinks into your pillow. Then . . .

Judy Evans: After being awakened at night many times so that awful feeling, you know, you've just gotten to sleep and then the alarm goes off.

NR: Each night hundreds of people like Judy Evans, a scenic designer and artist who lives in Brooklyn, are jolted out of their sleep by the nagging wail of a car alarm.

JE: You just wait it out but you don't know if that's going to happen again. You don't know when you're going to be reawakened for a second or third time even.

NR: Often she is, and sometimes a defective alarm will go on for hours.

JE: If one person were standing on the corner with a horn making that kind of noise, they would be arrested. They would be disturbing the peace.

Man: It slowly gets under your skin and eventually drives you nuts.

NR: A music producer and composer, this resident of Manhattan's Upper West Side got fed up with car alarms disturbing his sleep and his work. He got together with some similarly frazzled neighbors and formed a posse of sorts.

Man: We start out with a note saying, "Fix your car alarm, it's disturbed hundreds of people last night." If that doesn't help we quite often use some minor retaliatory step like breaking an egg on their windshield or on the front hood, which doesn't hurt anything but it's a little bit of a mess to clean up.

NR: The "egg man," who prefers to remain anonymous, says some vigilantes take even more drastic action. Like smearing axle grease on door handles.

Man: Another classic is to smear vaseline all over the windshield, which is incredibly hard to get off. So . . . I think in other neighborhoods there might even be broken windshields and things like that.

NR: Lucille DiMaggio was a target of vigilante retribution. It happened one night when, unbeknownst to her, the car alarm malfunctioned.

Lucille DiMaggio: I noticed something on the passenger front door. There were a lot of dent marks. It appeared to me that it looked like the heel of someone's shoe, as if someone had kicked my innocent car, because the alarm hadn't even been going off all night.

NR: The repairs cost her a couple of hundred dollars. To test the theory, Lucille DiMaggio set off her alarm for me in a restaurant parking lot. Not a single person bothered to see if a car was bring broken into. Which begs the question: Are car alarms really effective? Judy Evans says absolutely not, not even when she's called the police.

JE: One night, there was a real incredible racket, and a little MG was being mutilated to death. The alarm was going off. So I called 911. Well, about forty minutes later, the police drove up.

NR: Little remained of the car by then. Ms. Evans, who's taken to sleeping with earplugs and the windows closed, says car alarms should be banned in densely populated and already noisy neighborhoods.

Catherine Abate: The streets are much noisier than they were twenty years ago. Even ten years ago.

NR: New York State senator Catherine Abate represents Manhattan.

CA: The noise affects not only their ability to sleep at night, but for the most part their ability to work during the day. And even parents have come to me and said, "What is the impact on children?" And there are more and more studies that show that young people in particular, that are exposed to a sustained amount of loud noise, have hearing loss. So it's a health issue, it's a quality of life issue.

NR: Enforcement of existing laws, along with new regulations, may be cutting down noise in some neighborhoods. It's now illegal for alarms to run for more than three minutes. After that the police can break into a car to disable the alarm or even tow away a wailing vehicle. It's hoped these actions will motivate car owners to adjust their alarms, making them less sensitive so vibrations from passing trucks and the like don't set them off. Even the egg man admits the car alarm situation has improved, at least in his neighborhood. By the way, the egg man has a sidekick: his wife.

Man: When something happens outside she'll say, "Do you think that's eggworthy?" And I say, "That sounds like an egg candidate to me."

NR: For *Living on Earth*, I'm Neal Rauch in New York.

3C. *Listening for Details*

(repeat Section 3B)

3D. *Listening Between the Lines*

EXCERPT ONE

Judy Evans: You just wait it out but you don't know if that's going to happen again. You don't know when you're going to be reawakened for a second or third time even . . . If one person were standing on the corner with a horn making that kind of noise, they would be arrested. They would be disturbing the peace.

EXCERPT TWO

Lucille DiMaggio: I noticed something on the passenger front door. There were a lot of dent marks. It appeared to me that it looked like the heel of someone's shoe, as if someone had kicked my innocent car, because the alarm hadn't even been going off all night.

EXCERPT THREE

Catherine Abate: The noise affects not only their ability to sleep at night, but for the most part their ability to work during the day. And even parents have come to me and said, "What is the impact on children?" And there are more and more studies that show that young people in particular, that are exposed to a sustained amount of loud noise, have hearing loss. So it's a health issue, it's a quality of life issue.

EXCERPT FOUR

Man: When something happens outside she'll say, "Do you think that's eggworthy?" And I say, "That sounds like an egg candidate to me."

4. LISTENING TWO: Technology Talk

4A. *Expanding the Topic*

Host: Welcome to *Technology Talk*. Our topic today is "Technological Pet Peeves." What's one thing about modern technology that really drives you crazy? Our lines are open. Give us a call. . . . Hello. You're on the line with *Technology Talk*.

Caller 1: Hi. I'm Stanley from Chicago.

Host: Welcome, Stanley. As you know, we're taking complaints about technology today. What's one thing that really drives you crazy?

Caller 1: Well, what I really hate are automated phone systems. Everyone has them these days, but I . . . um . . . think they're a mixed blessing. It's awful to try calling somewhere and getting this. . . er . . . annoying recorded voice saying, "If you're calling from a touch-tone phone, press one." Then you spend the next ten minutes making choices and you never get to talk to a real person. After all that, half the time I don't get the information I want anyway. That system drives me crazy, and there doesn't seem to be anything I can do about it. In fact, I have to call my wife at work right now. But by the time I actually get through, she'll have already left.

Host: Uh-huh . . . I tend to agree with you, Stanley. But I don't know what we can do about it. Let's move on to Carol from Houston. Hi, Carol.

Caller 2: Hello.

Host: So, Carol, what's the one thing that really makes you frustrated with modern technology?

Caller 2: I'm happy to get a chance to speak out. I know that a lot of people like the convenience of cellular phones, but I find them truly irritating. People don't seem to know when to leave them at home. I hate it when people use their cell phones in a restaurant or a store. It's probably none of my business, but it drives me crazy. One night in a movie theater, some cell phone began to ring and a guy behind me began to have a conversation right there during the movie! And the people who talk on the phone while they drive, well, they're putting the rest of us in danger, aren't they? There should be a law against it!

Host: Well, Carol, maybe we'll be getting some response to your strong stand on cell phones. Stay tuned while we see what Jessica from Brooklyn thinks of all this. Jessica?

Caller 3: Good afternoon. I just had to call to share my frustrations with remote controls.

Host: Remote controls? I didn't realize they could be so problematic.

Caller 3: In my house, we have about five remote controls.

Host: *About* five?

Caller 3: Yes, we're always losing one of them, and then we have to search all over the house to find them just so we can change channels. I finally bought a universal remote, which is supposed to simplify life and control everything. But to be honest, it's so complicated to work, I've given it up. Where is all this technology taking us? That's what I want to know! It was so much easier in the good old days when you could just switch the channels by hand!

Host: But then, of course, we had to get up and walk over to the TV and um . . .

Caller 3: That's true, but . . .

Host: Let's take another call. Welcome, Arthur from Los Angeles.

Caller 4: Hello. I wanted to tell you about the one thing that drives me crazy. It's e-mail. I have hardly enough time already to answer letters and return calls, and now I'm supposed to answer e-mail, too? What happens is that when I do open my e-mail, most of it is junk—plus messages I don't really need to read. It takes me about an hour every day to sort through it. I wish we'd never gotten e-mail.

Host: I know what you mean! Well, the lines are open, folks. Let's hear what you think of our callers' comments today. . . . Who do we have next? . . . Betty from Atlanta . . . Hi, Betty!

Caller 5: Hello. I've been listening to your show all morning, and I just had to call and give a little historical perspective to this discussion. I'm eighty-eight years old, and I remember the so-called good old days before modern technology. And I want to tell you: they weren't so hot! When I was a child, we had no hot running water. We had to heat water in pans on the stove—for everything—to wash the dishes and clothes, to take a bath. And we had a big family! And we washed all the clothes by hand, too. And hung them out on the line all winter long. They'd be frozen on the line when we'd take them in. I love my washer and dryer, my modern refrigerator—instead of an ice box that we had to refill with ice every couple of days, etc., etc. I think you get my drift . . .

Host: I sure do, Betty. And thanks for the reminder. We needed that.

5. REVIEWING LANGUAGE

5A. *Exploring Language: Sound Words*

Listening Selections and Text Credits

Page 7, The National Public Radio program *On the Media,* produced by WNYC radio; **Page 22,** From *Newsweek on Air,* 5/14/89 ©1989, Newsweek, Inc., and Associated Press. All rights reserved. Used with permission; **Page 52,** a portion of the audio tape which accompanies this textbook is taken from the daily public radio program *The Connection,*® hosted by Christopher Lydon. The program is produced by WBUR-FM in Boston, and this excerpt is reproduced with their permission; **Page 97,** used with permission of David Winston, Herbalist AHG; **Page 100,** used with permission of Joseph Bruchac; **Page 121,** used with permission of BarWall Productions, Inc.; **Page 124,** used with permission of The Advertising Council; **Page 146,** Daniel Goleman, in *Utne Reader,* November–December 1995; **Page 164,** from *Newsweek on Air,* 9/15/96 © 1996, Newsweek, Inc. and Associated Press. All rights reserved. Used with permission; **Page 190,** as heard on PRI's *The World,* a co-production of the BBC World Service, Public Radio International, and WGBH Boston; **Page 213,** from *Living on Earth,* 9/27/96. Copyright 1996, World Media Foundation and Neil Rauch, by permission.

ANSWER KEY

UNIT 1 ◆ NO NEWS IS GOOD NEWS

2A. BACKGROUND

1. False. Americans get most of their news from TV.
2. False. Magazines and "other" are used less than radio.
3. True. Almost 70% (53% very interested plus 16% extremely interested) of Americans are very interested in local news.
4. False. More than 50% of Americans are interested in crime.
5. False. People are less interested in news about the arts and in political campaigns than they are in news about the environment and business.
6. True. More than 50% think that reporting on the government is good.
7. True. Almost 50% of Americans think that reporting on sports and crime is good.
8. False. Most people think that reporting on local and national news is good.
9. False. People trust newspaper reporters more than lawyers, but not much more!
10. False. It is true that people trust doctors more than they trust TV reporters, but they trust corporate executives less.

2B. VOCABULARY FOR COMPREHENSION

❷ 1. c
2. e
3. f
4. i
5. d
6. b
7. a
8. h
9. g

3B. LISTENING FOR MAIN IDEAS

Part One

1. a
2. c
3. b

Part Two

4. c
5. c
6. a

3C. LISTENING FOR DETAILS

Part One

1. D
2. A
3. A
4. A
5. D

Part Two

7. A
8. D
9. A
10. A
11. D

3D. LISTENING BETWEEN THE LINES

Excerpt One

1. c
2. *suggested answer:* Jones repeated "tune it out" and "fed up," probably to stress that the problem of dissatisfaction with the news is common.

Excerpt Two

1. a
2. *suggested answer:* Hamblin repeated "positive," probably to emphasize that his newspaper has a positive outlook.

Excerpt Three

1. b
2. *suggested answer:* Hamblin repeated "solutions," probably to emphasize his point that his newspaper reports on the positive ways people can deal with problems.

4A. EXPANDING THE TOPIC

suggested answers

Conversation One

Chen
1. He's fed up with bad news.
2. He doesn't think mainstream papers provide the whole truth.
3. Mainstream media is misleading.

Tanya
1. She's not sure if the coverage is objective.
2. She's afraid the coverage is misleading.
3. She thinks that readers like Chen might be lying to themselves.

Conversation Two

Rita
1. It has great stories.
2. She is interested in celebrities' lives.
3. She thinks it's fun.

Mark
1. Tabloids are a waste of time.
2. Tabloids are too sensational, and they provide gossip, not news.
3. Celebrities have a right to privacy.

5A. EXPLORING LANGUAGE: Using Idiomatic Expressions

❶ 1. right off the bat
2. first of all
3. in one sense
4. sugar-coated
5. go a step further
6. pick it up
7. narrow down
8. come up with

5B. WORKING WITH WORDS

❶ 1. sensational
2. negative
3. depressing
4. misleading
5. skeptical
6. superficial
7. alternative
8. innovative
9. objective

6A. GRAMMAR: The Passive Voice

❷ 2. were called
3. were flooded
4. have been treated
5. are being received
6. is predicted
7. be selected
8. was released
9. have been received
10. is being planned
11. will be followed
12. was rescued
13. had been warned
14. was interviewed
15. be given

3 1. was upset
2. are being cancelled
3. has not been marketed
4. is not reported
5. to be misled
6. is not reported
7. be controlled
8. are sold

UNIT 2 ◆ DO THE CRIME, SERVE THE TIME: TEEN BOOT CAMPS

2B. VOCABULARY FOR COMPREHENSION

1. a
2. b
3. c
4. b
5. a
6. b
7. a
8. a
9. b
10. c
11. a
12. a
13. c
14. a

3B. LISTENING FOR MAIN IDEAS

Part One

1. c 2. b 3. a 4. c 5. c

Part Two

6. b 7. a

3C. LISTENING FOR DETAILS

Part One

1. F
2. F
3. T
4. T
5. T
6. T
7. F
8. T
9. F

Part Two

10. T
11. F
12. T
13. F
14. F
15. T

3D. LISTENING BETWEEN THE LINES

suggested answers

Excerpt One

1. Anecdotal evidence is different from the other kinds because it is not based on fact, but on personal accounts.
2. Gonzalez would probably accept systematic evidence from a formal study.
3. He rejects anecdotal evidence because it may not be applicable to most cases.

Excerpt Two

4. The first group might see boot camps as a form of immediate punishment; politicians might see boot camps as an easy solution to a difficult problem and a way to win public support and more votes.
5. He seems to think retribution is not the long-term solution. He refers to people reacting on a "visceral level," not a carefully reasoned level.
6. He probably thinks many politicians may be more interested in public image ("it sells well") than in the welfare of the juveniles or society.

Excerpt Three

7. Hard evidence is factual; preliminary evidence is not yet complete; conclusive evidence is based on measurable, consistent information.
8. He would probably accept the results of long-term studies.
9. He would probably agree.

4A. EXPANDING THE TOPIC

1. a
2. a
3. b
4. b
5. b
6. b
7. a
8. a

4B. LINKING LISTENINGS ONE AND TWO

suggested answers

1 2. retribution; deterrence
3. reform
4. protection of the public; retribution
5. reform; deterrence
6. protection of the public; deterrence; reform

5A. EXPLORING LANGUAGE: Word Forms

NOUN	VERB	ADJECTIVE	ADVERB
analysis	analyze	analytical	analytically
anecdote	X	anecdotal	anecdotally
correction	correct	1. correctional 2. corrective	correctively
exertion	exert	X	X
insult	insult	insulting	insultingly
1. offender 2. offense	offend	offensive	offensively
1. politics 2. politician	politicize	political	politically
reassessment	reassess	reassessed	X
rigor	X	rigorous	rigorously
system	systematize	systematic	systematically

2 1. a. analysis b. analytical c. analyze
2. a. anecdotal b. anecdote
3. a. correctional b. correct c. correct
4. a. exertion b. exert
5. a. insult b. insult c. insulting
6. a. offenders b. offensive
7. a. politics b. politician c. political
8. a. reassessing b. reassessment
9. a. rigorous b. rigorously
10. a. systematic b. systematically

5B. WORKING WITH WORDS

1 a. 10
b. 3
c. 1
d. 9
e. 4
f. 5
g. 2
h. 6
i. 12
j. 14
k. 13
l. 7
m. 8
n. 11

6A. GRAMMAR: Gerunds and Infinitives

❷
1. pampering
2. solving
3. locking up
4. to know
5. to reform
6. to provide
7. supporting
8. to hear
9. to terrorize
10. to scare
11. releasing
12. to attack
13. dealing with
14. to commit
15. to serve
16. developing
17. to be
18. to reform
19. to do
20. sending
21. losing
22. giving

7A. SPEAKING TOPICS

❶
1. c
2. d
3. b
4. e
5. f
6. a
7. g

UNIT 3 ◆ THE DOCTOR-PATIENT RELATIONSHIP

2B. VOCABULARY FOR COMPREHENSION

❶
2. symptoms
3. dying breed
4. healing
5. long for
6. diagnosis
7. specialist
8. adverse reaction
9. hospitalization
10. array
11. chief complaint
12. inefficient
13. trivial
14. rough and tumble
15. critical
16. anxieties

❷
1. f
2. p
3. c
4. e
5. n
6. d
7. i
8. k
9. b
10. m
11. g
12. o
13. a
14. l
15. j
16. h

3B. LISTENING FOR MAIN IDEAS

1. a
2. a
3. b
4. a
5. b
6. a
7. a
8. a

3C. LISTENING FOR DETAILS

1. b
2. a
3. b
4. b
5. b
6. a
7. b
8. a
9. a
10. a
11. a
12. b
13. a

3D. LISTENING BETWEEN THE LINES

suggested answers

Excerpt One

1. The interviewer thinks the doctor-patient relationship is in trouble.
2. He compares it to the situation of a patient in an "intensive care" hospital unit.

Excerpt Two

1. He thinks machinery is not as important as the human contact a doctor can give a patient.
2. He uses a sarcastic tone when he says "such as it is," meaning that the examination is not adequate. He also emphasizes the importance of the human contact by using the word "touch" twice.

Excerpt Three

1. Norman Cousins thinks that Americans make too much of their medical problems. He shows this when he exaggerates, saying when Americans get a cold, "they think they'll be dead within the next ten minutes."
2. *answers will vary*

Excerpt Four

1. Dr. Lown thinks that the extra anxieties in modern times combined with the decrease in support and comfort from relatives has not been good for people's health.
2. His tone is complaining. He repeats that the doctor isn't there and doesn't listen. He repeats the words "listen" or "listening" six times.

4A. EXPANDING THE TOPIC

suggested answers

Shelley Travers: back pain / couldn't sleep; tests / X rays; no; yes—new cushion for desk chair; yes

Linda Jenkins: wart on foot; recommended operation; no; yes—acupuncturist recommended diet change and rest; yes

Ray Ishwood: arthritis in hands and wrists; series of shots; don't know; no

5A. EXPLORING VOCABULARY: Pronouncing Elongated Stressed Syllables

❶
2. acupuncturist
3. intensive
4. diagnosis
5. symptoms
6. medical
7. educated
8. trivial
9. anxieties
10. remedies
11. chiropractor
12. interesting
13. specialist
14. embarrassing
15. reaction
16. natural
17. ailments
18. allergies
19. physician
20. injections

5B. WORKING WITH WORDS

1. revolt
2. array
3. long for
4. chief complaint
5. diagnosis
6. ailment
7. alternative
8. acupuncture
9. put a premium on
10. hospitalization
11. treatment
12. tend to
13. allay

6A. GRAMMAR: PRESENT UNREAL CONDITIONALS

suggested answers

❷ 2. If my doctor were in the office more than two days a week, it would not be so difficult to make an appointment with her.
3. If my doctor weren't late for my appointments, I wouldn't miss so much time from work.
4. My doctor wouldn't rush during my appointment if she had more time to listen to me.
5. If my insurance paid for alternative treatments, I could try acupuncture.
6. If my doctor knew about alternative treatments, she wouldn't always recommend surgery.

UNIT 4 ◆ THE EYE OF THE STORM

1B. SHARING INFORMATION

These natural disasters are very common in the following areas:

Blizzards	United States, Northern Asia, Patagonia
Droughts	United States, West Africa, India, China
Earthquakes	United States (West Coast), Japan, Chile, Iran, Nicaragua, Serbo-Croatia
Floods	China (Huang Ho River), United States (Mississippi), Egypt (Nile), Bangladesh (Ganges)
Hurricanes	Caribbean, Gulf of Mexico, United States (East and West Coasts), Bay of Bengal (tropical cyclones), Arabian Sea
Tidal Waves	Philippines, Alaska, Hawaii, Japan
Tornadoes	United States (central, southern / Gulf states), Bangladesh
Volcanoes	Italy, Mexico, Indonesia, West Indies, Philippines

2A. BACKGROUND

❶

1. a	3. c	5. c	7. b	9. c
2. b	4. b	6. b	8. c	10. a

2B. VOCABULARY FOR COMPREHENSION

Part One

__4__ information-gathering
__9__ strength
__7__ easily hurt
__6__ radio waves to find the position of things
__8__ seemingly, but not in fact
__1__ the seashore; land next to the ocean
__3__ complicated; highly developed
__2__ away from the seashore
__5__ objects that circle the Earth

Part Two

__13__ move from a dangerous place
__14__ saving or buying extra amounts for later use
__16__ moved from one's normal place or home
__15__ supplies
__10__ feel a sudden fear or anxiety
__11__ staying on the surface of water
__12__ failure (usually electrical)

3B. LISTENING FOR MAIN IDEAS

__8__ a resident who almost lost her house
__3__ a resident who is not evacuating
__6__ a tourist who is scared
__7__ advice for tourists
__4__ how hurricane forecasts are made
__5__ supplies that people should buy
__1__ the mood in Pitsea Beach, Florida
__2__ the weather report

3C. LISTENING FOR DETAILS

1. c	4. c	7. c	10. b
2. a	5. b	8. a	11. a
3. c	6. a	9. b	12. b

3D. LISTENING BETWEEN THE LINES

*suggested answers for **Hurricane** column; answers for **Earthquake** and **Your choice** will vary*

Excerpt One

2. Be aware of the danger and people's vulnerability.

Excerpt Two

1. Stock up on supplies.
2. Get gadgets you will need (can opener, radio, flashlight)
3. Get a sturdy pair of boots.

Excerpt Three

1. Find out what plans the hotel has in case such an emergency happens.
2. Be prepared with extra cash.

4A. EXPANDING THE TOPIC

suggested answers

1. The Hurricane Hunters fly into the eye of the hurricane to gather information and relay it back to local authorities in towns in the hurricane's path. This helps the authorities decide what to do.
2. Outside the hurricane area the sky is blue and the sun is shining, but as they approach the hurricane, the weather changes.
3. Humans can tell certain things about the speed and direction of the storm that computers cannot by providing an eyewitness account and looking down at the surface of the water.
4. They say the experience is intense, but also exciting and heartening, since it helps save people's lives.

5A. EXPLORING LANGUAGE: Active and Passive Forms of Adjectives

1. a. exciting
   b. excited
2. a. amazed
   b. amazing
3. a. frightened
   b. frightening
4. a. heartening
   b. heartened
5. a. comforting
   b. comforted
6. a. surprising
   b. surprised

5B. WORKING WITH WORDS

❶

VOCABULARY	SYNONYM	ANTONYM
3. evacuate	X	stay in your home
4. flooded	X	dry
5. forecast	prediction	X
6. heartening	encouraging	X
7. manual	X	electrical
8. out of order	X	functioning
9. outage	stoppage	X
10. panic	X	stay calm
11. provisions	supplies	X
12. route	path	X
13. scared stiff	extremely frightened	X
14. second-guess	disbelieve	X
15. sophisticated	complicated	X
16. stock up on	X	get rid of
17. vital	X	unimportant
18. vulnerable	easily hurt	X
19. warning	X	reassurance

❷ Dialogue 1, Part One

Student A
1. vulnerable
2. sophisticated
3. out of order

Student B
1. panic
2. power outage
3. evacuate

Dialogue 1, Part Two

answers will vary

Dialogue 2, Part One

Student A
1. provisions
2. flooded
3. forecast

Student B
1. manual
2. stock up on
3. second-guess

Dialogue 2, Part Two

answers will vary

6A. GRAMMAR: Adjective Clauses

❷
1. who
2. which
3. where / in which
4. whose
5. that / which
6. whose
7. who / which
8. who
9. that / which
10. where
11. that / which
12. whose
13. who
14. who
15. that / which
16. which

❸ Group A
1. where / in which
2. that / which
3. that / which
4. who
5. that / which
6. where / in which

Group B
1. that / which
2. that / which
3. who
4. who
5. who
6. that

UNIT 5 ◆ YOU WILL BE THIS LAND

2B VOCABULARY FOR COMPREHENSION

1. j
2. f
3. e
4. d
5. a
6. h
7. i
8. b
9. c
10. g

3B. LISTENING FOR MAIN IDEAS

suggested answers

1. The First Law of Nature is that you don't take life without a real reason. For example, if you gather a plant, you should not take everything there.
2. The Second Law of Nature is that everything we do should serve the Great Life. An example is not to use an electric toothbrush because it uses energy.
3. The Third Law of Nature is that we don't pollute where we live. An example is not to pour chemical wastes down the drain because they end up in the water.

3C. LISTENING FOR DETAILS

1. b
2. b
3. c
4. c
5. c
6. b
7. c
8. a
9. b
10. c
11. a
12. a

4A. EXPANDING THE TOPIC

❶

with maps	Disagree
with eyes like birds	Agree
by walking on roads	Disagree
by walking where deer walk	Agree
by using all five senses	Agree

❷ maps / animal's / less eaten

see / rivers / streams / people / earth

roads / feet / follow

taste / see / you will be / you will be

❸
1. D
2. A
3. D
4. A
5. A
6. A

4B. LINKING LISTENINGS ONE AND TWO

suggested answers

1. Bruchac would probably agree with the Cherokee Laws of Nature.

First Law: In his poem, Bruchac suggests a great respect for animal life by speaking of animals we eat, eagles, and deer. He criticizes the practice of taking more than we need from nature ("always less eaten than thrown away").

Second Law: Bruchac emphasizes the importance and wisdom of the way animals might interact with nature (examples made by eagles seeing and deer walking and exploring), and he scorns the way most modern humans interact with nature (examples of "cutting" the Earth with maps, wasting food from animals, exploring with cars and roads).

Third Law: Bruchac's first stanza discusses the importance of regarding the Earth as a whole; the "wholeness" of the Earth is referred to in the second stanza (rivers linking the land).

2. The statement probably means that life goes on with or without humans, but that humans cannot exist without the other life around them. Bruchac would probably agree with it.

3. *answers will vary*

5A. EXPLORING LANGUAGE: *th* Sounds [θ] + [ð]

❶
1. three
2. they
3. there
4. think
5. so
6. ladder
7. worthy
8. dough
9. sued
10. they
11. bathe
12. other
13. breeze
14. Zen

5B. WORKING WITH WORDS

❶

NOUN	VERB	ADJECTIVE	ADVERB
benefit	benefit	beneficial	beneficially
1. competitor 2. competition	compete	competitive	competitively
electricity	electrify	1. electric 2. electrical	electrically
industrialization	industrialize	1. industrial 2. industrialized	X
nature	X	natural	naturally
pollution	pollute	polluted	X
1. protection 2. protector	protect	1. protective 2. protected	protectively
recycling	recycle	recycled	X
spirit	X	spiritual	spiritually
waste	waste	wasteful	wastefully

❷
1. c. benefit
2. a. competitive
   b. compete
   c. competition
3. a. electricity
   b. electrify
   c. electrically
   d. electrical
4. a. industrialization
   b. industrialized
   c. industrialize
5. a. nature
   b. natural
   c. naturally
6. a. pollute
   b. polluted
   c. pollution
7. a. protect
   b. protective
   c. protecting
8. a. Recycling
   b. recycle
   c. recycled
9. a. spiritually
   b. spiritual
   c. spirits
10. a. wastefully
    b. wasteful
    c. waste

6A. GRAMMAR: Past Modals—Advisability in the Past

❷
1. couldn't have known
2. shouldn't have poured
3. shouldn't have built
4. should have been
5. could have been
6. could have caused
7. could have stayed

UNIT 6 ◆ IT'S BETTER TO GIVE THAN TO RECEIVE

1B. SHARING INFORMATION

❸ Religious—46%
Educational—12%
Health related—10%
Human services—8%
Arts, humanities, etc.—7%
Public / society benefit—5%
Environmental / wildlife—3%
International—1%
Other—8%

2B. VOCABULARY FOR COMPREHENSION

a. 10	d. 9	g. 3	j. 6
b. 12	e. 5	h. 7	k. 4
c. 2	f. 8	i. 11	l. 1

3B. LISTENING FOR MAIN IDEAS

1. T
2. F (She tucked away $250,000.)
3. T
4. T
5. F (She wishes she had more to give.)
6. T

3C. LISTENING FOR DETAILS

1. c
2. b
3. a
4. c
5. b
6. b
7. b
8. b
9. c
10. a

3D. LISTENING BETWEEN THE LINES

answers will vary

4A. EXPANDING THE TOPIC

suggested answers

PSA 1: Asks us to volunteer time and money. / Not because we have to, but because we should, and many Americans do.

PSA 2: Asks us to volunteer our services. / This will make us feel something real.

5A. EXPLORING LANGUAGE: Consonant and Vowel Joining within Thought Groups

❷ *suggested answers*

The story of Oseola McCarty, a washerwoman who gave away her life savings, has touched the hearts of everyone who has heard it. This frail old woman has now become one of the most famous philanthropists in the nation.

❸ *suggested answers*

Mrs. Rich: Dear, let's talk about how we should donate our money.

Mr. Rich: That's a good idea, Sweetheart. Let's see . . . I admire the work of the Dinosaur Egg Association, don't you? They're trying to find out how to re-create dinosaurs from ancient DNA samples.

5B. WORKING WITH WORDS

❶
1. recipient
2. retired
3. volunteer
4. tucked away
5. nest egg
6. donation
7. stunned
8. touched . . . heart
9. fund
10. regret
11. benefactor

6A. GRAMMAR: Tag Questions

❷ Step 1

2. isn't it?
3. aren't they?
4. would they?
5. do they?
6. isn't it?
7. didn't he?
8. isn't it?
9. shouldn't they?

❸ ❹ *suggested answers*

1. Oseola McCarty was a hardworking woman who spent her life cleaning houses.
   (She washed clothes for a living.)
2. After finishing high school, she began to invest her money.
   (She didn't finish high school.)
3. She was careful about watching over her nest egg as it grew.
   (She herself was surprised at how much money she had.)
4. When her three children grew up and moved away, Oseola lived alone in her older years.
   (She had no children.)
5. Then she decided to make a contribution to help college professors.
   (She decided to help promising black students.)
6. She donated $100,000 to a university.
   (She donated most of her life savings.)
7. The first recipient of her scholarship didn't accept the money because she felt sorry for Oseola.
   (The first recipient of the scholarship accepted the gift gratefully.)
8. When she got older, Oseola couldn't afford to stop working.
   (Oseola no longer washes clothes for a living.)

UNIT 7 ◆ EMOTIONAL INTELLIGENCE

2B. VOCABULARY FOR COMPREHENSION

1. a
2. b
3. a
4. c
5. c
6. a
7. a
8. b
9. a
10. c
11. a
12. c

3A. INTRODUCING THE TOPIC

1. b
2. *answers will vary*

3B. LISTENING FOR MAIN IDEAS

suggested answers

Betty Cortina: Elementary school teacher; thinks EQ can help children overcome their frustrations and get along with their peers; thinks EQ can and must be taught and learned.

Jim McDonald: Management training executive; thinks EQ helps you work well with others; thinks it is difficult for adults to learn EQ, although it might be possible for children.

Jan Davis: Psychologist, marriage counselor; thinks EQ helps to keep your personal relationships strong; thinks it can be taught and learned.

3C. LISTENING FOR DETAILS

Checks on: 1, 3, 4,* 6, 8, 10, 11, 13,* 14,* 16, 17, 19

* *Note:* Some of these answers are inferred, not explicitly stated as belonging to people with high EQs.

3D. LISTENING BETWEEN THE LINES

suggested answers

Excerpt One

Self-Awareness (the child didn't understand her own feelings of frustration); Self-Control (she threw down the pencil); Self-Motivation (she should learn to redirect her energy)

Excerpt Two

Self-Control (it is important not to blame others); Empathy (it is necessary to consider the feelings of others)

Excerpt Three

Self-Awareness (the husband didn't realize his wife's success made him feel unsuccessful by comparison); Empathy (he didn't think about how his wife felt); People Skills (he made the situation worse instead of better)

4A. EXPANDING THE TOPIC

Step 2 *(with suggested answers for "Reasons")*

1. b
   Emotionally intelligent parents teach their children about emotions.
2. a
   Instead of dwelling on failures, we should think of specific ways to solve our problems.
3. c
   We should empathize with our friends but also suggest alternatives.
4. c
   If we act with respect, we can learn to control our negative feelings.
5. b
   People are more creative and work better together if they feel comfortable with one another.

5A. EXPLORING LANGUAGE: Pronunciation—Unstressed Vowels

❶

1. [ə] • con/trol
2. [ə] • ad/just
3. [ə] • suc/cess
4.* [ə] • [ə] pro/duc/tive/ly
5. • [ə] peo/ple
6.* • [ə] at/ti/tude
7.* • [ə] [ə] neg/a/tive
8. • [ə] re/sent/ful (sometimes pronounced [ə] • [ə] as re/sent/ful)
9. • [ə] em/pa/thize
10. • [ə] [ə] per/son/al
11.* [ə] • [ə] a/bil/i/ty
12.* • [ə] [ə] psy/chol/o/gist
13.* • [ə] [ə] in/tel/li/gence
14. • [ə] re/la/tion/ship (sometimes pronounced [ə] • [ə] as re/la/tion/ship)
15. • [ə] [ə] e/mo/tion/al (sometimes pronounced [ə] • [ə] [ə] as e/mo/tion/al)

**Note:* [i] as in *is* is often substituted for the schwa sound in the underlined syllable.

❸

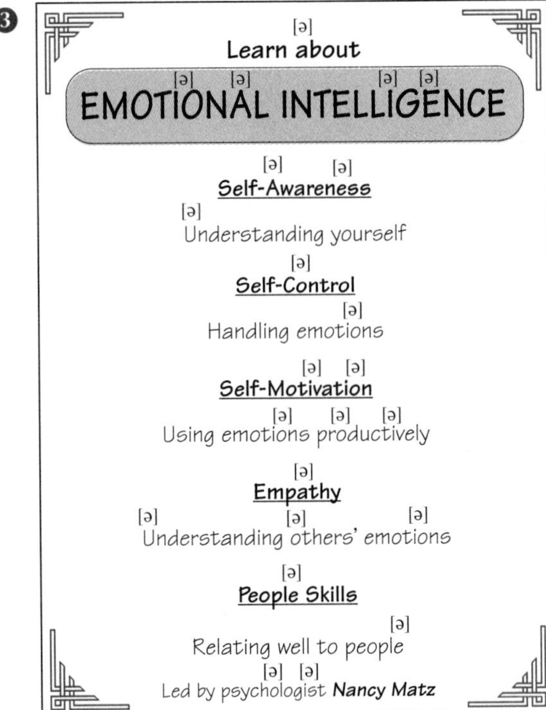

5B. WORKING WITH WORDS

❶

1. **a.** enthusiastic about
   b. respond well to change
2. **a.** be patient
   b. empathize with
   c. swallow their pride
3. **a.** spirited
   b. deal with setbacks
4. **a.** make a fuss
   b. put aside your negative feelings
5. **a.** put myself in my clients' shoes
   b. perceptive
6. **a.** swallow your pride
   b. take life in stride

UNIT 8 ◆ JOURNEY TO THE RED PLANET

2A. BACKGROUND

1. T
2. T
3. F (The diameter of Mars is about half that of the Earth.)
4. F (Mars is cold. The temperature drops to about –73° Celsius at night.)
5. T
6. T

7. T
8. F (Mars is called the "red planet" because of its strikingly red appearance.)
9. T
10. T
11. F (Gravity on Mars is only 38 percent that of the Earth.)
12. T
13. F (We have not found life on Mars yet.)
14. T
15. T
16. T

2B. VOCABULARY FOR COMPREHENSION

2. a	5. a	9. c	13. a
3. a	6. b	10. b	14. b
4. c	7. a	11. b	15. c
	8. c	12. a	16. b

3B. LISTENING FOR MAIN IDEAS

suggested answers

1. They are a group of scientists and engineers who believe that it's humankind's destiny to go to Mars.
2. They are keeping an eye on the Mars missions in the hope that humans can travel to Mars one day.
3. Humans are better at finding things than robots are.
4. It is similar to the past moon missions. It involves sending up a spacecraft and then sending astronauts to the planet's surface in a lander.
5. Another approach is to send up a spacecraft that doesn't have enough fuel to get back to Earth but can make rocket fuel out of the Martian atmosphere.
6. The second approach is very innovative and costs much less.
7. Scientists will focus on places where there was water and energy.

3C. LISTENING FOR DETAILS

1. b. T
   c. F
   d. T
2. a. F
   b. T
   c. F
   d. F
3. a. T
   b. T
   c. F
   d. T
4. a. T
   b. F
   c. T
   d. T
5. a. F
   b. T
   c. F
   d. F

3D. LISTENING BETWEEN THE LINES

answers may vary

4A. EXPANDING THE TOPIC

suggested answers

1. Terraforming is transforming the planet, making it more Earth-like.
2. To get more heat, we could redirect the sun's rays with mirrors or release some of Mars's internal heat.
   We would need to get frozen underground water to the surface of the planet.
   We would introduce life forms such as bacteria from the Earth.
3. Estimates vary between 50 and 100,000 years.
   In Robinson's novels, 300 to 500 years.
   Realistically, 500 to 1,000 years.
4. Benefits include more living room, a lesson in how to keep the Earth healthy, and ideas about solutions to environmental problems.

5A. EXPLORING LANGUAGE: The Stress-Changing Suffix-*tion*

❶ innovate, colonize, educate, adapt, recite; indicate, beautify, motivate, evolve

❷ The stress usually moves to the right. It then falls on the syllable *before* -tion, which is pronounced [ʃən] (or shŭhn).

innovation, colonization, education, adaptation, recitation; indication, beautification, motivation, evolution

❸ 1. a beautification program
2. a colonization project
3. indication
4. evolution
5. innovations
6. motivation

5B. WORKING WITH WORDS

❶ certain—inevitable
change—transform
develop—evolve
future—destiny
impractical—romantic
livable—hospitable
new—innovative

❷ 2. innovative
3. romantic
4. transform
5. inevitable
6. evolve
7. hospitable

❸ 2. a. new
   b. new/innovative
3. a. future
   b. destiny
4. a. impractical/romantic
   b. impractical
5. a. certain/inevitable
   b. certain/inevitable
6. a. develop/evolve
   b. develop
7. a. livable
   b. livable/hospitable

6A. GRAMMAR: Phrasal Verbs

2
2. e
3. b
4. l
5. h
6. d
7. a
8. g
9. c
10. i
11. k
12. j

3
3. get rid of it
4. hinted at it
5. keep it down
6. keep up with it
7. pick them out
8. run out of it
9. set them up
10. stick with it
11. think back on it
12. turn it down

UNIT 9 ◆ FINDING A NICHE: EXPERIENCES OF YOUNG IMMIGRANTS

1B. SHARING INFORMATION

suggested answers

Greece/Greek
Cuba/Spanish
Dominican Republic/Spanish
Russia/Russian
Japan/Japanese
Korea/Korean
West Indies (Trinidad, Tobago, Jamaica, etc.)/English
The Azores/Portuguese
Poland/Polish
Argentina/Spanish
Peru/Spanish
Israel/Hebrew
The Philippines/Tagalog
Cape Verde/Portuguese
Ecuador/Spanish
Pakistan/Urdu
India/Hindi
China and Taiwan/Mandarin, Cantonese

2B. VOCABULARY FOR COMPREHENSION

2
1. j
2. h
3. i
4. g
5. e
6. c
7. k
8. f
9. d
10. l
11. a
12. b

3B. LISTENING FOR MAIN IDEAS

Checks on: 1, 2, 3, 4, 6, 8, 9, 10 (item 10 is inferred)

3C. LISTENING FOR DETAILS

suggested answers

Jennifer Shenke: teacher; she likes the fact that students enjoy themselves, help each other, and learn at the same time

Priscilla Billarrel: student; she feels that the students understand, support, and correct each other without making fun of each other's mistakes

Aaron Listhaus: teacher; he thinks it is important that school is a "safe" place where students feel welcome and valued for who they are

Evelyna Namovich: student; she is relieved that at school she is encouraged not only to speak her own language, but also to study it

Kathy Rucker: teacher; school is providing valuable skills for students to operate bilingually in a modern society

4A. EXPANDING THE TOPIC

1
50% came from Asia
35% came from Latin America
3% came from Northern Europe
7% came from Southern and Eastern Europe

2
melting pot
salad bowl

5A. EXPLORING LANGUAGE: Discriminating between Similar Sounds

1
2. [dʒ]
3. [dʒ]
4. [dʒ]
5. [ʒ]
6. [tʃ]
7. [ʃ]
8. [tʃ]
9. [ʒ]
10. [ʃ]
11. [ʃ]
12. [dʒ]
13. [tʃ]
14. [ʒ]
15. [dʒ]
16. [ʒ]
17. [ʃ]
18. [dʒ]
19. a. [tʃ]
    b. [ʃ]
20. [ʒ]

5B. WORKING WITH WORDS

Part One

a. 8
b. 3
c. 5
d. 4
e. 2
f. 6
g. 1
h. 7

Part Two

i. 13
j. 10
k. 15
l. 11
m. 12
n. 16
o. 14
p. 9

6A. GRAMMAR: Present and Past—Contrasting Verb Tenses

2
1. came
2. was
3. didn't speak
4. went
5. weren't
6. had
7. was
8. didn't understand
9. was talking
10. asked
11. became
12. told
13. wanted
14. felt
15. thought
16. felt
17. doesn't speak
18. has changed
19. is
20. are
21. have changed
22. is
23. look
24. have spoken
25. are attending
26. learn
27. love
28. became/have become
29. teach
30. help
31. value
32. have also changed
33. was
34. wishes
35. is taking

3 *suggested answers*

2. How long has she been in the United States?
3. How did she feel about speaking German when she was a girl?
4. How does she feel about it now?
5. Why have her feelings changed? or Why did her feelings change?
6. What new technology has changed the way people learn other languages?
7. How do you feel when people speak a language you don't understand?
8. What is the author's native language?
9. What are the benefits of a bilingual school
10. How does the bilingual school help the author's children? or How has it helped . . .
11. How does the bilingual school help the immigrant children? or How has it helped . . .
12. What types of jobs require a bilingual person?
13. How do the author's views about language differ from her grandparents' views?
14. In your opinion, which type of education is better for immigrant children?

UNIT 10 ◆ TECHNOLOGY: A BLESSING OR A CURSE?

2A. BACKGROUND

1. c	4. b	7. a
2. a	5. d	8. c
3. c	6. d	9. b

2B. VOCABULARY FOR COMPREHENSION

2. a	7. a	11. a
3. a	8. a	12. a
4. b	9. c	13. a
5. c	10. a	14. b
6. a		

3A. INTRODUCING THE TOPIC

suggested answers

1. The noise is caused by a car alarm.
2. People probably feel angry and frustrated.
3. They might just go back to sleep, or call the police.
4. The report probably takes place in a city.

3B. LISTENING FOR MAIN IDEAS

1. F	3. F	5. F	7. F
2. T	4. T	6. T	8. T

3C. LISTENING FOR DETAILS

suggested answers

1. **a.** People are awakened often and don't know if they'll be reawakened.
   b. People are arrested for disturbing the peace.
2. **a.** They send the driver a note or break an egg on the windshield.
   b. They smear grease on door handles and vaseline on the windshield.
3. **a.** Her car was dented.
   b. No one bothered to see if her car was being broken into.
4. **a.** A car was being mutilated; the police came 40 minutes later.
5. **a.** It affects their ability to sleep and to work during the day.
   b. It can cause hearing loss.
6. **a.** The laws are now being enforced.
   b. Car alarms will not be set off by the vibrations of passing trucks.

4A. EXPANDING THE TOPIC

suggested answers

Caller 1: Stanley complains about automated phone systems; they drive him crazy because they take so long.

Caller 2: Carol is complaining about cellular phones; people use them in public places, and this disturbs others.

Caller 3: Jessica complains about all the remote controls in her house; they are so complicated to use, and they get lost.

Caller 4: Arthur complains about e-mail; it's mostly junk, and it takes so long to read.

Caller 5: Betty remembers that life was harder before we had modern appliances.

5B. WORKING WITH WORDS

Student A

Dialogue 1	1. getting under my skin
	2. jolts
	3. frustrated
Dialogue 2	4. irritated
	5. drive you crazy
	6. offense
	7. fine

Student B

Dialogue 1	1. go off
	2. defective
	3. frazzled
Dialogue 2	4. I've had it
	5. retaliatory steps
	6. disturbing the peace
	7. banned

6A. GRAMMAR: Future Perfect and Future Progressive

❷ Mystery Items Game

Item 1 (watch)
1. will have replaced
2. will have been made

Item 2 (toilet)
1. will have used
2. will have used

Item 3 (TV)
1. will have turned on
2. won't have become

Item 4 (bicycle)
1. will have asked
2. will have been invented

Item 5 (glasses)
1. will have had
2. will have introduced

Item 6 (radio)
1. will have been turned on
2. will have switched

❸ *answers will vary*